Aspects of American Poetry

Essays Presented to Howard Mumford Jones

Aspects of American Poetry

Edited by Richard M. Ludwig

71532

Ohio State University Press

Foreword

THE ESSAYS in this volume are assembled for presentation to a great scholar and teacher. The work of Howard Mumford Jones, during forty-three years of university teaching, has been distinguished for its competence and its catholicity of interest. From the year 1919, when he began teaching comparative literature at the University of Texas, to the day of his retirement in 1962 from Harvard University as Abbott Lawrence Lowell Professor of the Humanities, his scholarship has ranged from the history of ideas in British, French, and American literature through studies of seventeenth-century American history, Restoration drama, Victorian fiction, twentieth-century prose and poetry to a growing body of essays and books on the theory of education and the place of the humanities in our world. The size and scope of his bibliography, printed at the back of this book, attests to these interests. One book more than any other sums them up. In 1959, Professor Jones published *One Great Society: Humane Learning in the United States*. As chairman of a Commission on the Humanities of the American Council of Learned Societies, he was the spokesman in this volume for a group of twelve scholars. But the writing of this "statement about learning" was his task alone, and to it he brought eloquence and wisdom, as well as the knowledge of history, philosophy, literature, music, and the arts that has made his lectures over the years so stimulating to countless students.

It would be gratifying if his friends and former students could honor him with a volume that reflects the full latitude of his abilities. But that would have to be a large, heterogeneous volume, indeed. In lieu of that, we offer these critical essays on American poetry to a teacher who long ago instilled in us the belief that American literature was important enough to demand attention as a separate area of study but who, at the same time, made us see that our literature could be properly appreciated only in relation to its European backgrounds and to allied disciplines. We hasten to add that this volume is presented on behalf of his friends and debtors on college campuses throughout the nation.

RICHARD M. LUDWIG

Princeton, New Jersey
May, 1962

acknowledgments

The editor and the contributors wish to make grateful acknowledgment of the permission that has been granted them to quote from the following:

Conrad Aiken, *Scepticisms: Notes on Contemporary Poetry*. Reprinted by permission of Alfred A. Knopf, Inc.

A. Alvarez, *The Shaping Spirit*. Reprinted by permission of Chatto & Windus Ltd.

Sherwood Anderson, *Mid-American Chants* and *Marching Men*. Reprinted by permission of Harold Ober Associates.

The Sherwood Anderson Collection of the Newberry Library. Reprinted by permission of the Library and Mrs. Sherwood Anderson.

W. H. Auden, "Augustus to Augustine" and "The Means of Grace." Reprinted by permission of the *New Republic*.

W. H. Auden, "Balaam and the Ass: On the Literary Use of the Master-Servant Relationship," "The Dyer's Hand," and "The Fallen City: Some Reflections on Shakespeare's 'Henry IV.'" Reprinted by permission of *Encounter*.

W. H. Auden, "In Memory of W. B. Yeats" from *Another Time*, "For the Time Being" and "The Sea and the Mirror" from *For the Time Being*, "New Year Letter" from *New Year Letter* and *The Double Man*, "To Reinhold and Ursula Niebuhr" from *Nones*, "The Sea and the Desert" from *The Enchafèd Flood*, and *The Age of Anxiety*. Reprinted by permission of Random House, Inc., and Faber and Faber Ltd.

W. H. Auden and Norman Holmes Pearson (eds.), *Poets of the English Language*. Reprinted by permission of The Viking Press, Inc.

Herbert Bergman, "Ezra Pound and Walt Whitman." Reprinted by permission of *American Literature* and Herbert Bergman.

Cleanth Brooks, "The Teaching of the Novel: *Huckleberry Finn*," in *Essays on the Teaching of English*, edited by E. J. Gordon and E. S. Noyes. Reprinted

contents

Aspects of American Poetry

The
Meter-Making
Argument

Edwin Fussell

Ah, but our numbers are not felicitous,
It goes not liquidly for us.

JOHN CROWE RANSOM
"Philomela"

INDEED it does not. At first by default, more recently
by design, American numbers have continuously
been characterized by that "dissonance" with which
Ransom charges himself personally in this delightful poem, and of which he professes—such is the
casuistry of poets—to be sick. The lines containing
these mock complaints are by the most cunning
artistry metrically harsh. With obvious ironic relish, the poem also insists upon jarring our ears
with such studied cacophonies as "pernoctated,"
such unnecessary inversions as "To England came
Philomela with her pain." By diligent avoidance
of liquidity, "Philomela" achieves an undeniable
and unmistakably American felicity.

The poem tells first of the wanderings of Philomela ("lover of song," the spirit of poetry) from
Greece to Rome, thence to the continent, and finally to England—but not to America. In one
country after another she utters herself "in the

classic numbers of the nightingale." But "classic" can hardly refer with equal propriety to the meters of such various poetic traditions, and in fact Ransom himself seems dubious about both the French and German; moreover, as Ransom well knows, the nightingale is to the American imagination the arch symbol, both loved and hated, of the English tradition, whose notorious liquidity he professes to desire while in the act of demolishing it.

More specifically the poem tells of Ransom at Oxford hearing "from the darkest wood" the "fairy numbers" of the nightingale. (The tone suggests Keats, but "Philomela" is more significantly an Americanized version of Arnold's poem by the same name.) To his "capacious" *ear*—a pun, I think, intended in praise of the Americans' willingness to entertain a wider variety of musical delight—"her classics registered a little flat!" ("I rose, and venomously spat.") He pretends to lay the blame on the deficiencies of American sensibility, and declares with a devious innocence: "I am in despair if we may make us worthy." But the poem itself works the other way; it is eminently worthy, and entirely on its own terms, which are pointedly and persistently antagonistic to the English tradition. What "Philomela" tells us, finally, is that subject matter is of small importance, so far as the national quality of poetry is concerned (the poet shows no interest in the bird except as she sings), but that technique, and especially metric, is of the essence. "Philomela" tells us also, and shows us, that the American poet is indeed "inordinate," but can turn to account what he may not in any case avoid, a literary situation dominated by deprivation and therefore by excessive national self-consciousness, and manageable only by desperate remedies born of frustration and tension.

Modern American poetry is full of such jokes, which are pitfalls only for the unwary. William Carlos Williams' *Paterson* opens with an invocation describing itself as "a reply to Greek and Latin with the bare hands." Another trap for the innocent. How could it possibly be the ancients, with their dead languages, against whom the American poet must contend, except perhaps in a kind of harmless but revealing fantasy? For "Greek and Latin" read "British." "Bare hands" are the hard actualities of American life, the hardest of which (but also the most exhilarating) is the nearly impossible situation in which the American poet finds himself. Book One of *Paterson* concludes with a quotation from Symonds' *Studies of the Greek Poets,* dealing with the relations between metrical wrenching and distorted subjects ("as well as their agreement with the snarling spirit of the satirist"). Once more, felicity resides in dissonance; or, alternatively, in "looseness," for perhaps no important American poem is more deliberately chaotic in its meters.

All this dissonance and looseness ought to be very appealing to historians of American poetry, for in truth it goes not so liquidly for us either. Whenever we think of American poetry as a simple, separate subject, we find ourselves as balked and bewildered as the American poets whose story we try to tell. Except that we are less enterprising: faced with such queerly assorted poets as Whittier and Whitman, Robinson and Pound, Frost and Eliot, we incline either to pretend that some of these poets are "in the American tradition" (undefined) while others are not, or we panic, and declare the whole problem insoluble, saying, in effect, "There is no such thing as American poetry." What if instead we simply accepted the dissonance and the looseness of American poetry and tried to account for them? With these as starting points, a theory of American poetry immediately begins to take shape, and precisely from those paradoxical pairs of poets who otherwise most baffle our formulations. Naturally, the poets and the issues will never line up with perfect exactitude; still, the diverse, or even antithetical kinds of poem we associate with their names sufficiently suggest the fundamental divisions underlying the apparent confusion in American poetry. Some American poets are intensely nationalistic in their attitudes toward poetry, while others are scarcely national. Some American poets are in violent revolt against what they conceive to be the English tradition, while others are relatively comfortable—sometimes too comfortable—with it. As Wallace Stevens says, "Nothing could be more inappropriate to American literature than its English source since the Americans are not British in sensibility." Even though that statement requires considerable amplification and some modification, it is persuasive enough on the main point: no theory of American poetry can offer much unless it concentrates on the conflict between the aspirations of the American poet and the authority of the English tradition.

My own inclination is to press toward an understanding of that conflict by trying to talk about American poetry technically (metrically) and culturally (nationalistically) at the same time. For tutelary spirit I invoke Emerson, and especially seize upon his talismanic phrase about a "meter-making argument." For on close inspection, and imaginatively understood, that phrase turns out to be nationalistic as well as metrical. Even without Emerson's authority, I should still have elected the metrical emphasis, for a variety of reasons: first, because it is that element of poetic technique through which the American poet has directed most of his creative energy, especially when self-consciously engendering a native poetry, and it is therefore the metric of American poetry which differs most obviously from (while at the same time it most clearly relates to) English poetry; second, because metric is easier to discuss in short compass than more elusive qualities like metaphor or tone.

And of course, there is a much more important reason. Although prosodic descriptions, just because they are simplified, are comparatively crude, the poetic qualities they point to—rhythm and motion—are anything but crude. These are the soul of the poem, which comes into being only as language moves, in discernible and cumulative patterns of recurrence, from first word to last, through action to substance. The poem itself is *how* the language moves and where it arrives. Ideally, the poem arrives at a finality of statement (but different for every poem) wherein it is impossible to distinguish whether our satisfaction derives from its truth, or its beauty, or its goodness. Of these metaphysical properties, meter is the occasion and the investiture. If this is so of one poem, then it is so of all poems, or of any group of poems selected on reasonably homogeneous principles. Thus we can say that the soul of American poetry must dwell in its rhythm; and however imperfectly, we can approach that soul through metrical analysis.

So much for technique and transcendentals. If we approach American poetry from the opposite direction—from the national rather than the poetic side—we come to the same conclusion. Quite in addition to the fact that meters are always of the essence, American meters are strikingly and peculiarly symptomatic of the long-standing ambivalence in cultural (or political) relations between America and England. Indeed, it is not too much to say that American meters shift with the shifting harmonic overtones of the cultural relation between the two countries, or even, conversely, that a metrical shift on one side of the water may have political consequences on the other side—as in the latter nineteenth century, *Leaves of Grass* by its rhythms as much as its "message" induced in the British intellectual and workingman alike a kindlier and more respectful attitude toward the upstart States.

No matter how willfully idiosyncratic the poet, nor how unconscious of his involvement, the poems he makes are not atoms, but members of _a poetry,_ and poetries are for the most part distinctively national. Any of them—let us say the English—lies almost by definition within a tradition of shared sensibility and culture, expressed in a particular language, with a national bias derived from the deeply felt identity of a people. Ordinarily somewhat diffuse, this deeply felt sense of community is sharpened and articulated and stabilized by poets, with the consequence that in an actual national poetry, technique, sensibility, and culture are absolutely inextricable one from another, each being the intensified instrument and expression of the others.

But that description holds only when language and nation coincide, as in American poetry they assuredly do not. The American poet is a non-Englishman (often an anti-Englishman) writing in the English language. His feeling toward the common tongue must always be mixed and ambivalent; his poetic medium (with all its attendant implications for sensibility and culture) is at once a siren and an albatross. After all, it is his acute sensitivity to the stress and pace and tonality of his own culture that leads him to be a poet in the first place. Of course, ambivalence is more vocal in our early history. But if the anti-British, pro-American talk and animus have died away, the literary situation which initially caused them continues, in a disguised form, and will continue for the foreseeable future. No matter if English culture, English metric no longer directly threaten the American poet with foreign domination: the conservative, metrically "regular" tradition of England, at first both inescapable and unassimilable, has at length been introjected into the American poetic psyche in an almost Oedipal way (as we might have expected from the original "parent-child" relationship of England and her New World colonies) . Children must revolt against their parents; adolescents may, if they choose, revolt against themselves. So doing, they move toward maturity.

Our poetic history begins with the necessary emancipation from

English tradition, conceived as inherited but not quite wanted order and regularity. The American poet must liberate himself from an alien culture and sensibility; ultimately, he must liberate his art from an alien technique, or make it his own. Doubtless his problem was exacerbated by the fact that the catchword of the youthful culture was "liberty" and the catchword of the parent culture "order." Unfortunately for the English-speaking American poet, English "order" is nowhere more attractively enshrined than in English poetry; nowhere is the English poetic tradition more like a red flag to a bullheaded American poet than in its numbers. Given the nature of poetry, and the facts of American history, free verse was as inevitable as the Declaration of Independence.

There is simply no use arguing, against the sense of our poets in this matter, that "the English tradition" comprises a world of variety, or even calling attention to the existence of its several poetic periods, and their metrical differences from one another. The poet is not a historical prosodist, but a man whose ear must instruct him how to bring into being meters possible and appropriate to his actual situation. To the ear which has once responded to the obviously American cadences of Whitman, the metrical differences among Spenser, Dryden, and Wordsworth no longer sound startling. Compared with Whitman, they are all "regular," and their regularity consists in a general allegiance to the traditionally English syllable-stress metric, to a line most often made up of dissyllabic feet and measured out in pentameter length. To the American ear, this regularity tends to sound all of a piece. It smacks of the "foreign" and the "old." (Even in American poems otherwise conspicuous for native and modern flavor: Robinson is the perfect case in point.) Yet English regularity, before or after introjection, is *the* tradition with which the individual American talent must come to terms. In his *Fable for Critics,* Lowell called the English pentameter—the word

"English" being ambiguous—a "sham meter." Nearly a century later Frost compliments himself on having written his verse "regular all this time without knowing till yesterday that it was from fascination with this constant symbol I celebrate."[1] In Frost's view, the "constant symbol" seems to mean the discipline of form. But perhaps this "constant symbol" of his reveals more than he knows; at any rate, like Lowell's jibe, it points to the American conviction of English regularity.

Ironically, the best evidence that the English tradition seems all of a piece comes from the American poet-critic most comfortable in it. In "Poets and Poetry of the English Language" (1876 version), the essay introducing his anthology *A Library of Poetry and Song,* Bryant not only tells us that "our poetry" is synonymous with "English verse," but also that English prosody became "fixed" between Chaucer and Sidney, and that *The Faerie Queene* represents the English language ("so far as the purposes of poetry require") in a state of "perfection" not subsequently improved upon. So far as Bryant is concerned, the English tradition is *one* tradition, and that tradition is *ours.* Nearly all the American poets agree with him on the first point, I suspect, but few, or none, on the second. Clearly, Bryant's popular anthology was designed as a respectable repository for more or less uniform gems going "as far back as to the author who may properly be called the father of English poetry," Chaucer, and in the tradition thus asserted the American poet was expected to find his place. Longfellow, Lowell, Holmes, Whittier (even renegade Emerson) found generous places; Poe and N. P. Willis found smaller places; Whitman found none at all.[2] Given the

---

[1] From "The Constant Symbol" by Robert Frost. Copyright 1946 by Robert Frost. Used by permission of Holt, Rinehart and Winston, Inc.

[2] I am speaking of the first edition, 1871. For the second edition, five years later, Bryant excerpted passages from "Out of the Cradle Endlessly Rocking," hopelessly mangling the poem, retitled them "The Mocking-Bird," and placed this new creation among thirty-five other poems about birds, including "To a Waterfowl."

inherent problem of American poetry, Bryant's perpetual insistence on "models" (as early as 1825, as late as 1876) could have no other issue than an enforced and debilitating conformity with British tradition, and especially with British metric. "At the present day [1825] . . . a writer [whether English or American] of poems writes in a language [English] which preceding [English] poets have polished, refined, and filled with forcible, graceful, and musical expressions. He is not only taught by them to overcome the difficulties of rhythmical construction, but he is shown, as it were, the secrets of the mechanism by which he moves the mind of the reader."

So insensitive and uncomprehending a statement, coupled with the total rejection of Whitman's poems, immediately strikes us as an ominous sign how close American poetry came to being stillborn. But further reflection, along the lines of the theory of American poetry I have been trying to intimate, brings home to our minds an old and obvious truth: without a Bryant, a Whitman is unimaginable. Moreover, as we shall soon see, a Whitman conversely and consequently makes possible the existence of a later and better Bryant. American poetry emerges from a dialectic tension. Dialectic requires two opposing terms. Which is not to say that a Bryant—no matter how "improved"—commands 20–20 vision, or is in any respect the equal of a Whitman.

II

American poetry curiously resembles the two-party system of American politics, where one party invents (sometimes overstepping the bounds of reality) and the other alternately obstructs and then consolidates the inventions it obstructed. Both parties are necessary, and a kind of achievement is possible to either, but

in poetry as in politics the driving force behind historical development is nearly always attributable to the inventive, or active, party.
Cultural change originates with the sensibility which is disturbed
by the world it inherits and consequently avails itself of the courage and intelligence to change it. A theory of American poetry can
only begin with the isolation and definition of the radical tradition in poetic technique.

Fortunately, this radical tradition is easily identified; and ascription to it of primary importance accords with the most scrupu-
lously "critical" standards. The radical tradition immediately dis-
engages itself from the ruck of American poetry as soon as we ask
the question of questions: Who are the major and crucial American poets, both in literary excellence and in the difference they
make to their successors? Two American poets pre-eminently answer this description: Whitman and Pound. The other nineteenth-
century poets pass through Whitman's legs like Lilliputians.
Possibly he was endowed with more poetic talent than the rest;
but how can we tell, except as the talent proves itself in action?
The most persuasive proof of Whitman's genius is the perspicacity
with which he sensed the poetic needs of his time and place and
the almost flawless rectitude with which, in his theory and in his
finest poems, he rose to meet them. As he said in his 1855
Preface: "A heroic person walks at his ease through and out of
that custom or precedent or authority that suits him not . . . .
Nothing is finer than silent defiance advancing from new free
forms . . . . The cleanest expression is that which finds no sphere
worthy of itself and makes one." (The description is equally valid
for Pound, except that he had a model.) By common agreement,
even among those who cannot—because they will not—read his
verses, and therefore fancy a distaste for them, Pound is the insti-
gator of twentieth-century poetry in English. (But Pound does not
call it "English"; his term for the basic text of *The Cantos* is

"American.") T. S. Eliot has been telling us for years of his own dependence upon Pound (*il miglior fabbro*) ; unfortunately, he has also tried to conceal Pound's, and his own, indebtedness to Whitman.[3]

The most obvious, as well as the most significant characteristic of the major poetry of Whitman and Pound is metrical innovation carried to an extraordinary degree. No prosodist has come close to describing the basic metric of either man. Though by no means "undisciplined" or "formless," Whitman and Pound represent in American poetry the furthest reach of metrical rebelliousness, nationalistically inspired. As Pound says in Canto 81: "To break the pentameter, that was the first heave." Doubtless he was thinking of Whitman, who is repeatedly named in Canto 80, but in the lines immediately preceding he quotes a letter from one of the leaders of the American Revolution (John Adams) to another (Jefferson, who incidentally wrote a conventional treatise on English prosody) , and the subject of their correspondence is fear of political tyranny. Surely it is no accident that our two greatest poets place their prosodic radicalism—which is directed against the traditional order of English verse—in the context of American political thought. In the 1855 Preface to *Leaves of Grass,* which has much to say about "liberty," both literary and political, Whitman pointedly remarked: "The poetic quality is not marshalled in rhyme or uniformity." "Uniformity" can only mean the "regular" or syllable-stress metric of his English predecessors and American contemporaries. As his poems show, he totally rejected their assumptions and practices. Many years after the fact, holding court in Camden, Whitman delivered himself as follows (dis-

---

[3] It is difficult to conceive historical or critical judgments more clearly incorrect than Eliot's assertions that "Pound owes nothing to Whitman" and (in the wake of Arnold) that "Whitman was a great prose writer" (in his introduction to *Ezra Pound: Selected Poems;* other remarks of the same tenor, a decade earlier, in *Ezra Pound: His Metric and Poetry*) .

ciple Traubel reporting) : "I said to W.: 'I'm getting more and more dubious about rhyme and all that.' W. said: 'I got wholly dubious about rhyme long ago: as to the "all that," I dismiss it without a peradventure.' "

But our sense of the vital relationship between Whitman and Pound—which is indispensable to an understanding of the theory and history of American poetry—need not rest solely upon these parallels between their intentions and practices, no matter how impressive they are. We now have external evidence—in a 1909 essay which has only recently come to light—that Pound's poetic career began with specific emulation of Whitman.

> I honor him for he prophesied me while I can only recognize him as a forebear of whom I ought to be proud . . . . When I write of certain things I find myself using his rhythms . . . . Mentally I am a Walt Whitman who has learned to wear a colllar and a dress shirt (although at times inimical to both). Personally I might be very glad to conceal my relationship to my spiritual father and brag about my more congenial ancestry—Dante, Shakespeare, Theocritus, Villon, but the descent is a bit difficult to establish. And, to be frank, Whitman is to my fatherland . . . what Dante is to Italy . . . . Like Dante he wrote in the "vulgar tongue," in a new metric. The first great man to write in the language of his people.[4]

What could be simpler or more conclusive? The line from Whitman to Pound is the radical tradition of American poetry; the connection between them is quite as firm and unassailable as the

---

[4] There are observations to the same general effect in *Patria Mia* (written before 1913) , but the best statements are obviously these, from the 1909 essay, reprinted in Herbert Bergman's invaluable paper, "Ezra Pound and Walt Whitman," *American Literature*, XXVII (1955) , 56–61. Pound's later deprecations of Whitman notwithstanding, I fail to see him ever *as poet* recanting this youthful dedication to the Whitman tradition.

traditio from Chaucer to Spenser to Milton, which was also, among other things, a line of language and metric, with a powerful native bias.

Yet neither Whitman nor Pound has succeeded in establishing a continuing, general norm for American metric; rather, they indicate one of its possible limits. There is no agreement, but on the contrary much complaining, and more by poets than critics—e.g., in Karl Shapiro's *Essay on Rime*—that the achievement of Whitman, or of Pound, is not widely "usable," without endless modification and reversion. The reason for this failure is obvious: a radical poetry requires something to rebel *against,* a conservative tradition either foreign or introjected (but in either case productive of continuing discomfort). The norm of American poetry cannot possibly lie in the Whitman-Pound tradition alone, nor in what that tradition opposes, but only in the fact of opposition between them. Fortunately for the continuing health of our poetry, this opposition can never be entirely removed. The experimental American poet is wonderfully trapped between desire and necessity: the desire to be as free as possible of the English poetic tradition, and the necessity of maintaining at least an uneasy peace with his medium, the English language, which ineradicably embodies the English poetic tradition. It is no mere happenstance, then, but the logic of history (which is sometimes surprisingly "pure"), that the two explosive eruptions of American poetry (1855 and 1912) should be followed by long periods of gradually increasing conservatism, during which a succession of lesser poets carried American metric back nearer the traditional norms of English verse. The history of American poetry is the history of recurrent explosions, metrically centered, caused by the frustration of the American poet, who is and is not an "English" poet, alternating with longer periods of conciliation and consolidation. Behind this historical oscillation lies a discernible development, for after each explosion the American poet returns to "regularity" with a diminished sense of discomfort, a greater feeling of freedom and mastery, broader possibility, wider choice. What Bryant in 1876 implied had always been true was in fact at the very time he wrote in the process of becoming true, but in a very different sense from what he intended, and in ways of which he was totally ignorant. Sometime between Whitman and Pound, the English tradition became—insofar as we care to use it—"ours."

III

The crucial period in the history of American poetry is between Bryant and Whitman, the Age of Growing Discomfort and Inadequate Remedy. Except for Lowell, who was notoriously too facile for his own good, the poets of this age are almost unbelievably inept in their metrics; and the more ambitious, the more inept. Even Lowell, for all his over-facility in metric (of which he was so vain), is frequently very uncertain in this respect, especially in *A Fable for Critics,* as Poe noted in his review of it, responding, conceivably, to Lowell's charge in that poem that Poe talked "like a book of iambs and pentameters,/ In a way to make people of common sense damn meters." It will be noticed that (1) Lowell's objection to Poe's always harping on metric is itself metrically inept, and (2) whenever a poet of this period desires to insult a peer, he nearly always does so on the score of metric. (In his *Fable,* Lowell also called Emerson's verse "not even prose.") All the evidence suggests that the metrical problem was insistently pressing and not in the way of solution.

Poe, for one, was always riding to a lather what he called his "favorite horse of versification," not only in his most considered definition of poetry as "The Rhythmical Creation of Beauty," [5] but to more effect in his practical criticism, where his endless zeal for prosecuting metrical malefactors according to "the laws of verse, which are the incontrovertible laws of melody and harmony" sufficiently indicates his uneasiness. In the course of giving Bryant a thoroughgoing prosodic inspection, he wrote: "Upon a rigid attention to minutiae such as we have pointed out, any great degree of metrical success must altogether depend." His favorite words for lines he liked were "sweet" and "smooth"; for lines he didn't like, "rough" and "loose." His highest praise of another poet's versification was to call it "correct." Thus he moved readily from practice to principle: "In common with a very large majority of American, and, indeed, of European poets, Mrs. [Elizabeth Oakes] Smith seems to be totally unacquainted with the principles of versification—by which, of course, we mean its *rationale*. Of technical *rules* on the subject there are rather more than enough in our prosodies, and from these abundant rules are deduced the abundant blunders of our poets." Sadly, the indictment beautifully fits Poe himself, both as prosodist and poet. No more than the other blunderers could he discriminate rule from rationale. As in his criticism he increasingly tried by the autocracy of pure reason to reduce traditional English metric to an exact science, the meters of his own poems became ever more maladroit. (See "The Rationale of Verse," a model of theoretical arrogance, and such prosodic absurdities as "The Raven" and

[5] Taken by itself, the phrase is uncomfortably ambiguous, for it might equally mean only "a beautiful creation which is rhythmical" or "beauty created by—instigated by, promoted by—rhythm." The following passage, from Poe's 1843 review of Griswold's *Poets and Poetry of America*, may perhaps help fix his probable meaning (or perhaps not) : "POETRY, in its most confined sense, is *the result of versification*, but may be more properly defined as *the rhythmical personification of existing or real beauty*. One defines it as the 'rhythmical *creation* of beauty'; but though it certainly is a 'creation of beauty' in itself, it is more properly a personification, for the poet only personifies the image previously created by his mind."

"Ulalume.") Poe was hopelessly confused and distraught, responding to the American poetic situation with a kind of controlled
hysteria which he alternatively sought to suppress by fiat or escape through "originality" (mechanical fussing with inessential
details, alliteration, internal rhyme, refrains, trochaic jogs, ana-
pestic romps). He was never to realize that only through a significant break with English tradition might he relieve his discomfort.
This failure of perception is probably why his poetry came to so
little, after such early promise—as Poe himself conceded, pleading
lack of time.

> "Whose criticisms?" asked Emerson [of his young visitor from
> the West, William Dean Howells, who subsequently recorded the
> joke in his literary memoirs].
> "Poe's," I said again.
> "Oh," he cried out, after a moment, as if he had returned from
> a far search for my meaning, *"you mean the jingle-man!"*

The sage was obviously trying to dissociate himself from Poe,
and to discredit the verses which Whitman would call "melodious" and "morbid." Typically, he insulted Poe's metric. Yet
Emerson was not so purely Poe's opposite number as he liked to
think. Here is a poet of even greater talent who also finds it
nearly impossible to write good poems, who must needs "experiment," who almost never experiments to any successful purpose,
and whose most ambitious efforts regularly collapse on the rhythmical front. In a personal letter, criticizing Emerson's "Ode to
Beauty," Thoreau defines the trouble with his customary acuity
and candor: "The tune is altogether unworthy of the thoughts.
You slope too quickly to the rhyme, as if that trick had better
be performed as soon as possible or as if you stood over the line
with a hatchet . . . . It sounds like a parody." Like the other

American poets before Whitman, Emerson could be metrically conventional or he could dare to be (with what trepidation!) a little different. Either way—certain brilliant lines and passages excepted—he ended by sounding like a travesty of his transatlantic betters, whether of the nineteenth or of the seventeenth centuries.

Nearly every ambitious American poem before 1855 reveals this same unease in relation to the traditional techniques, and especially the traditional metric, of English poetry. The awkwardness is not the deliberate, and therefore successful, awkwardness of "Philomela." If the poems do not sound right, it is because the poets are trying to sound like English poets, and not succeeding, or self-consciously trying to sound like American poets, without having any adequate idea (auditory sense) what an American poet might sound like. For the most part, they do not sound like any poets at all, as Emerson confessed, when he wrote in a personal letter: "My singing be sure is very 'husky,' & is for the most part in prose. [Was he alluding to his essays or his poems?] Still am I a poet . . . . "

Yet Emerson came closer than any other critic to articulating the poetic problem for American culture. In "The Poet," after complaining of those minor versifiers for whom "the argument is secondary, the finish of the verses is primary" (Poe?) , he declared: "It is not meters, but a meter-making argument that makes a poem." That he was thinking of American poetry—and not of "romantic" or "modern" poetry, or poetry in general—is borne out by his subsequent elaboration in the same essay of that brilliant (if slightly ambiguous) phrase. "We have yet had no genius in America, with tyrannous eye, which knew the value of our incomparable materials [catalogue follows] . . . . Yet America is a poem in our eyes . . . and it will not wait long for meters. If I have not found that excellent combination of gifts in my country-men which I seek, neither could I aid myself to fix the idea of the poet by reading now and then in Chalmers's collection of five centuries of English poets." Thus by 1844 at least one American poet was at least now and then face to face with his poetic problem (clearly identified as both metrical and national). And neither his American colleagues nor his British predecessors were of the slightest use to him. The American poet had arrived at the end of his tether; plainly, that tether would have to be broken.

"Meter-making argument": the greatness of the phrase lies in the way it enables us to bring into single focus the metrical and cultural problems of American poetry, considered as a whole, by joining in exactly the right relationship American nationality (as in the prompting "matter" of American life, or even the broadly political intention to create a specifically "American" poetry) and an answering technique. "America"—by which we must understand the representative situation of poetry in this country—is the "argument" (the substance and the intention) which "makes" the "meters" appropriate to it. Subsequently, of course, as Emerson failed to add, the meters make the actual American poems which slowly begin to create that national sensibility and culture out of which further meters may arise (in order that poets may continue to sharpen and articulate and stabilize a developing sense of community). There is an obvious difference between English and American poetry, of course; but it is probably sentimental to dwell overmuch on the natural and easy development of the English poetic tradition in comparison with the American poet's conspicuous discomfort and struggle and self-conscious intentions. We see these things clearly in our own poetry because it is so recent; because the English poetic tradition was initiated so long ago, we tend to overlook the likelihood that the creation by such poets as Chaucer and Spenser of the English heroic line was quite as difficult and self-conscious an affair as Whitman's liberation of American metric from foreign domination. The important difference is that the English poet, for all the difficulty of his technical problem, was at least in sensibility and culture one with a people who were scarcely able to remember a time when they had not been a people; the Americans had simultaneously to create their poetry and themselves.

With Emerson's insight that verse techniques are for the most part the effects of poetic motives, and not, as Poe thought, their direct and mechanical causes, together with his understanding (if only tentative and partial) that the relation between meter and culture could not possibly be quite the same as in England, but must equally depend on a national literary situation, American poetry was in position to make its first major breakthrough. And perhaps the most amazing quality of Emerson's insight is the fact that more than a century later it remains as true as it ever was, if not truer. The longer American poetry goes on, the more complicated it gets, the more difficult it is for the historian to articulate a coherent theoretical understanding of it, the more obvious it seems that Emerson's way of defining the American problem in poetry is not merely the best, but the only way of defining it. Let me drive that point home in the fewest possible words by restating Emerson's fundamental proposition in terms of the Aristotelian theory of form, and from the vantage point of today. The *efficient cause* of "our poetry" is the whole group of American poets, radical and conservative, taken *ensemble* (the gangs of kosmos) ; the *material cause* is the dilemma of American poetry, caught between the desire for cultural freedom (equality) and the necessities of language (including the incorporation of poetic tradition) ; the *formal cause* is the total and exceedingly various response to this challenge actually made by American poets; the *final cause* is the fact that an unmistakably American poetry now exists. Such an explanation, oriented toward the overriding question of metric (considered both poetically and nationalistically), seems to me to cover the ground—including, as it does, the poets, their problem, their responses to it (poems), and, finally, the entire field of American poetry—and to provide the only practical and realistic basis for a theory capable of eliciting an intelligible history of the art of poetry in this country.

IV

By a kind of historical logic—which would of course include the impact of Emerson's ideas on Whitman—the period of metrical discomfort was consummated by the first major explosion, or reflex,[6] of American poetry, *Leaves of Grass*. This explosion was followed by a long period of conservative reassertion. In their metric, Dickinson, Lanier, Moody, Robinson more nearly resemble Bryant, Lowell, Poe, and Emerson than Whitman. But they no longer sound so ill at ease, so awkward in their meters, even when the meters are most traditional. Emily Dickinson refurbished the old common measure so sensitively (and yet with a marvellous harshness) as to earn a place in several anthologies as the first "modern" American poet. Perhaps no other contemporary poet handles so wide a variety of traditional meters with such unobtrusive mastery as Frost, a feat all the more impressive in view of the fact that his theoretical understanding of the metrical problem of American poetry shows little or no advance over Bryant. (The poet "has been brought up by ear to choice of two metres, strict

---

[6] In *Patria Mia,* Pound calls Whitman a "reflex" and himself, by implication, another. "Whitman was not an artist, but a reflex, the first honest reflex, in an age of papier mache letters. . . . [But] his 'followers' go no further than to copy the defects of his style. They take no count of the issue that an honest reflex of 1912 will result in something utterly different from the reflex of 1865."

iambic and loose iambic.")⁷ Once the American poet knew freedom was available, and where to look for it, constraint was no longer constraining. The traditional meters were no longer exclusively "English," nor absolutely inescapable either, but a choice of discipline, though choice might still be affected by the *Zeitgeist*. In 1892, Robinson, as a very young poet, wrote an elegy on Whitman, nostalgically, and perhaps too passively, contrasting the freedom and energy of the poetic situation then and now. Robinson's poem hauntingly suggests at least a halfhearted inclination to follow in the Whitman tradition, together with a mild sense of frustration that the times should prevent his doing so. Although his elegy was in blank verse, he singled out for special praise Whitman's "piercing and eternal cadence." ("Too pure for us," he added.) That cadence was not to be "eternal" for him. In 1900, working on what he was always to consider his most "experimental" poem, *Captain Craig*, he was pleased to announce that it ended with a brass band and opened with a line that didn't scan. (It does, but only barely.) From that point, his meters (and his substance) became gradually less piercing. But at least he had a choice.

So the first period of conservative reassertion ran into the sand (as might have been predicted), to be followed, in the years around 1912, by a second major explosion. This time the force of the explosion was greater, because Pound had at his disposal not only his own power but Whitman's flowing through him; more efficiently directed toward a more stringently conceived poetic achievement, because Pound had learned much from Whitman's mistakes; more widespread, not only for these two reasons, but also because the poets affected by Pound were more disposed to be affected than Whitman's contemporaries were. Pound's "heave"

⁷ From "The Constant Symbol" by Robert Frost. Copyright 1946 by Robert Frost. Used by permission of Holt, Rinehart and Winston, Inc.

("to break the pentameter") was not, after all, the first heave but the second. On the other hand, the Poundian revolution also met a powerful resistance, of a sort quite different from what prevented Whitman's example being followed in the mid-nineteenth century. As Bryant's attitudes indicate, Whitman was rejected because he failed to conform to standards of metrical decorum assumed to be universally binding on all poets using the English language. By 1912, metrical regularity had become thoroughly introjected into American poetry and therefore a viable alternative native tradition. Embedded within the American sensibility, more or less purified of its noxious "English" implications, it proved a worthy opponent. Thus the succession of poets after Pound—Williams, Eliot, Crane, Ransom, Stevens, Shapiro, Lowell, Wilbur—show Pound's example first being imitated, then assimilated, then modified, then causing a considerable discomfort of its own. The poets began gradually to return to the time-honored norms of English metric, no longer buttressing themselves with "English" authority but taking heart from American examples (I suspect the chief ones were Robinson and Frost).

This was the second conservative reassertion. In thirty years American poetry returned from Pound, whose Imagist manifesto demanded composition according to the musical phrase (and to hell with the metronome), to Stevens, with his "Virgilian cadences, up down, up down," which sound almost "eighteenth century." As Stevens adds, not quite on our subject but nearly, "It is a war that never ends." It is the inevitable American civil war between meter like this (still quoting the conclusion of "Notes toward a Supreme Fiction"):

> How simply the fictive hero becomes the real;
> How gladly with proper words the soldier dies,
> If he must, or lives on the bread of faithful speech.

and meter like this (from another war poem, *The Pisan Cantos*) :

> Whitman liked oysters
> at least I think it was oysters
>   and the clouds have made a pseudo-Vesuvius
>   this side of Taishan
> Nenni, Nenni, who will have the succession?

Today nearly everyone seems to sense that we approach the end of a long period of conservative reassertion, judging from the way our lesser poets divide all too neatly into elegant formalists and pseudo-Whitmanians, while the better poets are torn and floundering. Perhaps another reflex is imminent.

V

Like all his countrymen provincially isolated from the centers of civilization, the American poet is periodically compelled to assume the defiant stance, to ward off too much—too much of the wrong kind of—influence. This is obvious in the poems and prefaces of Whitman. Yet these poems and prefaces insistently proclaim the American poet's need to involve himself with Europe. Few poets have regarded their forerunners, especially the greatest ones—all of them European—whom we might have expected him to fear, more generously or with a closer affection. Pound's devoted search for models through all cultures in all ages shows the same generosity, but also, come to think of it, the same animus as Whitman's smashing of English metric. A plethora of models (few of them English) is an excellent way of fending off the tradition whose closeness makes it dangerous. But the generosity of Whitman and Pound primarily stems from their greatness, which is their radicalism, the greatness which belongs only to those with sufficient daring (and ability) to be wholly themselves. Poe, who was a slave to convention, despised the best poets of the past. Poor Emerson found them short of his "ideal." ("Milton is too literary, and Homer too literal and historical.")

But Whitman, Pound, and, *a fortiori*, the more conservative poets are still more deeply implicated in European—specifically English—tradition than these merely cultural or emulative considerations imply. As usual in the arts, this more practical and realistic involvement arises from the nature of the medium, and is thus, once again, best seen in metric. The American poet may mutter to himself, "and as for those who deform thought with iambics," as Pound does in Canto 98 (the ghost of Whitman cheering him on), yet Pound no less than Whitman is frequently caught deforming thought with what look suspiciously like iambics: in *The Cantos,* e.g., "To have gathered from the air a live tradition/ or from a fine old eye the unconquered flame"; in *Leaves of Grass,* e.g., "As fill'd with friendship, love complete, the Elder Brother found,/ The Younger melts in fondness in his arms." It appears that even those who campaign most actively against iambics find it desirable to return to them from time to time, quite often because of a temporarily conciliatory mood toward the traditions they customarily oppose (as suggested by these quotations), but nearly always, ironically, for their most splendid effects (high emotion or the climax of an argument). In "Song of the Exposition," a poem beautifully blending Whitman's aspirations for a national American poetry with his passionate adoration of the European past ("not to repel or destroy so much as accept, fuse, rehabilitate"), a long passage of loose and falling rhythm, which is not only markedly (and I think deliberately) anti-English in technique but also includes the flat statement that "the stately rhythmus of Una and Oriana" is dead, surprisingly

ends with a sudden reversion to English regularity (iambic tetrameter) : "Blazon'd with Shakspere's purple page,/ And dirged
by Tennyson's sweet sad rhyme."

Thus even the radical poet is lured back time and again toward
the metrical practices he professes to despise (because he fears
them) by his ingrained respect for the English tradition. The
poems of Chaucer, Spenser, Shakespeare, Milton, Pope, Wordsworth—quite apart from their more obvious use as "cultural
heritage"—press upon the American poet realistically, as words,
sounds, measures. Despite his antagonism, poems sound that
way; or, more accurately, since we increasingly possess poems of
our own that do not sound quite that way, that is what poems may
sound like, or have sounded like. Many of them are simply too
great to be altogether ignored or rejected. Among the answers to
the question, "What do you hear Walt Whitman?" (in "Salut au
Monde"), we find the telltale evidence (and indeed the entire
theory of American poetry) : "I hear continual echoes from the
Thames." Perhaps that is one reason why Eliot in *The Waste
Land* admonishes that "sweet" river to "run softly" till he ends
his song.

It goes without saying that the American poet can never abandon the English language either, nor radically modify it, except as
the speech of his own people may in the course of centuries modify
it. But the more restless American poets are always trying to out-
run natural development. I have already alluded to the fact that
Whitman's fondness for falling rhythm is an obviously anti-
British gesture. "Out of the cradle endlessly rocking,/ Out of
the mocking-bird's throat, the musical shuttle . . . . " Out of
that musical shuttle—and often with a little mockery—American
poetry has recurrently tried to rock. Even Longfellow had given
us, eight years before the first edition of *Leaves of Grass,* such an
imperishable line as: "This is the forest primeval. The murmur-

ing pines and the hemlocks" (for which intransigence trochee-loving Poe promptly rapped his knuckles, in the revised version of "The Rationale of Verse"). Significantly, we hear of his temporarily putting aside falling rhythm in the midst of composition, to try how *Evangeline* might sound in iambic pentameter couplets, but quickly returning to his dactyls. (Even more significantly, perhaps, the passage in question was referred to by Longfellow as "the song of the mocking-bird"; Longfellow's final version sounds suspiciously like a crude sketch of "Out of the Cradle.") Neither Whitman, Pound, nor Eliot, of course, would ever commit the error of writing an entire poem in a meter so awkward and unnatural. But used sparingly, flexibly, and with genuine delicacy—as Whitman so often uses it—falling rhythm is undeniably one of the most rewarding metrical maneuvers for the American poet; simply because it strikes the ear (even the American ear) as unusual, it immediately frees him from the nervous apprehension of being overwhelmed by English lilt, and leads to his dearly beloved dissonance and freedom from constraint. American metric is never so enticing as when a basically rising rhythm is overlaid with heavily falling cadences and loaded with dactylic and trochaic words. All considerations of "rising" and "falling" fade from the mind, as the ear responds to a rhythm absolutely *sui generis;* for example, in the opening lines of *The Cantos:*

> And then went down to the ship,
> Set keel to breakers, forth on the godly sea, and
> We set up mast and sail on that swart ship,
> Bore sheep aboard her, and our bodies also
> Heavy with weeping, and winds from sternward
> Bore us out onward with bellying canvas,
> Circe's this craft, the trim-coifed goddess.

Indeed the craft is Circean, for the passage begins regularly enough and only gradually transforms itself into another movement. The same American music is everywhere in Eliot:

> Where is there an end of it, the soundless wailing,
> The silent withering of autumn flowers
> Dropping their petals and remaining motionless;
> Where is there an end to the drifting wreckage,
> The prayer of the bone on the beach, the unprayable
> Prayer at the calamitous annunciation?

(Paradoxically, this passage from "The Dry Salvages" also loosely imitates the age-old sestina.)

The greatest metrical moments of American poetry customarily arise from this tension between the American poet's desire respectfully to wrench the English tradition out of its course and the disinclination of the English tradition, or the English language, to be too rudely forced. Falling rhythm fails except as offset or overlay of a generally rising rhythm. Introduction of too many unstressed syllables in rising rhythm does not really eliminate iambic meter but leads to prose. So, beyond a certain point, does too reckless a mixture of rising and falling feet. Nor can the American poet write entirely in spondees, though sometimes it sounds as if he were trying to. A similar tension manifests itself with respect to line length. The standard length for serious poetry in English is five feet, as any collection quickly confirms. But taken as a whole, American poets give a queer impression of being exceedingly anxious to run to either extreme in order to avoid what obviously seems to them an oppressive (or prescriptive) norm. The unduly short line is a common American phenomenon as early as Emerson and Thoreau; it recurs in Dickinson and in Imagism; conversely, the inordinately long line is a common

American phenomenon as early as Bryant and Poe and Long-fellow, and is, of course, the hallmark of most of Whitman and Pound, and much of Eliot. Yet a surprising number of fine American poems are five-stress, and in times of conservative reassertion, pentameter easily and naturally re-establishes itself as the accepted length (Robinson, Stevens). Tetrameter and hexameter lines tend to break in the middle. Trimeters are too gnomic, fourteeners too walloping, for most poetic purposes.

Obviously there are a great number of other prosodic factors at work, constraining and annoying and stimulating the American poet, but even these brief remarks may suggest in what practical sense we are entitled to say that the American poet may never entirely escape his metrical past, nor ever rest entirely easy in it, though he tends to rest *easier* as he gradually assimilates it to his own needs and purposes. The American poet has not been able to resolve his dilemma, and our frequent wish that he might—that he once and for all achieve a purely "American" solution of poetic problems—is a foolish chauvinistic wish. If it is impossible for our poets to innovate as freely as some of them would like, it is equally impossible for them to continue humming the same old monotone (as too many British poets do). If it is a "meter-making argument" we want—that is, a literary situation incessantly pressing toward the improbable resolutions of rhythm and harmony and form, out of the most intractable materials—then we are lucky enough. A "meter-making argument" is exactly what the American poet has as his birthright, because that is what America, poetically speaking, most fundamentally is. Possibly that is what Whitman meant when, following Emerson, he referred to the United States as essentially the greatest poem. At the end of his career, he said it more plainly: "I consider 'Leaves of Grass' and its theory experimental—as, in the deepest sense, I consider our American republic itself to be, with its theory." But experiment—in poetry as in politics—is valuable only insofar as it leads to practicable and pluralistic actualities—not *modus* but *modi vivendi*—and under the constant pressure of change. This is the real achievement of American poetry: that the desperate experiments of our poets, tormented by a deep-seated conflict of loyalty between culture and medium, have in the course of time eventuated in a specifically American tradition, which is neither the "English way" nor its opposite, but both, in provocative antithesis, and alternation, and occasionally, on halcyon days, in strange and delightful harmony; and yet a harmony continuously on the verge of dissolution and re-articulation, so that even as we try to fix its essence in a formula, American poetry is almost certainly undergoing a further metamorphosis.

Some
Varieties of
Inspiration

G. Ferris Cronkhite

To use the word "inspiration" in connection with American poetry may evoke the association of virtuous "uplift" exerted on the reader of such poetry. But what I refer to by the term "inspiration," in its literary application, is a psychological experience in which a writer, without the conscious operation of his will, finds ideas, images, and relationships flooding into his mind. Perhaps a main theme or the essential shape of a contemplated work is given to him in one of these moments. All this centers on matters that deeply concern the writer, but it is a very different process from his thinking his way through the problems of composition. It may, in fact, occur when such effort has reached an impasse and been suspended. Then, strangely and unforseeably, a new and convincing way out of the difficulty may present itself, or perhaps an entirely new conception replaces the earlier muddle. In this vision of new possibilities, parts of the work may even seem to dictate themselves. Incoherence and groping are replaced by order and conviction. What is envisioned seems peculiarly "right." In intensity the experience may range from moments akin to the mystic's ecstasy down to a gentle surprise, and in literary outcome it may shade from the conception of a major work down to the happy turning of a few crucial lines. The experience is strangely exciting and compels the writer eventually, if not immediately, to literary composition. This is the psychological phenomenon which occurred to a number of American poets in the nineteenth and twentieth centuries. Their divergent interpretations of it and some of its effects upon their poetic manner constitute my subject.

Drawing first on Emerson's testimony, I want to distinguish two different levels of inspiration (which will show up again in some of the later poets), and I also want to point out that Emerson regarded the subjective qualities of inspiration as symptoms of its divine source. Then, drawing on both Emerson and Whitman, I wish to show how the subject matter conveyed by inspiration affected their poetic stance. Next, I will outline how belief in the divine source of inspiration faded, even among "inspired" poets like Holmes and Stedman, until in the twentieth century Hart Crane was convinced that inspiration came in part from his unconscious.

Inspiration may take two main forms—"dictation" and "illumination"—and both are illustrated in Emerson's work. The first is shown in the way a short poem, which Emerson came to regard as among his best, took shape so effortlessly that he commented in his *Journal* for January 1852:

> I find one state of mind does not remember or conceive of another state. Thus I have written within a twelvemonth verses ("Days") which I do not remember the composition or correction of, and

could not write the like to-day, and have only, for proof of their being mine, various external evidences, as the MS. in which I find them, and the circumstance that I have sent copies of them to friends . . . .

This little poem of eleven lines presents a single, sharply imaged conception: the poet's failure to seize upon the richest possibilities that the days offer him and his taking instead some lesser gifts. However quickly and effortlessly this conception may have taken on poetic form sometime in 1851, elements of it had occupied Emerson's thought before, as attested to by a letter in 1840 to Margaret Fuller (in which he pictured the days as gods muffled in disguises) and again by an 1847 entry in his *Journals:* "if we do not use the gifts they bring, they carry them as silently away."

In contrast to the very specific content of "dictation" is a second pattern of inspiration, which may be called "illumination." In a famous prose passage, strikingly parallel to Wordsworth's recorded expression in "Tintern Abbey" of a "sense sublime of something far more deeply interfused," Emerson writes, in "Nature," of those moments when he enjoys a "perfect exhilaration" and becomes "glad to the brink of fear." In the woods,

> Standing on the bare ground,—my head bathed by the blithe air, and uplifted into infinite space,—all mean egotism vanishes. I become a transparent eyeball; I am nothing; I see all; the currents of the Universal Being circulate through me; I am part or parcel of God.

Rather than producing such immediate or explicit literary expression as does "dictation," this second form of inspiration supplies Emerson with what Wordsworth would call "the master light" of all his seeing—a sense of spiritual direction and of an ultimately happy destiny.

Three subjective qualities of Emerson's inspirational experience are worth enumerating, since they represent so well those felt by any "inspired" writer: (1) inspiration is involuntary and peremptory; (2) it imparts confidence and a conviction of the "rightness" of whatever it reveals; and (3) it compels one to give expression to his insight.

Emerson interprets these qualities in the light of assumptions derived from the surrounding climate of opinion, from literary and religious tradition, or from his own conceptions of Over-Soul, the nature of the mind, and poetry. The imagery in which he records his sensations and the language in which he reflects upon them show that for him they indicate a lofty and super-human source for the whole experience.

In "Instinct and Inspiration" Emerson testifies to the involuntary and peremptory nature of inspiration: "It is not in our will. That is the quality of it that it commands, and is not commanded. And rarely, and suddenly, and without desert, we are let into the serene upper air." The poet, he says, "works to an end above his will, and by means, too, which are out of his will . . . . The muse may be defined, *Supervoluntary ends effected by supervoluntary means.*" Further reflection on the strange involuntariness of the experience led Emerson to comment in "Inspiration" that

all poets have signalized their consciousness of rare moments when they were superior to themselves,—when a light, a freedom, a power came to them, which lifted them to performances far better than they could reach at other times.

This aiding power is more explicitly seen in "The Divinity School Address" as divine in origin, and thus as ample authentication for whatever message inspiration carries:

The divine bards are the friends of my virtue, of my intellect, of my strength. They admonish me that the gleams which flash across my mind are not mine, but God's; that they had the like, and were not disobedient to the heavenly vision.

A second characteristic of inspiration, the feeling of confidence which springs from the experience itself and the sense of the absolute rightness of what it reveals, is recorded by Emerson in "The Over-Soul" when he speaks of those moments of moral and spiritual insight which are the sources of our faith: "Yet there is a depth in those brief moments which constrains us to ascribe more reality to them than to all other experiences." Or again, referring to "the inspiration which uttered itself in Hamlet and Lear," he observes, "from that inspiration the man comes back with a changed tone. He does not talk with men with an eye to their opinion. He tries them." Persons thus inspired are not concerned with opinions; they speak not as spectators but *"from within,* or from experience, as parties and possessors of the fact." Indeed, Emerson is so sure that all revelations are discoveries or recognitions of some truth in the universal order that it does not occur to him to make a possible distinction between the euphoric confidence which arises as the immediate psychic tone of the experience and the intellectual confidence which may arise from conscious retrospective appraisal of what is revealed. He is sure, however, that literary men do not attain such insights by mere will or simply through having sensitive faculties. "They are poets by the free course which they allow to the informing soul." For Emerson the ultimate source of inspiration is divine energy.

The third subjective characteristic of inspiration—the way it compels one to give expression to his insight—is noted by Emerson in "The Poet." Whether artist, orator, composer, or poet, each man visited by inspiration

hears a voice, he sees a beckoning. Then he is apprised, with wonder, what herds of daemons hem him in. He can no more rest; he
says, with the old painter, "By God it is in me and must go forth
of me."

The same compulsion is felt too by those whose insights are more
directly moral and spiritual:

It is very certain that it is the effect of conversation with the
beauty of the soul, to beget a desire and need to impart to others
the same knowledge and love. If utterance is denied, the thought
lies like a burden on the man. Always the seer is a sayer.

In Emerson's view the inspired person feels not just a psychological urge to impart the burdening thought but a conscious obligation to do so. Since he knows his inspiration comes from the
divine mind and conveys an undeniable truth, he feels he must
express it, even though his doing so may awaken hostility in his
audience. In "Inspiration" Emerson observes, "When the spirit
chooses you for its scribe to publish some commandment, it makes
you odious to men, and men odious to you, and you shall accept
that loathsomeness with joy. The moth must fly to the lamp, and
you must solve those questions though you die."

Emerson based the foregoing interpretations on the subjective
feelings that accompany inspiration. Further interpretations both
he and Whitman drew from the subject matter which inspiration
communicates. It seems legitimate to disregard chronology in this
instance and examine both men together, since Whitman so clearly
followed the direction Emerson established. But first let me
point out that Whitman as well as Emerson seems to have experienced two forms of inspiration.

His most notable record of inspiration is, no doubt, that contained in the fifth section of *Song of Myself:*

> Swiftly arose and spread around me the peace and knowledge
>   that pass all the argument of the earth,
> And I know that the hand of God is the promise of my own,
> And I know that the spirit of God is the brother of my own,
> And that all the men ever born are also my brothers, and the
>   women my sisters and lovers,
> And that a kelson of the creation is love,
> And limitless are leaves stiff or drooping in the fields,
> And brown ants in the little wells beneath them,
> And mossy scabs of the worm fence, heap'd stones, elder,
>   mullein and poke-weed.

In its all-absorbing intensity the total experience parallels Emerson's feeling of becoming a "transparent eyeball" and shows the same near-mystical "illumination."

A second, and less overwhelming, kind of inspiration seems to be recorded in "The Mystic Trumpeter." The phrase "some wild trumpeter . . . Hovering unseen in air" may possibly refer to nothing more than the faint noises of the night wind, but, whatever the reference, the experience reveals the salient characteristics of "dictation":

> That now ecstatic ghost, close to me bending, thy cornet
>   echoing, pealing,
> Gives out to no one's ears but mine, but freely gives to mine,
> That I may thee translate.

Several scenes then flood in upon him, pageants of the feudal world and "terrible tableaus" of war and violence, but also a sense of love, "the enclosing theme of all." The self and the conscious will disappear, just as in Emerson's rapture, swallowed up in the vision: "O trumpeter, methinks I am myself the instrument thou playest,/ Thou melt'st my heart, my brain—thou movest, drawest, changest them at will." Finally, with an invocation to the mystic trumpeter to "Rouse up my slow belief, give me some vision of the future," Whitman rounds off the poem with an exultant ode to joy, a glimpse of time to come, in which "A reborn race appears . . . Women and men in wisdom innocence and health."

Whitman's visions were similar to Emerson's not only in the subjective states which accompanied them but in their very substance. In the *Song of Myself* passage, Whitman has an intuitive view of the cosmic order; he is assured of his spirit's relation to God ("the brother of my own"), of his own relation to other men and women, and of his relation to nature; he becomes aware of a pervasive moral force ("a kelson of the creation is love"). Though Whitman's ideas are here more comprehensive and more explicit than Emerson's finding that "the currents of Universal Being circulate" through him and that he is "part or parcel of God," they have the same spiritual focus. Both "The Mystic Trumpeter" and "Days" are essentially about man's use of the possibilities which the universe offers him. The substance conveyed, then, by the inspired moments of both men is characteristically a vision of a moral and spiritual cosmos under a benevolent God. This subject matter in itself undoubtedly reinforces the belief which each poet draws from his subjective feelings that inspiration emanates from a divine source.

Taken as a whole, the work of both Emerson and Whitman constitutes, in its author's eyes, a gospel—not a set of doctrines to be preserved, but a set of convictions providing a basis for action. Always the tone is one of certainty and the motive is to acquaint others with the gospel—which is not so much disclosed as proclaimed. It is when one sees how the corpus of Emerson's and Whitman's work functions as gospel that the crucial role of inspiration, particularly in the form of illumination, becomes clear. Gospel may be drawn, of course, from various sources—historical fact, observation, intuition, reading, meditation—but if it is to become more than just a body of personal beliefs, if it is to impel one to preach it abroad as the Word, then it requires some special authentication. For Emerson this is supplied by those moments of illumination which make him feel he is "part or parcel of God." For Whitman, the authentication comes from occasions such as he testifies to in "The Mystic Trumpeter" and *Song of Myself,* when he experiences an unwilled inrush of ideas, impressions and—most importantly—a feeling of assurance that there *is* a plan, that there *is* a harmony, that man's destiny may open into a wondrous future.

Inspiration thus serves both to authenticate the "gospels" of Emerson and Whitman and to turn each poet into a seer or prophet. If the prophetic tones carry over into other works than those which explicitly record inspiration, it is not necessary to postulate that each poem is prompted by inspiration. One does not need to authenticate his gospel afresh each time he preaches a sermon out of it. Though the timbre of his poetic voice may be peculiarly his own, he feels he is not speaking solely for himself. Nor is he merely proclaiming the traditional beliefs of a congregation or the public philosophy of a community. He has, he feels, been granted special insights into the workings of the soul, the spiritual relation of man to other men or to God, or the moral meaning of the universe itself. For example, Emerson announces, in his "Ode Inscribed to W. H. Channing," "Law for man, and law for thing"; or Whitman sings, in "When Lilacs Last in the Dooryard Bloom'd," his praise to death, the "strong deliveress." What most characterizes their poetic address as essentially hierophantic, however, is their speaking for or interpreting God—or their assuming the voice of some elemental or supernatural force. Emerson, for instance, speaks in the guise of Nature, the Sphinx, Over-Soul, Brahma, or Earth. Whitman speaks as the bringer of a new courage, dropping "in the earth the germs of a greater religion," exhorting others to receive his lesson of the spiritual oneness of mankind, his assurance that the soul will find God its Elder Brother and melt "in fondness in his arms." In "Chanting the Square Deific" he speaks in turn as the Father, Christ, Satan, or Santa Spirita. In a number of poems he takes on another larger-than-life role: he becomes the collective consciousness, projecting himself omnisciently into all sorts and conditions of men ("I am the man, I suffer'd, I was there"). He is "Walt Whitman, a kosmos."

This foregoing view, that the poet functions under inspiration, commanded great prestige in the first half of the nineteenth century. It became the ideal pattern for a poet to follow—if he could. This does not mean all poets did so: Lowell certainly saw himself much more as a "maker" than as one of the "possessed"; so too, probably, did Longfellow. Poe was, of course, very self-consciously the craftsman, claiming in "The Philosophy of Composition" an exaggeratedly calculative method. Let us, however, put aside the "makers" and confine our attention to certain poets of the next eighty years who experienced inspiration in some form or other and who responded to it in a variety of ways, which depended ultimately upon differences in temperament, training, or intellectual climate.

Oliver Wendell Holmes—who began writing poetry at about the same time that Emerson did and shared much the same New England intellectual climate—had a mind much more inclined to exactitude and detail than Emerson's and was trained for medicine rather than the ministry. His description of inspiration in

The Autocrat of the Breakfast Table (1857) shows a characteristic combination of impressionistic physiological detail and traditional literary allusion:

> A lyric conception—my friend, the Poet, said—hits me like a bul-
> let in the forehead. I have often had the blood drop from my
> cheeks when it struck, and felt that I turned as white as death.
> Then comes a creeping as of centipedes running down the spine,
> —then a gasp and a great jump of the heart,—then a sudden
> flush and a beating in the vessels of the head,—then a long sigh,
> —and the poem is written . . . . The soul of it is born in an
> instant in the poet's soul . . . . It is enough to stun and scare
> anybody, to have a hot thought come crashing into his brain,
> and ploughing up those parallel ruts where the wagon trains of
> common ideas were jogging along in their regular sequences of
> association. No wonder the ancients made the poetical impulse
> wholly external. . . . Goddess,—Muse,—divine afflatus,—some-
> thing outside always.

Though his account of inspiration in *Mechanism in Thought and
Morals* (1870) points out, just as Emerson's did, the involuntary
nature of the experience ("a creating and informing spirit which
is with us, and not of us") and its way of impelling one to expression ("it frames our sentences; it lends a sudden gleam of
sense or eloquence to the dullest of us all"), Holmes does not feel
Emerson's awe in the face of the experience. Rather than being
swallowed up in it to the point where he loses a sense of self and
becomes "part or parcel of God," he is characteristically a little
detached from it and almost in control of it. During the composition of "The Chambered Nautilus," though writing under inspiration, he is as much aware of method as of content, mention-
ing in a letter

the highest state of mental exaltation and the most crystalline clairvoyance, as it seemed to me, that had ever been granted to me—I mean that lucid vision of one's thought, and of all forms of expression which will be at once precise and musical, which is the poet's special gift, however large or small in amount or value.

Although Holmes clearly felt "dictation" ("the poet always recognizes a dictation *ab extra;* and we hardly think it a figure of speech when we talk of his inspiration"), apparently he did not feel "illumination." Perhaps if his experience had been closer to those nearly mystical ones of Emerson and Whitman, he too might have felt it proceeded from a divine or spiritual source. But Holmes was by temperament and training much more akin to the urbane and rational neo-classicist than to the romantic, and the fact that he pays even as much attention as he does to "dictation" attests to the prestige in his literary milieu of the doctrine of inspiration. As it is, when he uses the term "divine afflatus" in the passage from *The Autocrat,* he is not stating a personal conviction but merely citing literary tradition. Without explicitly denying the possibility of divine origin, he gravitates to the conclusion that, though inspiration may be a mystery, it is not a *divine* mystery. In *Mechanism in Thought and Morals* he speculates:

> After all, the mystery of unconscious mental action is exemplified, as I have said, in every act of mental association. What happens when one idea brings up another? Some internal movement, of which we are wholly unconscious, and which we only know by its effect. What is this action, which . . . in men of wit and fancy, connects remote ideas by partial resemblances; in men of imagination, by the vital identity which underlies phenomenal diversity; in the man of science, groups the objects of thought in sequences of maximum resemblance? Not one of them can answer. There is a Delphi and a Pythoness in every human breast.

Emerson too implies a Pythoness in every human breast (refer-ring in "The Over-Soul" to "the spirit of prophecy which is in-nate in every man"), but Emerson is more sure of the ultimate source of her pronouncements. The scholar, the poet, or the ora-tor, Emerson says in "The American Scholar," who follows his spontaneous thoughts and dives deep "into his privatest, secretest presentiment" finds there what is universally true—because he has touched the pervasive substratum of Over-Soul. But, since Holmes regards the nature of the depths within as simply a psy-chological mystery, susceptibility to this "internal movement" does not mean that a poet has tuned in on Over-Soul or that he may assume a prophetic stance and speak for God. He speaks only for himself. Whereas Emerson's commitment to a divine source for inspiration placed him in the position, apparently, of respecting any authentic inspiration, Holmes felt no such sweep-ing respect for inspired utterances—even his own. His skepticism has not only a theoretical basis but also a practical one. As a pa-tient reader of unsolicited manuscripts, Holmes exclaims in " 'Exotics' " about the delusion of writers that "their vascular and nervous excitement is the index of their power."

> What a pity that the passion and the fever and the delirium are
> not a measure of the excellence of the poetic trance! It is mourn-
> ful to think how many rhymes have been written in tears of ec-
> stasy and self-admiration, which have been read with the smile of
> pity or the sneer of contempt.

His appraisal of the poetic result of the "trance" seems based at least as much on its shaping as on its content. In his own poetic practice he rarely commits himself to the serious personal lyric, such as "The Chambered Nautilus" or "Musa"; the bulk of his work is occasional or light verse, always carefully, sometimes exquisitely, turned. Such a manner is appropriate: if even an inspired poem originates simply as a mystery of psychology and instead of a gospel offers only traditional truths, it may at least command respect by its artistry.

Emerson and Whitman, on the other hand, with their reverence for the vision, feared that its power might be impaired by too careful consideration to formal or stylistic matters. Whitman declares in his Preface to the 1855 *Leaves of Grass,* "What I tell I tell for precisely what it is. . . . What I experience or portray shall go from my composition without a shred of my composition." In a similar vein Emerson cautions, in "Natural History of Intellect," that "Inspiration is coy and capricious; . . . and in order to win infallible verdicts from the inner mind, we must indulge and humor it in every way, and not too exactly task and harness it." In "The Poet" he goes further, asserting that "the poet knows that he speaks adequately then only when he speaks somewhat wildly, . . . not with the intellect used as an organ, but with the intellect released from all service and suffered to take its direction from its celestial life." Both the stylistic modes of Emerson and Whitman and their theory of "organic form" are, of course, largely outgrowths of their having experienced "illumination" and their consciousness of possessing a "gospel."

Indeed, Emerson's remark that "nothing great or lasting can be done except by inspiration, by leaning on the secret augury" might be taken as indicating the high respect in which inspiration was held not just by poets but also by readers and men of action in the first half of the nineteenth century. One reason for this, no doubt, was that inspiration had for so long been associated with the doctrine of the divine inspiration of the Scriptures, with an image of the Hebrew poets and prophets of the Old Testament and with a sense of the religious zeal of the New Testament. This association persisted, of course, even after mid-century, but increasingly in the latter half of the century inspiration was accorded a more secular interpretation—one more in line with Holmes's view that mysterious, unconscious action occurs in even the ordinary processes of the mind. It was not something exhibited only on occasions of high solemnity or expressed chiefly in literature. The man of science, too, might have sudden intuitions and insights. The reasons for this shift are complex, and I shall only point out that underlying it was the general extension of scientific thought or investigation into areas in which "explanations" had traditionally been religious ones. In addition to the pervasive effect of evolutionary thought, the Higher Criticism spread specific doubt that the Scriptures were the literally inspired word of God. Among the laity generally there was a lessening of belief that a personal God intervened directly in human matters. There was, concurrently, a growing interest in philosophic and scientific study of the mind and its actions—ranging from Eduard von Hartmann's *Philosophy of the Unconscious* in 1868 to William James's *Principles of Psychology* in 1890 and "The Will to Believe" in 1896. An individual writer's own discoveries and experience in religious, philosophical, and psychological matters were carried along like surface currents on the surge of this ground swell.

One poet-critic reluctantly borne along on this increasingly secular drift was Edmund Clarence Stedman, whose *Nature and Elements of Poetry* was given as a series of lectures in 1891. Stedman was clearly predisposed to believe that inspiration is the central force in poetry. The poet "utters, reveals, and interprets what he sees with that inner vision, that second sight, the prophetic gift of certain personages . . . through which the poet is thought to be inspired." Looking back, in 1892, on his earlier experience, he declares in a letter, "I rarely wrote a poem that did not first write me, and compel me to give it out." His remark reveals two of the familiar subjective qualities of inspiration—its involuntary nature and its compulsion to utterance. To the third subjective characteristic of inspiration, however—that instantaneous conviction of its "rightness," its truth—Stedman gives no firsthand testimony. He merely takes the position of an observer, remarking that the insight "is the inward light of the Quaker, the *a priori* guess of the scientist, the prophetic vision of the poet, the mystic, the seer. If it be direct vision, it should be incontrovertible. In occult tradition the higher angels, types of absolute spirit, were thought to know all things by this pure illumination." The reasons that the "prophetic vision" and the "pure illumination" did not visit Stedman may lie partly in his temperament and partly in his milieu. The urbane and practical disposition of the head of a brokerage house in Wall Street was perhaps not the sort that fosters "illuminations." Nor was he a man of strong religious instinct, which might have increased his sensitivity to such impulses; he remarks in a letter, "I believe in God, in a quiet way." His surrounding intellectual climate seemed to him not to nourish strong religious belief, and he specifically felt that the time of the prophetic bard had passed. "We cannot have, we do not need, another Ezekiel, another Dante or Milton. Hugo, the last Vates, was the most self-conscious, and his own deity."

Not experiencing, then, that "illumination" which impels some poets to take the stance of a prophet with a new gospel, Stedman became, in effect, a custodian of certain traditional literary values and attitudes which he characterized as "Ideality." Poetry, he believed, presents an idealized view of things—things "as they are or may be at their best," emotions which are noble or romantic, material that is lifted above the commonplace and shaped to express Truth and Beauty. Though he held these values sincerely, he did not hold them with the zeal one might show for "gospel"— in large part, no doubt, because they were an inheritance and not his own discovery. In strong contrast to Emerson's or Whitman's ringing declarations on human destiny or cosmic law, Stedman's mood is cautiously "literary." Rarely in his poetry, and only softly, is Stedman a spokesman of personal ideas or feelings. Of his collected poems, roughly a third are occasional or laudatory verse in which he voices the prevailing sentiment on such national subjects as Gettysburg or Lincoln, pays tribute to such literary respectables as Hawthorne, Whittier, or Bryant, or commemorates such events as Yale commencements and reunions.

Poetic inspiration was one of the literary traditions Stedman most revered, though his explanation of it seems prompted in part by a certain lack of self-confidence and a wish to find some overarching sanction for what his inspiration (i.e., "dictation") impelled him to say. Ironically, the more he pursued his search, the more his reading in philosophy and psychology led him away from any assurance that the poetic impulse was divine. Eventually he was left to face the strong possibility that this force may be human in origin and may in fact depend upon one's individual nature. He cited Eduard von Hartmann, for instance, who, in his *Philosophy of the Unconscious* (1868), classified the creative insight as "the activity and efflux of the Intellect freed from the domination of the Conscious Will." When, in an article on "genius" in the *New Princeton Review* in 1886, Stedman says, "the intuitionists, if not the inspirationists, are right," he admits a distinction which virtually means capitulation, since the intuitionist conceives of creative insight (i.e., what is "seen," plus the impulse to express it) as a personal force from within, rather than a suprapersonal or divine force from without. Stedman again acknowledged the intuitionist view in 1892 when, defending the existence of genius, he incorporated into *The Nature and Elements of Poetry* a statement from F. W. H. Myers' recent remarks on "Subliminal Consciousness" (a concept which corresponds roughly to what we now call the "unconscious") : "Perhaps we seldom give the name of genius to any piece of work into which some uprush of subliminal faculty has not entered."

Still, Stedman never wholeheartedly accepted the intuitionist point of view. For one reason, it was, particularly in the form of "subliminal consciousness" which Myers championed, incompatible with his own presuppositions about the workings of the poetic impulse and about poetry as ideality. Though he seemed to agree with Hartmann that creative insight is the "spontaneous, involuntary force of the untrammelled soul," the "soul" which Stedman had in mind was, of course, Victorian "soul"—a complex of elevated conceptions and refined emotions. Consequently he distrusted the unselective nature of "uprushes" from murky subliminal or subconscious depths. They may not tend toward Ideality at all, and rather than making for universal Beauty and Truth, they may be capricious, irrational, and even improper. Moreover, because the intuitionist view interprets the creative impulse as simply a personal force, emanating solely from the artist's "self," it deprives the poet of a higher authority for what he says—whether in the form of suprapersonal inspiration from without or some element of the divine dwelling within, such as soul or Over-Soul. For example, Myers' assertion that it is the "fuller self-revelation" of the genius' mind which in part distinguishes its work from that of ordinary minds, may imply that the poet's "vision" is *only* self-revelation, and has behind it only the poet's personal authority. This makes the poet individually responsible for both the quality of his verse *and* the quality of his vision. Psychically, Stedman was not braced to be this much on his own. Failing to establish a divine or absolute sanction for poetry, he contented himself with what was at least a suprapersonal sanction and consequently spoke as a custodian of literary tradition, not in prophetic tones, of course, but occasionally in pontifical ones.

As Stedman's intellectual maneuverings show, by the end of the nineteenth century the theory of poetic inspiration came into conflict with new knowledge and new beliefs. In the early twentieth century, George Edward Woodberry attempted a theory which would satisfy two aims: to explain, in acceptably "modern" terms, how inspiration functions, and, at the same time, to establish some higher authority for the poet's insights. More willing than Stedman to envisage inspiration as proceeding from a psychic rather than a spiritual source, Woodberry nevertheless sought to enlarge its authority beyond that of the individual. In a series of eight lectures, published in 1910 as *The Inspiration of Poetry*, Woodberry describes "poetic madness" as "no more than the common emotional experience of men in a form of higher intensity." In this state a man is

> an instrument, a voice, not personal but oracular . . . . Do we not all have such moments, so charged with emotion that we seem taken out of ourselves, . . . moments when new truths come with a physical flash on the eye, when perceptions of beauty illuminate the soul with sudden and ample glory, when motions of love expand the spirit and pour it abroad . . . ?

But Woodberry is careful to establish the pedigree and respectability of this emotional force. He speculates that emotion may have had a significant role in man's evolution, "that the emergence of man from the brute-stage of life was accompanied by an immense outburst and increase of emotional power. . . . that such emotion was a main condition of the gradual advent of intellectual life." This was not raw and unqualified emotion but, indeed, took on value as it "passed into the intellect." The "wasteful and destructive" Dionysiac elements are avoided so that the "creative emotion" issues "in harmonies of the mind."

But the question remains, do all the forms of this "madness" proceed "from one infinite power that prompts them"? Here, reflecting contemporary skepticism, he treads circumspectly:

> the source of inspiration is no more known than the source of the other moods by which our being is sustained. It belongs to our sense of the infinite in which man feels he vaguely shares, that the inspiration is inexhaustible, and continually puts forth a new form.

Even when Woodberry is content, as here, to by-pass the question of inspiration's divine source, he is wary of letting its authority rest simply on the individual. After assuring his hearers that "inspiration resides in the infinite, in emotion," he ends his lecture series by picturing how, when the light begins to die off after any particular outburst of genius, "then emotion, which is of the infinite, again supervenes, still brooding in itself some new world, some new gospel of gladder tidings of greater joy." Though he ignores any specifically religious source for inspiration, Woodberry instinctively, if illogically, pictures inspiration (i.e., emotion) as a force larger than any single individual. His view of emotion, "brooding in itself" (with the poet hardly in sight) suggests, if not an Over-Soul, at least an Over-Psyche. He seems to be trying to translate the subjective feeling—that "something greater than the man speaks through the man, and there is a virtue in his works that his own unaided power never placed there" —into some more generally current concept which will convey the awe of the experience. In *The Inspiration of Poetry* the concept is "the infinite." In his 1913 lecture on "Aesthetic Criticism" it is "our immortal part," the soul, which "transcends nature, and reconstitutes the world in the image of its own finer vision and deeper wisdom, realizing ideality in its own consciousness."

"The infinite," "the soul," "ideality"—these are the concepts on which he falls back. Some of them are the same "sanctions" which Stedman had sought to attach to poetry in 1890. Already hazy in Stedman's day, their meaning—and to some extent even their evocative power—had been left even more indefinite and uncertain in the intervening twenty years by the general drift away from traditional religious belief and, more particularly, by certain lines of philosophical and psychological inquiry. For example, though William James, in *Principles of Psychology* (1890), is willing to posit such a thing as "soul," its meaning becomes simply "the *ground of possibility of thought*"—hardly a concept which can be invoked as a sanction for a particular pattern of feelings and values in a poem. Another favorite sanction, invoked by Emerson and a long succession of other poets, was "Truth." Though "Truth" was not the private preserve of the inspired poet, still it constituted the chief aim of Emersonian insight or revelation. Such "Truth" was generally conceived as it would be by philosophical idealists, not just as an attribute of statements or propositions but as an ultimate reality, eternal and unchanging. In "Pragmatism's Conception of Truth," however, James denies to truth this absolute quality: "It is useful because it is true or it is true because it is useful," James declared. "Both these phrases mean exactly the same thing." This line of attack against a doctrine of absolutes was continued, of course, by John Dewey in the twentieth century.

At the same time that these abstract, spiritual sanctions were losing status, the rising study of psychology directed more and more attention to the inner mental state of the individual. William James's *Principles of Psychology,* with its sensitive probing of such matters as "the stream of thought," may be cited as typical of the exploration being made near the end of the nineteenth century. Freud's work was introduced into the United States by his five lectures at Clark University in 1909, but it was not until the 1920's that his concepts of the unconscious, the ego, and the superego began to be widespread. Further emphasis was given to the depths within the individual by the theories of Carl Jung, which expanded the concept of the unconscious to include a "racial memory." The ideas and terminology of these psychologists began to pervade the intellectual atmosphere and to offer new modes of explaining or accounting for the subjective states that accompanied poetic insight and composition. In 1912, F. C. Prescott's *Poetry and Dreams,* drawing on Freud's theory of the "dreamwork," suggested that poetry written under inspiration is an expression of unconscious rather than conscious mental activity.

This new consciousness about the unconscious finally engendered a new respect for the unaided self as an originating force in poetry. In 1919, Conrad Aiken pointed out, in a review of John Gould Fletcher, that the poet's abandonment to "these automatically, unravelling verbal reflexes" allows impressions to "come up shining from their long burial in the subconscious." The writer "learns the trick of shutting his eyes and not merely allowing, but precisely inviting, his subconscious to take possession of him." Aiken disapproves of this passive method—not, however, because it draws on the subconscious but because, in Fletcher's case, the resulting poetry "contains no thought" and "extraordinarily little of the sort of emotion which relates to the daily life of men and women." What Aiken sees in another article, entitled "Magic or Legerdemain?," as a more fruitful state is "a sort of dual consciousness, heightened no doubt on its ordinary plane, but conspicuously different from the usual state of mind in that the many passages which lead downward to the subconscious are thrown open, and the communications between the two planes, upper and lower, are free and full." Whether this condition is deliberately or accidentally evoked,

> during this state of dual consciousness there is a sense in which it is true that the poet has his subconscious under control. Even when working at most rapid intensity, he is sagacious of his quarry, and . . . his decisions themselves are largely conscious, but the logical train by which he reaches any such decision has . . . been to all intents obliterated.

If he should pause in partial dissatisfaction with the result, "his salvation is only in an adamantine command to the whole conscious realm of his mind to be silent, and at once his entire attitude is that of one who listens."

"One who listens" suggests immediately the traditional posture of the inspired poet, but the voice he hears is now felt to come not from the Muse or Apollo or God or the Over-Soul, but from the self. Whether the voice expresses something fine or something inferior depends on the poet. As Aiken comments, "One cannot dig up jewels from a commonplace sensibility." Aiken's image, "digging up," was symptomatic of a shift in the way inspiration was visualized. Instead of being thought of as flowing or breathed into the poet from outside and frequently, indeed, as descending from above, the originating impulse was now seen as arising from the depths within the poet.

Hart Crane, the last of the poets here under examination, was representative of this new conception of the poetic process. For Crane inspiration is central to poetic composition, which will not be brought about by contemplating aesthetics or studying other poets: "These theories and manoeuvres are interesting and consolatory,—but of course, when it comes right down to the act it-self,—I have to depend on intuition, 'inspiration' or what you will to fill up the page." For Crane, too, the subjective qualities of the experience are basically just what they were for the earlier poets who attributed inspiration to some celestial force. First, the advent of inspiration is involuntary, though its operation may be selective:

> The actual fleshing of a concept is so complex and difficult, how-ever, as to be quite beyond the immediate avail of will or intel-lect. A fusion with other factors not so easily named is the condi-tion of fulfilment. It is alright to call this "possession," if you will, only it should not be insisted that its operation denies the simul-taneous functioning of a strong critical faculty. It is simply a stronger focus than can be arbitrarily willed into operation by the ordinarily-employed perceptions.[1]

Second, "inspiration" fills Crane with confidence and conviction. He wrote to Gorham Munson: "At times, dear Gorham, I feel an enormous power in me—that seems almost supernatural. If this power is not too dissipated in aggravation and discouragement I may amount to something sometime." [2] Finally, this state of mind seems to generate expression. In sending a friend a manuscript copy of the last part of *The Bridge,* done, as he said, "in a lump," he commented that

> It was written verse by verse in the most tremendous emotional exaltations I have ever felt. I may change a few words in it here

[1] Hart Crane to Gorham Munson (April 5, 1926) , in Brom Weber, ed., *The Letters of Hart Crane: 1916–1932* (New York, 1952) , pp. 244–45.

[2] *Letters,* p. 91.

and there before the entire poem is finished, but there will be practically the same arrangement as what you see.[3]

Though Crane shows the same subjective responses and attitudes toward inspiration as had earlier poets, he explains the experience in terms of the new psychology. In 1922 he wrote,

> I am going through a difficult readjustment right now, besides meeting a period in my so-called "creative life" where neither my conscious self nor my unconscious self can get enough "co-operation" from the other to do anything worth while.[4]

Given Crane's reliance on inspiration, both for getting work started and for "fleshing the concept," and given his assumption that inspiration grows out of a co-operative merging of the conscious and the unconscious self, it is small wonder that he tried to induce that state by various means—by music, by drink, by love. Malcolm Cowley describes, in *Exile's Return*, how Crane might be "meditating over [a] particular poem for months or even years, scribbling lines on pieces of paper that he carried in his pockets and meanwhile waiting for the moment of genuine inspiration when he could put it all together." (One recalls how Emerson's notations in letters and journals later flowered in "Days.") Then might come a session of drinking and laughing with friends, followed by his retirement to another room, where he would type out his verses to the loud accompaniment of a Cuban rumba or Ravel's *Bolero* on the phonograph. This burst of composition would be succeeded by a sober and persevering revision—a tireless search for the right word to clarify the vision.

---

[3] Hart Crane to Charlotte Rychtarik (July 21, 1923), *Letters,* p. 141.
[4] Hart Crane to Gorham Munson (February 25, 1922), *Letters,* p. 80.

Crane's effort, as Cowley puts it, "to charm his inspiration out of its hiding place with a Cuban rumba and a pitcher of hard cider," grew ever more frantic and ever less productive in the few years before his death.

Ironically enough, though disregarding the advice Emerson gives in his essay on "The Poet" ("the air should suffice for his inspiration, and he should be tipsy with water") and taking too literally Emerson's poetic exhortation to "Pour, Bacchus! the remembering wine," Crane at times achieved an ecstasy much like that of the Emersonian bard. Apparently under the impetus of "almost supernatural" power moving in him he conceived *The Bridge,* a poem to embody "the myth of America," or "a new cultural synthesis of values in terms of our America." Its materials are "organic and active factors in the experience and perceptions of our common race, time and belief." In a letter to Otto Kahn, Crane saw the work as "an epic of modern consciousness." It is beside the point that his poem finally contains more of Crane than of his country, and that, in failing to sustain its myth it fails to achieve any real unity; what is significant here is that Crane's conception of his poem attests to the presence of a "vision" or a "gospel." That is, his work springs from, or is at least authenticated by, moments of great emotional exaltation. Its theme and scope, moreover, are cosmic and its overtones considerably more spiritual than a "myth of America" might suggest. In the "Proem: To Brooklyn Bridge," for instance, Crane invokes the bridge to "lend a myth to God"—that is, its structural beauty ("curveship") suggests a celestial beauty and a communication from God. And in the last section of the poem, "Atlantis," the bridge is "Forever Deity's glittering Pledge." These are but two of many references which imply some vision of a final harmony in the creation. In writing to one of the reviewers of *The Bridge* who had noted in the poem an "essential religious motive," Crane admitted, with qualification, this strain: "I have never consciously approached any subject in a religious mood; it is only afterward that I, or someone else generally, have noticed a prevalent piety." By "piety" I think Crane refers to the afterglow of "illumination." What he felt was probably a faint sense, lingering from the euphoria of inspiration, that he had glimpsed a harmonious order in the universe. This is the same feeling that underlay Woodberry's implication that, somehow, infinity (in the form of emotion) moved through him; that evoked Whitman's expectant vision in "Passage to India" that "the Elder Brother found,/ The Younger melts in fondness in his arms"; or that led Emerson to say, in "Each and All," that "Beauty through my senses stole;/ I yielded myself to the perfect whole."

This feeling, linking Crane to a succession of poetic "prophets," should furthermore be a corrective to the temptingly easy assumption that inspiration has all along been merely a matter of literary fashion, and that the conception of it in the twentieth century, as not external and divine but internal and human, means that the poet now finally knows he speaks only for himself. Theoretically, this should mean, too, that, though the poet may still speak for a "cause" or from intellectual conviction, he will no longer speak from the prophet's stance of discovery and supreme confidence. Yet *The Bridge* shows precisely this sense of exaltation and discovery; it proclaims, however indirectly, "some Word that will not die"; it evokes a vision, however obscure, meant for the enlightenment of all men. Moreover, the poem was written at a time when inspiration had ceased to be the fashion; in the age of the Imagists, Pound, Frost, and Tate, the cult of the "maker" had become dominant. The reason for this divergence between the poem and its milieu is, I suggest, simply that Crane experienced a full measure of inspiration—both dictation and illumination. As earlier examples show, a poet so imperiously moved may actually distrust literary fashion and literary form. The very intensity of Crane's vision led him to believe that it had far more than personal import and must be expressive of modern American culture in general. Indeed, as we look back at the poetic manner of Emerson and Whitman and glance aside at that of Blake and Shelley, we may be led to ask whether it is not a distinguishing mark of any "prophetic" poet to fuse certain elements of epic and lyric: to give to a subject matter which is epic—at least in its grandeur of conception and its cultural con-notations—a stylistic expression which is, both in its subjective intensity and its musical quality, essentially lyric.

Poe:

Journalism and the
Theory of Poetry

William Charvat

THE SUBTITLE of *Eureka* is "A Prose Poem." In his
Preface Poe states that it is for dreamers; that it is
an "Art-Product"—a "Romance"; and finally and
flatly, that it is a "Poem."

It is not a poem at all. It is not even a prose
poem, as some of Poe's tales are. Edward Davidson
ably demonstrates that it is "a central statement"
of the symbolist theory that "art is man's one instrument for making some order out of the infinitude of empirical formlessness." [1] True: in *Eureka* Poe makes order of a kind, but it is not a
poem's kind.

I am not concerned with the worth of *Eureka* as
an essay (as Poe properly calls it in a second subtitle), but rather with how it became possible for
him so to change his conception of the poem that
he could put his lyrics and this work of "scientific
detail" [2] (as he also described it) in the same

[1] Edward H. Davidson, *Poe, A Critical Study* (Cambridge,
Mass., 1957) , p. 252.

[2] John Ward Ostrom, ed., *The Letters of Edgar Allan Poe*
(Cambridge, Mass., 1948) , II, 366.

genre-category. The reasons are complicated. I limit myself here to those that have to do with professional influences and pressures —those that transformed a natural lyricist into the author of a treatise on the universe.

I suggest that at least by the middle of the 1840's Poe became impatient of the limitations of the lyric, and even a little contemptuous of it, and came to realize that he could not afford to put his professional energies and talents into it. His alienation from formal verse increased as he committed himself to journalism as represented by the monthly magazine. The essential characteristic of the general monthly magazine was variety. In offering a widely varied fare of amusement and information, editors were responding, in part, to the American public's admiration of expertise—of specialized knowledge of disciplines, of how things work or are done. Through magazine writing and editing (perhaps especially through reviewing a wide variety of books), Poe discovered the versatility of his own mind,[3] and came to think of the magazine, rather than the book, as the appropriate expression of American culture. At the same time, he came to feel the need of a literary form of broader scope than the lyric and the tale— one in which both imagination and erudition could be allowed free play. In part, his wish to create such a form was a reflection of the nineteenth-century poet's desire to find a modern equivalent of the epic. *Eureka*—a mixture of philosophy, religion, mathematics, physics, and scientific theory in general, all serving as a vehicle of his private vision of the universe—was Poe's attempt to make a modern epic. Its modernness, in part, consisted of his effort to journalize scholarship, to make knowledge and theory diverting. Pathetically, he believed his "poem" (which

---

[3] The long list of subjects in which Poe was, or pretended to be, an expert includes modern foreign languages, Oriental linguistics, classical culture, Egyptology, physics, astronomy, mathematics, philosophy, logic, phrenology, seamanship, landscaping, music, painting, cryptography, and duelling.

had a slow sale of 750 copies) would be immensely popular.

In his last years Poe had two obsessions, and they were related. One was with the *idea* of *Eureka,* the theme of which was, to him, so "solemn," "august," "comprehensive," and "difficult" that it awed him into "humility." The other was a determination to establish what he envisioned as the ideal monthly magazine (which he entitled, first, "The Penn Magazine," later, "The Stylus"). The latter was the more important to him: he hoped to put his earnings from the book, and from lectures on it, into the magazine.

II

His magazine project, like his tales and poems, was dream work, inspired by revulsion against the realities of American journalism. In spite of his reputation as editor of magazines (the legend of his success as editor needs careful re-examination), it is a question whether Poe was suited for the commercial magazine world at all. Harper & Brothers—shrewd, thoroughly business-minded, and certainly one of the foremost publishers of fiction—thought his magazine tales "too learned and mystical. They would be understood and relished only by a very few—not by the multitude. The numbers of readers in this country capable of appreciating and enjoying such writings . . . is very small indeed." [4] Poe's reputation as editor is based largely on his management of *Graham's,* but the owner, George R. Graham, one of the most astute magazine publishers of the 1840's, wrote after Poe's death: "The character of Poe's mind was of such an order, as not to be very widely in demand. The class of educated mind which he could

[4] Arthur Hobson Quinn, *Edgar Allan Poe* (New York, 1941), p. 251.

readily and profitably address, was small—the channels through which he could do so at all, were few . . . . " [5] In introducing Poe's "For Annie" to *Home Journal* readers under the heading "Odd Poem," N. P. Willis, the most successful of magazinists, made the interesting suggestion that "Money . . . could not be better laid out for the honor of this period of American literature—neither by the government, by a society, nor by an individual—than in giving Edgar Poe a competent annuity, on condition that he should . . . never dilute his thoughts for the magazines, and never publish anything till it had been written a year." [6]

These judgments came from both the book world and the magazine world, which were by no means identical. Poe's professional fate to a certain extent was determined by the position he took in the squeeze between the book and magazine economies in the 1840's, when publishers' rivalry in the reprinting of foreign works was at its height. During most of the first ten years of his writing life (1827–37) Poe was essentially book-minded— that is, he thought in terms of the permanence of the book as opposed to the transience of the periodical. The prestige of the book was infinitely greater than that of the periodical, a fact that most American writers were keenly aware of, and one that determined the form and the tone of much that they wrote.

Of course, there was no clear physical distinction between the two kinds of artifacts, and works published as pamphlets (Poe's *Tamerlane,* for example) belonged to neither. Periodicals took forms as different as the daily newspaper and the booklike annual, and between these were the weekly, the monthly, and the quarterly. The longer the interval between issues, the greater the prestige of the periodical. But by the 1830's the book and the

---

[5] Quinn, *Poe,* p. 664.

[6] Killis Campbell, ed., *The Poems of Edgar Allan Poe* (Boston, 1917), p. 288.

magazine were borrowing each other's characteristics: some books were issued in paperbound parts, periodically, and some of the worst of these looked as bad as the weeklies.

Yet, despite the blurring of distinctions, the book maintained its superior status in the minds of writers and readers, and was imitated by those magazine publishers who were ambitious of prestige. The best magazines boasted fresh, unbroken type, good paper, wide margins, and finely tooled illustrations. Burton, the owner of the *Gentleman's Magazine,* wrote Poe that competition was forcing him toward book standards: "expensive plates, thicker paper, and better printing than my antagonists." [7]

In a letter of 1844 to Charles Anthon, Poe made an extraordinary statement: "Thus I have written no books . . . . " [8] Since by that date he had published three collections of verse, a two-volume collection of tales, a romance, and a textbook, the statement invites speculation. Some curious phrases in his book reviews are relevant: "absolutely bound volumes" and "absolute book." Sometimes he used them invidiously. "As the author of many *books* [Poe's italics], of several absolutely bound volumes in the ordinary 'novel' form of auld lang syne, Miss [Catharine Maria] Sedgwick has a certain adventitious hold upon the attention of the public, a species of tenure that has nothing to do with literature proper . . . . " He would not allow the hard covers of her works "to bias . . . critical judgment." [9] In his "Literati" papers he rarely neglected to state whether a writer's magazine work had been collected or to comment on the format and typography of such collections. When he favored a writer's work, its book publication was evidence of its quality; when he did not,

[7] Quinn, *Poe,* p. 278.

[8] *Letters,* I, 270.

[9] Edmund Clarence Stedman and George Edward Woodberry, eds., *The Works of Edgar Allan Poe* (New York, 1903), VIII, 120; hereafter cited as *Works.*

the hard binding occasioned a sneer that such trash should be so honored. Thus, a complimentary article on Willis refers to the "handsome edition of his poems . . . with portrait." But of Longfellow he wrote that the "country is disgraced by the evident toadyism which would award to his social position and influence, to his fine paper and large type, to his morocco binding and gilt edges, to his flattering portrait of himself, and to the illustrations of his poems . . . that amount of indiscriminate approbation which neither could nor would have been given to the poems themselves." [10] The point is sharpened by the circumstance that in 1839, long before the publication of the elegant, illustrated edition of Longfellow referred to, Poe had begged the publishers of his *Tales of the Grotesque and Arabesque* to print a few copies on fine paper. They refused because Poe could not afford to pay for the luxury.[11]

If "absolutely bound" means simply hard binding, Poe's *Tamerlane* (1827, forty pages, 12¼ cents) was not a book. But *Al Aaraaf* (1829, seventy-two pages) was in boards, and *Poems* (1831, 124 pages) in cloth.[12] (Purchasers complained of the bad printing of the latter.) Poe probably paid for the printing of all three, and could not afford attractive book-making.[13] Certainly

[10] "Sarah Margaret Fuller," *Works*, VIII, 76.

[11] George Edward Woodberry, *The Life of Edgar Allan Poe* (Boston, 1909), II, 376.

[12] "Second Edition" on the title page of this work was either a common false claim, or it means that *Poems* was to be considered a second edition of *Al Aaraaf*. Poe said that *Tamerlane* had been withdrawn from circulation. He wrote Lowell, July 2, 1844 (*Letters*, I, 258): "I have [not preserved] copies of any of my volumes of poems—nor was either worthy of preservation," as if he had produced not three but two volumes of verse.

[13] Jacob Blanck to the writer, May 16, 1960: "Many [small collections of verse in the 1820's] were issued as pamphlets; many in printed boards; . . . it is generally agreed that board binding was meant only as protection of the sheets until the sheets were put into permanent custom binding. But plenty of these slim productions were issued in cloth . . . frequently highly decorated and surely meant to be permanent."

"The Prose Romances of Edgar Allan Poe, Number One," issued by a Philadelphia publisher of cheap books in 1843 as part of a "Uniform Serial Edition" at 12½ cents per miserably printed number, did not qualify as a book. Even at this price and in this format (halfway between book and magazine), there were few purchasers. There is no reference to this title in Poe's correspondence, but in his review of Sedgwick he said that the binding of her works gave her "a very decided advantage . . . over her more modern rivals [who are condemned] to the external insignificance of the yellow-backed pamphleteering." Graham had this circumstance in mind when he said in the article on Poe previously quoted that the "tendency to cheapen every literary work to the lowest point of beggarly flimsiness in price and profit" made "even the well-disposed" reader recoil from works so repulsively presented.

What of the *Tales* of 1840 and *The Narrative of Arthur Gordon Pym,* which were hardbound? (Indeed, the two-volume *Tales* was in the same format as Sedgwick's early novels.) We must now fall back on possible meanings of "absolute book." If the phrase refers to some standard of form or unity, or to seriousness of content, he may have excluded *Pym* because, loose and episodic, it had none of the unity he strove for in his tales and expected in good novels. In a sense, he wrote *Pym* to order, and in a hurry. In June, 1836, the Harpers told him that "Readers . . . have a . . . strong preference for . . . a single connected story," occupying a "whole volume or a number of volumes." [14] Within six months of that date Poe began to serialize his first and only "novel." In the whole of his correspondence, the only word about it is that it is a "silly book." Obviously, he wished it to be forgotten.

[14] Quinn, *Poe,* p. 251.

His unwillingness to let the 1840 *Tales* qualify as a book is harder to explain. From the early thirties he had wished to present his tales in a framework, which, he may have thought, would have given them book status as far as organization was concerned. The tales were to be recited by members of a club, and each tale was to be followed by a critical discussion. In 1836 he proposed a volume of three hundred pages, one-quarter of which would consist of connective tissue between tales. His claim that the tales were "originally written to illustrate a large work 'On the Imaginative Faculties,' " [15] if it is true at all, probably represented the all but universal tendency at that time to disguise fiction as something else more respectable—to give it dignity by associating it with history or philosophy or psychology or something equally "useful."

In his Preface to the *Tales,* Poe said, rather evasively, "I may have written with an eye to this republication in volume form, and may therefore have desired to preserve a certain unity of design. This is, indeed, the fact." The word "fact" must refer to "desired," for the collection has no design whatever. The publishers apparently rejected the critical interludes, and Poe, to fill up the customary two volumes, simply gathered together all the stories he had written, including eight late ones which had nothing to do with the "club" pattern.

III

Sometime between 1839 and 1842, Poe's conception of book unity changed. During the latter year he drew up a plan for a new two-volume edition of his tales to be entitled *Phantasy-Pieces.*

[15] *Letters,* I, 103.

All twenty-five of the 1840 *Tales* were to be included, together with ten uncollected ones. The significant feature of the new collection was to be the order of the pieces, a matter he pointed up in the margin of the Table of Contents: "To Printer—In printing the Tales preserve the order of the Table of Contents."[16] The "order" is simply that of variety. The first five tales, for example, are, successively, a detective story, a burlesque, an adventure tale, a satire, and a speculative dialogue on death.

The principle of variety is again emphasized in the 1844 letter to Anthon: "Unless the journalist collects his various articles he is liable to be grossly misconceived & misjudged [by those] who see . . . only a paper here & there, by accident . . . . He loses, too, whatever merit may be his due on the score of *versatility* —a point which can only be estimated by collection of his various articles in volume form and altogether." And again, in 1846: the 1845 tales, selected by E. A. Duyckinck for the publisher, did not succeed in *"representing* my mind in its various phases . . . . In writing these Tales one by one . . . I have kept the book-unity always in mind—that is, each has been composed with reference to its effect as part of *a whole.* In this view, one of my chief aims has been the widest diversity of subject, thought, & especially *tone* & manner of handling. Were all my tales now before me in a large volume [their merit] would be the wide *diversity and* variety."[17]

The implication here is that the unity of the whole derives from the totality of the mind of the writer in all its diversity, a conception which certainly owes something to Poe's commitment to journalism. Yet Poe perceived that by its very nature magazine writing encouraged ephemerality and courted oblivion. Only the book offered the possibility of recognition and of a passport to posterity. On the other hand, he was convinced that the "ener-

[16] Quinn, *Poe,* pp. 336–40.
[17] *Letters,* II, 328–29.

getic, busy spirit of the age [tends] wholly to the Magazine literature—to the curt, the terse, the well-timed, and the readily diffused, in preference to the old forms of the verbose and ponderous & the inaccessible." If Anthon would persuade Harpers to publish his *Phantasy-Pieces,* the groundwork would be laid for public acceptance of his ideal monthly, which would attract the "best intellect and education of the land, . . . the true and permanent readers." [18]

He would invest his magazine with the physical dignity of well-printed books [19]—clear new type, hand-press work, good paper, wide margins, French stitching (so that "the book" would lie fully open), thick covers, and woodcuts in the style of the best illustrated European books. It would acquire "caste" through contributions by men of wealth and status—Nicholas Biddle, Judge Conrad, Judge Upshur—and President Tyler's son! He would escape the domination of commercial publishers by seeking private capital, and of Eastern critical cliques by getting subscribers in the South and West, where the influence of the cliques was slight. He would address the "aristocracy of talent" in America. His estimates of the circulation of such a serious journal ran as high as 100,000—at a time when the maximum circulation of *Godey's* was 40,000.

In Poe's more euphoric moods his dream took the form of a crazy conspiracy. His magazine would "control" American literature. The editors would be a "coalition" of a dozen influential men of letters; their names would be kept secret to protect them from the commercial press; the "elite" of our writers would "combine" secretly; new candidates for the staff would be subject

[18] *Letters,* I, 268.

[19] Lowell's *The Pioneer,* 1843, was said to have been physically an imitation of "the page, the type, the width of the columns of Chapman's and Moxon's pamphlet editions of the British poets." See Sculley Bradley's Preface to the facsimile of *The Pioneer* (New York, 1947), p. xi.

to exclusion by blackball; and the profits would easily provide an income of $5,000 a year for each member, even if the circulation were only 20,000.[20] Toward the end of his life the dream became megalomania. In 1848 he wrote Mrs. Whitman, the middle-aged widow and poetess to whom he was briefly engaged: "It would be a glorious triumph, Helen, for *us*—for *you & me*. I dare not trust my schemes to a letter . . . . Would it *not* be 'glorious' . . . to establish, in America, the sole unquestionable aristocracy —that of intellect— . . . to lead & to control it? All this I *can* do . . . if you bid me—and aid me." [21]

Yet Poe put some real thought as well as wishful thinking into his project. One of the commonest phrases in his criticism is "the many and the few," and his use of it is almost always condescending to the many. Nevertheless, though he defined the mass as "the uneducated," "those who read little," and "the obtuse in intellect," he further divided these groups into two classes— "men who can think but who dislike thinking" and "men who either have not been presented with the materials for thought, or who have no brains with which to 'work up' the material." [22] Perhaps his dream of a large audience was sustained by the hope that some of the mass could be trained to like to think, and that some others would be hospitable to the materials for thought. This possibility seems to be confirmed in his statement that "the career of true taste is onward—and now moves more vigorously onward than ever." [23] His contempt for the mass is further mitigated in his Hawthorne review of 1847, where he refers to "the

---

[20] *Letters,* I, 247, 265–66.
[21] *Letters,* II, 410. "Aid" apparently refers to the Whitman family property, which Poe hoped to use to finance the *Stylus.* Within a month after the engagement he was obliged to sign papers which put the property out of his reach. See Quinn, *Poe,* pp. 582–83, and *Letters,* II, 420–21.
[22] "Henry Cockton's *Stanley Thorn,*" *Works,* VII, 97.
[23] "Lever's *Charles O'Malley,*" *Works,* VII, 78.

few who belong properly to books, and to whom books perhaps do not quite so properly belong. . . . The few . . . through a certain warping of the taste, which long pondering upon books as books never fails to induce, . . . are prone to think the public not right rather than an educated author wrong. But the simple truth is that the writer who aims at impressing the people is *always* wrong when he fails in forcing that people to receive the impression." [24]

The point of view expressed here is obviously that of an editor (or publisher) rather than an author. In the next sentence he turns author again and relieves Hawthorne (whose genius he generously admits and demonstrates) of the charge of failure because Hawthorne does not aim to impress "the people," who are, indeed, incapable of comprehending him. The passage is but another example of the doubleness of Poe's mind; yet, in the later years, Poe thought more and more like an editor and less and less like an author. Not only are his later works more calculated attempts to catch a wide audience than his earlier ones, but he repeatedly defends authors who, like Dickens and Bulwer, deliberately write for the many as well as for the few.

The defense becomes offensive when he says that Charles Fenno Hoffman's ability "to use the tools of the rabble when necessary without soiling or roughening the hands with their employment" is an "unerring test of the . . . natural aristocrat." [25] But he makes his point more objectively when he argues (in discussing Dickens) that "the writer of fiction, who looks most sagaciously to his own interest, [will] combine all votes by intermingling with his loftier efforts such amount of less ethereal matter as will give general currency to his composition." Indeed, "the skill with which an author addresses the lower taste of the populace is

---

[24] "Hawthorne's *Tales*," *Works,* VII, 26–27.
[25] "Charles Fenno Hoffman," *Works,* VIII, 126–27.

often a source of pleasure . . . to a taste higher and more refined." [26]

Thus, though Poe thought all his life of the mass audience as "rabble," he tended increasingly to dwell on the "skill" which succeeds in "uniting all the suffrages," and, inferentially, he came to believe that such skill is superior to that which is appreciated only by the few. This belief must have entered into his hopes for the *Stylus*, which he was most certainly thinking of when he said of Duyckinck's magazine, *Arcturus*, that it was a "little *too good* to enjoy extensive popularity," though "a *better* journal might have been far more acceptable to the public." [27]

IV

Most of Poe's thinking about the potentialities of magazine literature had to do with prose, but his attitudes toward poetry and the audience for it changed radically too as he became more deeply committed to an elevated journalism.

His early books of verse and his letters of the time contain a standard set of postures, many of which he borrowed from the elite tradition in England. Expecting to become, through inheritance, a man of independent means, he would address the cultivated few, ignore the rabble, and wait for fame. The postures are complicated and often conflicting. (1) One does not write for publication, and if one prints, it is for one's peers. *Tamerlane* was "of course not intended for publication," and the 1831 volume was "printed . . . for private circulation." (2) The gentleman is not "busy" or ambitious, and poetry is a product of "hours of idleness." "I am and have been from my childhood an idler,"

---

[26] "Lever's *Charles O'Malley*," *Works*, VII, 67.
[27] "Evert A. Duyckinck," *Works*, VIII, 59.

and thus it cannot be said that "I left a calling for this idle trade." (The "idler" pose was a commonplace among writers of the early nineteenth century.) (3) Maturity has nothing to do with the poetic gift. He wrote *Al Aaraaf*, he claimed, when he was ten, most of the other early pieces before he was fifteen. (4) Learning has little to do with the imagination, and poetry is not subject to intellectual analysis. Yet the gentleman-poet is erudite, and he assumes that his peers will understand his arcane allusions and his quotations from foreign languages. (5) The poet is indifferent to popular opinion. "I would be as much ashamed of the world's good opinion as proud of your own." (6) The poet is a rare, exalted creator, with gifts denied to ordinary mortals, and a poem cannot be judged except by poets. If Shakespeare is praised by the many, it is because the world has accepted the opinions of a "few gifted individuals, who kneel around the summit, beholding, face to face, the master spirit who stands upon the pinnacle." Artists, he wrote in 1836, are the "gifted ministers to those exalted emotions which link us with the mysteries of Heaven," and are infinitely superior to the "vermin" who "crawl around the altar of Mammon." [28]

Some of these attitudes recur in the Preface to *The Raven and Other Poems* (1845). The poems are "trifles," collected and republished to restore the correct text. They are not in accord "with my own taste" or "very creditable to myself," or "of much value to the public." He denies that he has ever made "any serious effort" in poetry. Yet he insists that he holds it in too great reverence to write it "with an eye to the paltry compensations, or . . . commendations of mankind." Three years earlier he had written a friend that the "higher order of poetry . . . always will

---

[28] Jay B. Hubbell, *The South in American Literature* (Durham, N. C., 1954), p. 539.

be, in this country, unsaleable," [29] but publicly he argued that the public had an appetite for verse, that we are a "poetical people," and that our practical, utilitarian talents and the love of poetry are not incompatible.[30]

It is difficult to make sense of all this (especially if we put all the statements in chronological order), but it is likely that the success of "The Raven" with the general reader made him revise his concepts of the nature of verse and begin to consider the possibility of "suiting at once the popular and the critical taste" in verse as well as in prose. Though he could, in his lecture on "The Poetic Principle" in 1848, repeat his 1842 statement that poetry is a "wild effort to reach the Beauty above," there is little recognition of the "wild" in his published criticism of verse after 1845. Rather, he tends to play down the "romantic" order of poetry, to defend the "accuracies and elegancies of style" which were associated with Pope, to admit that he had underrated the value of Bryant's polish, and to argue the necessity of "reconciling genius with artistic skill." "Nine tenths" of prosody "appertain to the mathematics; and the whole is included within the limits of the commonest common-sense." [31] "The Raven," he claimed in "The Philosophy of Composition," was composed "with the precision and rigid consequence of a mathematical problem."

This celebration of the role of precision, logic, mathematics, and common sense in poetry, this denigration of "fine frenzy," "ecstatic intuition," and "accident," was in part a journalist's attempt at a rapprochement with the common reader to whom he had once denied any capacity for the understanding of poetry.

[29] *Letters*, I, 216.

[30] "Mr. Griswold and the Poets," *Works*, VIII, 150.

[31] These statements are in the 1848 version of "The Rationale of Verse" (*Works*, VI, 47), not in the version of 1843 (*The Pioneer*).

Poe was investing the poet with qualities that the reader admired, and divesting him of those that set him apart from the non-literary person.

His major effort to narrow the gap between poet and reader was his analysis of "The Raven" in "The Philosophy of Composition" (which, we must remember, was published in *Graham's,* the most popular of middle-class magazines). This essay caters to the American appetite for the "inside story" of how something is done, and makes the reader feel that he can do it too. In a sense, it deflates the romantic poet, who, Poe was sure, would shudder at this "peep behind the scenes," at this exposure of the backstage gadgets which constitute the "properties of the literary *histrio."*

The poetic "laws" which Poe stresses in this essay are those most readily comprehended by the common reader. The insistence on brevity, on a poem's suitability for a reading at a "single sitting," Poe supports with the practical argument that in this land without leisure or repose two sittings would allow "the affairs of the world [to] interfere." His dicta that "melancholy is . . . the most legitimate of all the poetical tones" and that "the death of a beautiful woman is, unquestionably, the most poetical topic in the world," especially if a "bereaved lover" is involved, must have been acceptable to the sentimental reader. His argument for the "intrinsic value" of the refrain is based on the "universality of its employment" (he had kept "steadily in view the design of rendering ['The Raven'] *universally appreciable"*). The "thirst for self-torture" was an idea readily grasped by the consumers of misery-novels. And, finally, he recognizes the popular desire for an explicit and useful meaning in his admission that the last stanza disposes the reader "to seek a moral."

To what extent Poe persuaded himself that his essay could serve as a blueprint for the making of true poetry is questionable.

We cannot trust entirely his statement to a friend that " 'The Raven' has had a great 'run' . . . —but I wrote it for the express purpose of running—just as I did the 'Gold-Bug' . . . [but] the bird beat the bug . . . all hollow." [32] Yet this private statement is echoed in the essay itself: " . . . irrelevant to the poem *per se* [is] the circumstance—or say the necessity—which in the first place gave rise to the intention of composing *a* poem [is there significance in the italic?] that should suit at once the popular and the critical taste."

If he believed that he had found a formula for writing poems both good and popular, why did he not use it more often in the last years of his life? He attempted to do so once more, in "Ulalume" (1847), a poem so mechanically constructed, so similar to "The Raven" in theme and tone, and so closely in accord with the general prescription offered in "The Philosophy of Composition" that one wonders why it has been such a riddle to commentators, and why it is considered "private" and obscure. Poe obviously planned a popular poem, and carefully "promoted" it as such. The original title was journalistic: "To ——— ——— ———. Ulalume: A Ballad." He first published it anonymously; got a friend to reprint it, again anonymously, but with a prefatory puff and the query, "Who is the author?"; planted it twice again, with his name; and read it into a public lecture. Five printings yielded much publicity but few dollars. Perhaps this was why he wrote no more "Ravens."

After the 1831 *Poems* he wrote few lyrics—a total of twenty-eight in eighteen years—and the public was rather indifferent to most of those he produced. We tend to be impressed by the number of reprintings [33] of the individual poems—"The Raven," 11; "The Haunted Palace," 10; "To One in Paradise," 8; "Sonnet—

[32] *Letters,* I, 287.
[33] The figures are based on a rough count of listings in Campbell, *Poems.*

To Science," 8; "The Coliseum," 7. Of fifty-one poems, twenty-eight were reprinted more than three times. But these figures include reprintings in his own four collections (some poems were printed in all four). Moreover, three-fifths of the reprintings were in periodicals with which Poe had a close connection, editorial or other, and some were reprinted at his request in magazines edited or controlled by friends. Most of the reappearances, therefore, do not represent a genuine response to public demand, and he was rarely paid for them. Even first printings were not highly valued by editors: when he was paid, his rates were among the lowest offered to poets who were paid at all.

Yet the necessity to be a poet remained, and he never quite gave up hope that he would be generally accepted as one. *Eureka* was an attempt to realize that hope: he predicted the need of a first edition of 50,000 copies. It was his last and most dismally unsuccessful effort to "suit at once the popular and the critical taste."

The

Problem of Structure
in Some Poems by Whitman

Marvin Felheim

IN 1953, LIONEL TRILLING, editing *Perspectives, U. S. A.*, a publication designed to interpret American literature and life to the world, selected for inclusion an essay from the *Kenyon Review* entitled "Some Lines from Whitman" written by Randall Jarrell.[1] A happy combination: one of our more interesting twentieth-century poets and a stimulating critic, Jarrell, discussing the poetry of a great nineteenth-century writer. Jarrell's article is appropriately enthusiastic; in addition, it offers the reminder that "Critics have to spend half their time reiterating whatever ridiculously obvious things their age or the critics of their age have found it necessary to forget." In the case of Whitman, the purport of this reiteration is to remind us

---

[1] First published in *Kenyon Review*, XIV (1952), 63–79, under the title "Walt Whitman: He Had His Nerve," this essay was reprinted in Jarrell's collection of critical essays, *Poetry and the Age* (New York, 1953), pp. 112–32, with the title "Some Lines from Whitman."

that he was a poet, not a political philosopher. To support this claim, Jarrell not only recalls the admiration of Hopkins and James for Whitman, but he also adds his own appreciation: "To show Whitman for what he is one does not need to praise or explain or argue, one needs simply to quote."

But is "simply to quote" enough? A hundred years after the first edition of *Leaves of Grass* shocked the literary world of two continents, the modern critic cannot be content merely to point out what many of the most violently anti-Whitman critics have always been willing, even though grudgingly, to admit: that he wrote original and lovely lines.

Much of the criticism of Whitman as a poet has always centered about his "lines." Santayana's comment is typical of the negative criticism; he speaks of "this abundance of detail without organization, this wealth of perception without intelligence and of imagination without taste . . . . " On the whole, however, critical investigations of this kind have led to the conclusion that Whitman had an amazing facility. John Erskine and Floyd Stovall pointed to his many rhythmic successes; even Paul Elmer More spoke of his "magical power"; and Fred Newton Scott, Sculley Bradley, Killis Campbell, and Gay Wilson Allen, to name only the most prominent, have analyzed in minute detail the various distinctive techniques which characterize the Whitman line.

Distressing enough is the myopia of those critics who have so entangled themselves in the vines that they have never seen the whole plant. Perhaps even more to be deplored is that criticism which has been concentrated exclusively upon the content of Whitman's poetry. It began with contemporary reactions: Whittier threw his copy of *Leaves of Grass* on the fire; Emerson dashed off a spontaneous letter of encouragement; and some years later, Amy Lowell wrote, "We need Whitman's message as he meant it, rather than as he said it." This tendency to praise Whitman because his poetry somehow mystically incorporates Emersonian ideas is a baffling one. But even such distinguished critics as Norman Foerster and F. O. Matthiessen have done so. For the sake of the record, it should be pointed out that many of these critical estimates of Whitman's philosophy have done him and the study of American literature much good. One outstanding example is Joseph Warren Beach's *The Concept of Nature in Nineteenth-Century English Poetry*. Here Beach does Whitman the deserved honor of placing him properly in the list of nature poets; particularly significant are these conclusions: "The position of Whitman in relation to other nature-poets is rather peculiar. On the whole he belongs with Coleridge and Emerson by virtue of his transcendentalism . . . . In richness of sensual outfit, in devotion to the concrete, he is most like Wordsworth and Goethe . . . . Whitman's democratic passion links him with Wordsworth and Shelley, with Swinburne and Meredith . . . . " Distinguished company, indeed. But, one notices, the basis of the association is on philosophical principles, not, unfortunately, on poetic practices.

What is needed for Whitman, as for any poet, is an aesthetic on the basis of which we may make meaningful judgments. And since my contention is that Whitman was a great poet, obviously my task is to isolate those critical principles which will serve not only for Whitman (although it is true that every poet is, in a sense, unique) but for all poets. A poem is not merely a "collect" of ideas. Nor is it simply "the spontaneous overflow of powerful feelings." Like all works of art, it must be compounded of both these elements. But for true artistry it must also have been shaped by the intellect. In Coleridge's words, it is not only the "graceful" but the *"intelligent* whole." This is what, I take it, Suzanne Langer means by her definition of art as "the symbolic expression of feeling." "Here," she says, "we stand before a conception of art that accounts for its seriousness, its distinctness from practical interests, its intimate relation to feeling, yet its complete freedom from passion, and indeed its mastery over the whole gamut of emotions. This view shows the artist's activity as work, not play; as an intellectual conquest of the deepest and most difficult reality, instead of a flight from reality into a world of dream."

By virtue of such activity the poet makes the great poem. One remembers Goethe's statement that a distinguishing mark of the great poet is his ability to build. A minor poet—Edgar Allan Poe can write an exquisite song, but he cannot create a long poem —does not have this architectural capacity. While he was correcting proofs on the seventh edition of *Leaves of Grass* in 1881, Whitman said to a reporter on the *Boston Globe:* "This edition will complete the design which I had in my mind when I began to write. The whole affair is like one of those old architectural edifices, some of which were hundreds of years building, and the designer of which has the whole idea in his mind from the first." So, Whitman had in mind this quality, this control, this structure. His chief aim, he once wrote, was "to construct a poem on the open principles of nature," for "the cleanest expression," he said in his first Preface, "is that which finds no sphere worthy of itself and makes one." ("The organic form," wrote Coleridge, "is innate; it shapes, as it develops, itself from within, and the fulness of its development is one and the same with the perfection of its outward form. Such as the life is, such is the form.") "The fruition of beauty," Whitman claimed, "is no chance of hit or miss," but as "exact and plumb as gravitation," the product of man's "beautiful blood and beautiful brain."

One must admit, at this point, that it is comparatively easy to find such dicta as these in the huge bulk of Whitman's prose works. It remains now to analyze the poems. Are they, as has often been asserted, utterly formless, at best an assembly of poetic themes and a disorganized collection of lines? The problem has caused considerable anguish. Basil de Selincourt's experiences with the opening lines of "When Lilacs Last in the Dooryard Bloom'd" are instructive. "On the very threshold" of the poem, he wrote in *Walt Whitman, a Critical Study,* "a sheer barbarism confronts you":

> Ever-returning spring, trinity sure to me you bring.

"What does this betray," he asks, "if not a childish, under the circumstances a fatuous and even wanton, pleasure in a silly jingle of words?" But this was not to be De Selincourt's final judgment. In a lengthy footnote, he reverses himself. "After a long turning over in my mind, tasting and retasting, the tercet of which this is the first line, I have come to suspect in it a concealed rhythmical intention which would make such harsh terms unjustifiable." De Selincourt then goes ahead to give a masterly interpretation of the tercet, finding in it a "conformation" which is "the result of scrupulous and delicate adjustments." Then he hedges: "But the uncertainty attaching to all this is instructive. Whitman seems to be trying here to obtain effects to which a scheme is indispensable." A "scheme" in Whitman? Unthinkable! If the lines are magnificent by accident, well and good; but if they achieve distinction because they are part of a significant pattern, then there is some mistake in our reading of the poem. Even with a short poem like "Tears," De Selincourt has difficulties. "The form here," he admits, "is of such exquisite sensitiveness that it is with an effort we remember the offenses its author could commit." Why bother with such "an effort"? one is prompted to ask. Do the lapses of other poets (such pieces as make up *The Stuffed Owl,* for example) keep us from wholeheartedly enjoying their great works?

If Whitman has suffered unduly at the hands of detractors, he has also had his defenders. We are not concerned here with the many loving and exciting analyses of the shorter works. Mark van Doren's treatment of "A Noiseless Patient Spider" is a good example. The major poems have also been subjected to *explication de texte*. Two excessively ambitious students have addressed themselves to "Song of Myself": Henry W. Wells found it a series of lyrics in a "well-arranged sequence" which made the poem "virtually an effusion in five acts and fifty-two scenes"; [2] Carl F. Strauch also discovered a five-part organization to the poem, beginning with the "Self" and concluding with "the larger questions of life—Religion, Faith, God, Death." [3] Stephen Spender's comment on *Leaves of Grass* is a happier one; he observed that it is "the only successful contemporary epic" and lamented that its technique and style have not been adequately analyzed.[4] And James E. Miller, Jr. has approached the problem of meaning and form in terms of recurring images, of which he finds the bird image to be typical as well as particularly significant: the mockingbird (associated with *love* in "Out of the Cradle") ; the mountain hawk (associated with *democracy* in "Thou Mother with Thy Equal Brood") ; and the hermit thrush (associated with *religion* in "Lilacs") ; "by identifying the birds with these three themes, Whitman appears to be dramatizing a basic three-part thematic structure of *Leaves of Grass*." [5]

Of all of Whitman's major poems, "Out of the Cradle Endlessly Rocking" has been most conscientiously and rewardingly

[2] *The American Way of Poetry* (New York, 1943) , p. 36.

[3] "The Structure of Walt Whitman's 'Song of Myself,' " *English Journal* (College Edition) , XXVII (September, 1938) , 597–607.

[4] Quoted in Charles B. Willard, *Whitman's American Fame* (Providence, 1950) , pp. 212–13.

[5] In a paper, "Recurring Images in *Leaves of Grass*," delivered at the annual meeting of the Modern Language Association, 1955.

studied. Charles Walcutt's article [6] is helpful, but it pales to insignificance beside the masterly *explication de texte* applied by Leo Spitzer.[7] Spitzer finds the poem divided into three parts: a proem (lines 1–22), the tale of the bird (lines 23–143), and the conclusion (lines 144 to the end) in which the influence of the bird on the outsetting bard is stated. One is perhaps presumptuous to attempt to add to the vast knowledge which Spitzer brings to the poem. Yet his three divisions can be further classified. The first section is one long sentence; it is introductory, descriptive, physical, sensual; it corresponds to childhood, that of the boy or of any child; it deals with the subject of birth. The second section of the poem is narrative; it incorporates three lyrics sung by the bird ("Shine! shine! shine!" "Blow! blow! blow!" and "Soothe! soothe! soothe!"; the vowel sounds in these three opening lines are distinctly significant for the whole movement of the poem); its whole mood is emotional; its subject is love, mature passion. The final section of the poem is an intellectual, philosophical, and spiritual poetic statement; the lines are long; the feeling is lofty, dedicated, resolved as the coda of a great symphony; the subject is death, the final meaning of life. Whitman has created unity here: the three pinnacles of human life—birth, love, death—are so magnificently interrelated that no word or section is out of place. The lines and the poetic devices are all apt and appropriate. For example, the lines

> Whereto answering, the sea,
> Delaying not, hurrying not,
> Whisper'd me through the night, and very plainly before
>   daybreak,
> Lisp'd to me the low and delicious word death,

[6] "Whitman's 'Out of the Cradle Endlessly Rocking,'" *College English,* X (February, 1949), 277–79.

[7] "'Explication de Texte' Applied to Walt Whitman's 'Out of the Cradle Endlessly Rocking,'" *Journal of English Literary History,* XVI (1949), 229–49.

incorporate the mood exactly—the liquid consonants, the predominantly long vowels, the caesuras, the suspenseful phrasings. The word "death" and the whispering sea which informs the poet are both marvellously captured in Whitman's phrase, "hissing melodious," two lines later.

The poet has, indeed, "gained not only an emotional, but an intellectual triumph" (Spitzer's words). Further, he has (in line 31) given us the very terms to describe what he has done: the poet tells us,

> . . . every day I, a curious boy, . . .
> Cautiously peering, absorbing, translating.

"Peering, absorbing, translating"—the words not only describe, they are the activity: peering, the physical experiences of the child; absorbing, the emotional and intellectual reactions of the man; translating, the philosophical and artistic activities of the poet. The parallel with the scheme of "Lines Composed a Few Miles above Tintern Abbey" is too obvious to need further comment. (F. O. Matthiessen, in *American Renaissance,* has pointed out some of the significant similarities between Whitman and Wordsworth, but only in terms of their statements about the aims and materials of poetry, not in terms of the structure of individual poems.)

Spitzer has appropriately fixed the poem's category. "To what sub-genre does our lyrical poem belong? It is obviously an *ode* . . . if an ode may be defined as a solemn, lengthy, lyric-epic poem that celebrates an event significant for the community." Now George N. Shuster in his definitive study, *The English Ode from Milton to Keats,* explicitly rejects the notion that any of Whitman's poems could be termed odes. His attitude is reminiscent of De Selincourt's. He points out that "Whitman was the first of the poets whom a craving for unhampered emotional expression sundered completely from classicism." "Formally," he admits, "some of Whitman's dithyrambs consort well with the Pindarick idea . . . . Perhaps analysis would show that 'When Lilacs Last in the Dooryard Bloom'd' is not unlike other Romantic threnodies in structure. Nevertheless, this and other Whitman poems could be termed odes only on the basis of the eighteenth century feeling that any primitive—or pseudo-primitive—impassioned uttering in verse is an ode; and to that idea the historian of the ode cannot, of course, subscribe." Yet his definition of the form nowhere could be constituted as excluding Whitman's major works. English odes, he points out, "are characterized by their stanzas"; they have "patterns which reveal the organic relationship which usually exists between inspiration and expression." The definitions of Edmund Gosse ("We take as an ode any strain of enthusiastic and exalted lyrical verse directed to a fixed purpose, and dealing progressively with one dignified theme"), Lawrence Binyon ("An ode is a poem of address written about a theme of universal interest"), J. F. A. Pyre ("Primarily, it [the term *ode*] refers to the content and spirit of a poem, implying a certain largeness of thought, continuity of theme, and exalted feeling"), and Carol Maddison ("The vernacular ode . . . was basically a formal, public or social poem, usually occasional, celebrating something. It was of moderate length, stanzaic, eulogistic, and philosophic or learned, reflecting on life by means of highly wrought imagery, mythology, and aphorism.") —all encourage the use of the term "ode" to describe Whitman's major poems.[8] Indeed, Whitman has, as Spitzer concluded, "acclimated the ode on American soil and democratized it."

---

[8] See Edmund Gosse (ed.), *English Odes* (New York, 1886); Lawrence Binyon, "The English Ode," *Essays by Divers Hands,* ed. W. R. Inge (London, 1919); J. F. A. Pyre, *A Short Introduction to English Versification* (New York, 1929); and Carol Maddison, *Apollo and the Nine: A History of the Ode* (Baltimore, 1960).

Other major poems of Whitman can be similarly analyzed to illustrate the shaping intellect behind them. We can pursue this line of investigation a bit further on philosophic grounds. For instance, Alfred Marks has taken a surprising choice, "Chanting the Square Deific," as the basis for his thesis that Whitman made "poetic use of the logical technique which Hegel popularized, the Dialectic." [9] And he finds that the poem is "dependent on the triadic method." He cautions us, however, that "it is not entirely fair" to this method or to this poem "to examine it only for intellectual values. 'Chanting the Square Deific' is a powerful and unique poem; it represents as complete and complex a poetic statement of a philosophy as one may easily find. But the poem does not represent Whitman's great abilities in handling drama, mood, natural imagery, and word music, abilities which may be shown to derive a great deal of power from the triadic method." For this purpose, he then analyzes "Out of the Cradle."

In the analysis of Whitman's poems, it has also been customary to refer to recurrent analogies. In *American Renaissance,* Matthiessen lists three: oratory, Italian opera, and the sea (other critics add the Bible). In terms of these images, Matthiessen gives a masterful interpretation of "When Lilacs Last in the Dooryard Bloom'd." But while he succeeds in elucidating many of the symbols which Whitman uses in the poem, he was not at all interested in exploring the ways in which Whitman organized and incorporated the symbols.

"Lilacs" has the same basic structure as "Out of the Cradle." Its opening movement, a statement of the situation and an enunciation of the themes and images, runs through the first five sections of the poem. The mood varies from tenderness (Section 1) to exclamation (the apostrophe to the star in Section 2) to calm de-

---

[9] "Whitman's Triadic Imagery," *American Literature,* XXIII (March, 1951), 99–126.

scription (of the procession of the coffin in Section 5). The poet wants to introduce his subject; this he accomplishes both by the use of descriptive terms ("In the dooryard fronting an old farm-house near the white-wash'd palings,/ Stands the lilac-bush tall-growing with heart-shaped leaves of rich green" or, "In the swamp in secluded recesses,/ A shy and hidden bird is warbling a song") and by the use of the three natural images he has chosen: lilac, star, bird. The sections are significantly objective; Whitman uses the pronoun "I" only five times in these thirty-two lines. Sections 6 through 14 then make up the central, or lyric, portion of the poem. These sections are emotionally charged; the emphasis is on feeling and understanding. This middle part of the poem opens dramatically in Section 6 with another description of the passage of Lincoln's coffin, but a significant detail has been added: human beings appear. This section begins also a reiteration of the symbols, but this time they are not just stated; they are expanded, as is Lincoln's death to include all death ("O sane and sacred death"; the apostrophe to death in Section 7 parallels the apostrophe to the star in Section 2). The star and bird now convey something to the poet; they are no longer static; they bring feeling and knowledge ("I understand you," says the poet in Section 9). Sections 10 and 11 add a rhetorical quality, with a series of questions representative of the intellectual search on the part of the poet. In addition to the questions, there are answers, provided by nature ("sea-winds blown from east and west") and by men (pictures of men will adorn the "burial-house"). This portion of the poem concludes in a magnificent blending of images:

> O liquid and free and tender!
> O wild and loose to my soul—O wondrous singer!
> You only I hear—yet the star holds me, (but will soon depart,)
> Yet the lilac with mastering odor holds me.

The sensual qualities of the images are received, ecstatically, and understood. The only way in which the poet can encompass the understanding and the emotion is to break into song, which he does through the bird, his alter ego. The lyric moment is now completed. (Whitman's use of the lyric—a bird's song—both here and in "Out of the Cradle" is a stunning device to reinforce the emotional part of the poem.) The conclusion of the poem (Sections 15 and 16) is calm, resigned, spiritual. The lines are direct and long. Section 15 brings the war dead into the threnody:

> And I saw askant the armies,
> I saw as in noiseless dreams hundreds of battle-flags,
> Borne through the smoke of the battles and pierc'd with
>   missiles I saw them,
> And carried hither and yon through the smoke, and torn and
>   bloody,
> And at last but a few shreds left on the staffs, (and all
>   in silence,)
> And the staffs all splinter'd and broken.

And Section 16 emphasizes peaceful acceptance:

> Passing the visions, passing the night,
> Passing, unloosing the hold of my comrades' hands,
> Passing the song of the hermit bird and the tallying song
>   of my soul,
> Victorious song, death's outlet song, yet varying
>   ever-altering song,
> As low and wailing, yet clear the notes, rising and falling,
>   flooding the night,
> Sadly sinking and fainting, as warning and warning, and yet
>   again bursting with joy,

Covering the earth and filling the spread of the heaven,
As that powerful psalm in the night I heard from recesses,
Passing, I leave thee lilac with heart-shaped leaves,
I leave thee there in the door-yard, blooming, returning
  with spring.

The symbols are now spiritualized. The bird's song has become a "powerful psalm," the star is the "silver face" of the comrade, and the lilac "with heart-shaped leaves" remains "blooming, returning with spring," made into myth and promise:

Lilac and star and bird twined with the chant of my soul,
There in the fragrant pines and the cedars dusk and dim.

"Lilacs" thus embodies Whitman's basic triadic structure. From its physical beginnings, objectively rendered in pure description, to its central lyrical (the bird's song) and intellectual portions, the movement is unswerving; the concluding section moves into the spiritual, and the pattern is complete, fulfilled.

"Crossing Brooklyn Ferry," "Song of the Broad-Axe," and "Passage to India" are other poems which I find incorporate the same three-part structure of peering, absorbing, and translating. All three begin with great emphasis upon physical description, move to the emotional and intellectual apprehension of a central idea (the continuity of space and time in "Crossing Brooklyn Ferry," the relationship between democracy and nature in "Song of the Broad-Axe," and the oneness of the world in "Passage to India"), and conclude with a spiritual affirmation, a "certain heroic ecstasy," as Whitman called it.

The ferry in "Crossing Brooklyn Ferry" represents three levels of meaning. First of all, of course, it is the literal ferry crossing and recrossing the East River between Manhattan and Brooklyn, serving a physical function, real, tangible, observable. On the next level, the ferry is the poet, the "representative man" of his time, speaking to the generations to come, communicating between present and future in the form of projected questions and answers, the poet's body serving as the physical "identity" to give reality to his intellectual journey. The poet's body also carries the seeds of life, and is a ferry crossing between the shores of life and death. Finally, the poem itself is a ferry, a spiritual as well as hortatory message bridging the gap between Whitman and his readers, creating thereby a mystical, perfect union.

These three meanings are not just ideas to be extracted from the poem by an imaginative reader; they are embedded in and inseparable from the form and rhetorical devices of the poem itself. Three descriptive sections form the proem. Lines consist of long, positive statements. The pronouns used are I and you, and the you is explicit: the "flood-tide," the "clouds of the west," the "crowds of men and women," and "you that shall cross from shore to shore years hence." Section 3, the climax of this first part, a typical Whitman catalogue, consists of two stanzas, the first of seven lines, five of which begin with "Just as you" and set up a literal, physical comparison between the poet and future generations; the second stanza, of twenty-two lines, consists, first, of a series of verb phrases all of which use verbs of "peering" ("Watched," "saw," "had my eyes dazzled," and "look'd"), then of a series of noun phrases, all objects of the final verb "saw." Verbs and nouns, then—this is the way in which the poet incorporates physical realities. Section 4 is a one-stanza, five-line transition, a typical Whitman interlude, marked by a dramatic parenthesis in the concluding line, an aside from poet to reader, an intimate, frank moment. The whole stanza is merely one sentence.

The central, intellectual, "absorbing" portion of the poem includes Sections 5 through 8. The chief rhetorical device throughout is appropriately the question. Two short questions begin Section 5, then there are random questions in Sections 6 and 7, but Section 8, the climactic section of this part, is made up entirely of questions: indeed, every line in this section ends in a question mark. A new pronoun also appears, the first person plural: "we" and "us" are strategically placed, at the beginning of Section 5 and in the last stanza of Section 8.

The characteristic terminal punctuation of the first part of the poem (Sections 1 to 4) is the period (there are only three exclamation marks in a total of fifty-three lines) ; of the second part (Sections 5 to 8) , the question mark (actually fifteen of the forty-seven lines terminate in question marks) ; of the third part (Section 9) , the exclamation point (of thirty-two lines, exactly half end in exclamation marks, while there are ten more exclamations used internally) .

The concluding part of the poem is, in the first stanza of Section 9, exhortatory and, in the second stanza, calm and deliberative (in the final seven lines there are three dashes used to expand the content of the lines) . Another striking feature of Section 9 is the complete absence of any pronoun used in the singular. Section 9, like Section 3, is, in large part, a catalogue, consisting of verbs and nouns. But with a difference: here the verbs are those of command, of exhortation, of ecstasy; these verbs are not used for descriptive purposes but for "translating" description into action. Stanley K. Coffman, Jr. has made some remarks on the two catalogues which are pertinent here. In his "Note" on "Crossing Brooklyn Ferry," he found that these are "by no means 'bare lists,' " but that the "words" of the lists create "a pattern of motion and light." Further, he sensed a "difference in tone" between Sections 3 and 9—"the force of the imperative"—but the two catalogues "occurring as they do at the middle and end of the poem . . . provide an over-all framework, a structural basis upon which the poem rests." Just as does Marks in his reading of "Chanting the Square Deific," Coffman allows for a "dialectic technique": he finds "a thesis (sympathy) " in Sections 1 to 3, "an antithesis (pride) " in Sections 4 to 9, and "a synthesis expressed in the closing lines of Section 9." [10]

The key to the final meaning of the poem is the poet's suggestion that the "dumb, beautiful ministers," those "objects" of the world which he had just addressed, commanded, pleaded with, at last are seen to "furnish your parts toward the soul." The whole process from physical objectivity (peering) to spiritualization is summed up here, having been understood and organized and made beautiful for us (absorbed, translated) by the poet.

Triadic imagery also underlies "Passage to India," which Whitman once planned as a major poem of a projected companion volume to *Leaves of Grass*. The initial physical trio which Whitman celebrates in the poem are "the great achievements of the present": the completion of the Suez Canal in the Old World and the transcontinental railroad in the New, as well as the laying of the Atlantic Cable ("The seas inlaid with eloquent gentle wires") . Matching these wonders are, first of all, "the antique ponderous Seven" wonders of the ancient world and, secondly, "a worship new": "Trinitas divine shall be gloriously accomplish'd and compacted by the true son of God, the poet," for "Nature and Man shall be disjoin'd and diffused no more,/ The true son of God shall absolutely fuse them." To accomplish this magnificent poetic exercise, the poet uses some of his most striking rhetorical devices.

[10] " 'Crossing Brooklyn Ferry': A Note on the Catalogue Technique in Whitman's Poetry," *Modern Philology*, LI (1954) , 225–32.

The first part of the poem, Sections 1 through 4, celebrates the physical achievements of the present. Whitman takes the reader on actual sightseeing trips to the Suez and along the Platte to the Pacific. The second unit of the poem embraces Sections 5 through 7 and stresses the intellectual nature of the journey; it is, indeed, "to wisdom's birth." Finally, in Sections 8 and 9, we see the poet's ultimate concern: to make this a spiritual pilgrimage, the journey of the soul "to more than India!"

As usual, the first stanzas tend to be made up of long sentences filled with physical details, expressing sensual delight. So, in Section 1, the first stanza is a nine-line sentence, suspended in a participial construction which conveys the very essence of physical reality, and in Section 2, stanza two is a long periodic sentence, reminiscent of the opening stanza of "Out of the Cradle." In Section 3, the second stanza consists of seventeen long lines setting forth the poet's joy in lush physical details; eleven of the seventeen lines begin with "I" followed by the verbs "see," "hear," "cross," "span." The first part of the poem concludes in Section 4 with a forthright statement that America was "born"

> For purpose vast, man's long probation fill'd,
> Thou rondure of the world at last accomplish'd.

There is no rhetorical or philosophical mysticism here. The basic idea is incorporated in a sentence which concludes with the past tense of the verb. This is affirmation embodied. The poet is not suggesting; he is stating.

The second part of the poem begins with both a change in mood and an appropriate rhetorical change too. The poet picks up a word, "rondure," from the preceding line, but he capitalizes it and puts it in the vocative—"O vast Rondure,"—and further, he puts it in suspension—"swimming in space." Then he adds the notion, tentatively expressed, that there is an intellectual problem connected with this magnificent physical world: "Now first it seems my thought begins to span thee." And he concludes "with that sad incessant refrain," appropriately phrased as questions and, one notes, neatly italicized: " . . . *Wherefore unsatisfied soul?* and *Whither O mocking life?*" There follows a whole stanza made up of six questions and a dramatic parenthesis. Section 6 continues the intellectual emphasis of this middle portion in lines in which the poet pours out his erudition about the past, both oriental and occidental. This section then concludes with a short, five-line parenthetical stanza. The parentheses again act as a dramatic device; they not only suggest a stage-aside but also bring a change of pace and mood in the poem. Section 7 provides a brilliant conclusion to the central, intellectual element of the poem by stressing the nature of the passage ("to primal thought") and by summarizing the whole poem: the soul's journey started as a physical activity—"Thy circumnavigation of the world begin"— and continued as an intellectual passage—"Of man, the voyage of his mind's return." But it was, always, a spiritual quest as well, a search for "paradise" and a return "to innocent intuitions."

The final portion of the poem (Sections 8 and 9) triumphantly celebrates the poet's passage with his soul "to more than India!" Whitman employs various devices to elevate his style: the use of "O"; the use of a variety of punctuation devices, including parentheses, the dash, the exclamation point; rhetorical instead of actual questions are posed; repetition and capitalization are fully exploited. Indeed, the overwhelming effect is one of sheer ecstasy. The final section of the poem is truly a climax; its tone has been made really distinctive by concentration of all the poetic devices into a crescendo. Such skill must command our admiration. We are impelled, then, by more than the ideas to "sail forth,"

> For we are bound where mariner has not yet dared to go,
> And we will risk the ship, ourselves and all.

Ezra Pound's
London Years

Richard M. Ludwig

> I think one work of art is
> worth forty prefaces and as
> many apologiae.—*Pavannes
> and Divisions,* 1918.

IT IS TOO EARLY for apologiae and too late for the
kinds of prefaces Pound's fellow poets—Eliot,
Aiken, Flint, Aldington, Sandburg—were writing
when "the good Ezra" was living in London: appreciation and censure following hard upon the
publication of a new collection of poems. Ezra
Pound's major work has been on our shelves for so
many decades he is in no need of prefaces. But if we
wish, by our criticism, to send readers back to the
poems, and that is all a good poet asks of good
criticism, we need to look closely at these London
years, 1908–20, putting aside for the moment
Pound's later work, the *Cantos,* the economic
pamphlets, and the critical writings.

By looking closely I do not mean *explication de
texte.* Pound has had more than his share of exe-
gesis in the last ten years. It has not, even Hugh
Kenner's exhausting efforts have not, brought him
more readers. He is still the formidable *collagiste,*

compiler of an endless epic which remains largely unread. Mr. Kenner asks early in his book "why Eliot, Joyce, and Yeats are thoroughly assimilated" and "Pound's reputation alone remains so much a matter of inert convention." [1] The reason is patent, but Mr. Kenner will never accept it. F. R. Leavis spelled it out for him in 1932 in his *New Bearings in English Poetry*. T. S. Eliot hinted at it in his contribution [2] to *An Examination of Ezra Pound*, Peter Russell's collection of essays published for Pound's sixty-fifth birthday. Alfred Alvarez says it more justly, and more eloquently, in his essay on Pound in *The Shaping Spirit*. For too long, he believes, we have been asked to accept the *Cantos* as a masterpiece of structure, as the culminating work in Pound's stormy career, whereas "his most expressive form is the short poem. Both *Mauberley* and *Propertius* are a series of these; the finest parts of the *Cantos* have the same singleness and concentration." [3] Whether the *Cantos* are a masterpiece or a failure I shall not argue here. We know where Mr. Kenner stands. What I share with Mr. Alvarez is the strong feeling that "one of the main troubles with the *Cantos* is not their obscurity but their remoteness." [4] Pound's work from 1908 to 1920 was neither obscure nor remote, and it consisted chiefly of short poems. They deserve revaluation.

When Pound came up to London from Venice in 1908, he brought with him not only his first published book but a whole armful of poetry. With his own money he paid for the printing of one hundred copies of *A Lume Spento,* a collection of forty-four poems. He had been fired from Wabash College at the age of

[1] *The Poetry of Ezra Pound* (London, 1951) , p. 18.

[2] First published in *Poetry,* LXVIII (September, 1946) , 326–38.

[3] *The Shaping Spirit: Studies in Modern English and American Poets* (London, 1958) , p. 68; published in the United States under the title *Stewards of Excellence.*

[4] *Ibid.,* p. 59.

twenty-three [5] and had left America in disgust for the part of Europe he has loved ever since: Spain, France, and Italy. But he could not have chosen, even as an ex-instructor of Romance languages, a more unlikely city than Venice in which to publish poems in English. He had come to Europe, after all, to be near Yeats, and within four months he was writing from London to his old friend, William Carlos Williams. This long letter (the first of hundreds Williams received over the years) is one of the most revealing Pound has ever written. Among other things, he says:

> I am very sure that I have written a lot of stuff that would please you and a lot of my personal friends more than A L[ume] S[pento]. But, mon cher, would a collection of mild, pretty verses convince any publisher or critic that *I* happen to be a genius and deserve audience? I have written bushels of verse that could offend no one except a person as well read as I am who knows that it has all been said just as prettily before.[6]

During the next ten years, Pound winnowed these bushels of verse in a way that may delight a bibliographer but maddens the general reader who admires a single poem and then tries to find the rest of the volume in which it appeared. Before we can judge the London years, we need to set the publishing record straight. It is less complex than it looks at first glance.

A Lume Spento was not reprinted in London, although Yeats called the collection "charming" and Pound told Williams that "Mosher is going to reprint." Instead, a second volume, *A Quinzaine for This Yule,* appeared in London late in 1908. It contained only twenty-seven pages, probably for private circulation, and to-

[5] The details are recorded in Charles Norman's biography, *Ezra Pound* (New York, 1960), pp. 22–24.

[6] *The Letters of Ezra Pound: 1907–1941,* ed. D. D. Paige (New York, 1950), p. 4.

day it is as rare as *A Lume Spento*. Pound's third volume, *Personae*, appeared in April, 1909. He had written Williams in February that he was "by way of falling into the crowd that does things here. London, deah old Lundon, is the place for poesy." [7] With this fifty-nine-page volume, Pound had indeed found his place. Elkin Mathews, the Vigo Street bookseller, was the publisher. The reviews could not have been better had Mathews written them himself. In Ford Madox Ford's *English Review*, Edward Thomas said that "from the first to the last lines of most of his poems he holds us steadily, in his own pure, grave, passionate world." Rupert Brooke praised the book in the *Cambridge Review*, R. A. Scott-James in the *Daily News*. *Punch*, the *Observer*, the *Bookman* nodded full approval. No one mentioned the fact that almost half of *Personae* had been first published in Venice.

Mathews issued another volume of Pound's work in the fall of the same year, 1909, twenty-seven new poems called *Exultations*. America was now ready to recognize this expatriate. In spite of his feelings about the moribund American audience, Pound did not object. He spent ten months in America (from summer, 1910, to spring, 1911) seeing his parents in Wyncote, Pennsylvania, getting to know New York City, and arguing about poetry with Williams and his wife, out in Rutherford, New Jersey. In Boston, he arranged for the publication of *Provença*, technically his fifth book but actually a collection reprinted from *Personae* and *Exultations*, plus a few new poems. His fifth and sixth volumes appeared in London: *Canzoni*, in 1911, and *Ripostes*, in 1912. He later called *Canzoni* "many false starts never reprinted." Actually, he had exhausted his experiments with Pre-Raphaelite subjects, imitations of Browning, Provençal forms, self-conscious diction ("olde-

---

[7] *Letters*, p. 7.

worlde" diction, it has been called) , and transmogrifications of Latin and Italian poems. *Canzoni* is the end of a cycle. With *Ripostes,* Pound began the second stage of his poetic career.

Ripostes is dedicated to William Carlos Williams, whose approval he cherished although they quarreled over theory. One wonders if Williams recognized the sharp break Pound was making here with his past enthusiasms. The collection includes "translations," it is true, notably "The Seafarer," but it also gives us Pound's own authentic voice: sharp images, overt satire, polished epigrams, and free-verse lyrics. The last five pages of the book contain the "complete poetical works of T. E. Hulme" which Pound claimed were "reprinted here for good fellowship . . . a custom out of Tuscany and Provence." Pound owed much to Hulme, the reactionary philosopher whose career was tragically brief, and to F. S. Flint, the talented linguist. They were the instigators of the Thursday evening meetings in Soho restaurants of a poetry club at which Pound, early in 1908, discovered congenial companions and attentive ears. Moreover Hulme was a spokesman for the "new" poetry. He was certain that "images in verse are not mere decoration, but the very essence of an intuitive language." [8] In a two-page introduction to these poems by Hulme, Pound uses for the first time in print the term *Les Imagistes* to describe the poets writing what Hulme later called "dry, hard, and classical verse." The whole history of Imagism cannot detain us here,[9] but it is significant that in *Ripostes,* 1912, Pound was ready to announce the direction he and some of his friends were taking. In January, 1913, Harriet Monroe's magazine, *Poetry,* published H. D.'s first work and Pound's notes from London:

[8] *Speculations,* ed. Herbert Read (London, 1958) , p. 135.

[9] F. S. Flint published *A History of Imagism* in 1915. For a recent, detailed account of the movement, see Stanley K. Coffman, Jr., *Imagism: A Chapter for the History of Modern Poetry* (Norman, Oklahoma, 1951) .

Space forbids me to set forth the program of the *Imagistes* at length, but one of their watchwords is Precision, and they are in opposition to the numerous and unassembled writers who busy themselves with dull and interminable effusions, and who seem to think that a man can write a good long poem before he learns to write a good short one, or even before he learns to produce a good single line.[10]

Precision continued to be Pound's watchword long after he had lost interest in the Imagist school.

This same year his new direction was luckily bolstered by the gift of Ernest Fenollosa's notes and translations, sent to him by the widow of this former Imperial Commissioner of Arts in Japan. *Cathay,* 1915, Pound's seventh volume of verse, is the result. The title page calls the work "translations for the most part from the Chinese of Rihaku, from the notes of the late Ernest Fenollosa, and decipherings of the Professors Mori and Agira." Rihaku is the Japanese name for Li T'ai Po, the eighth-century Chinese poet. On the last page of *Cathay,* Pound appended this strange note, an early sign of what in a few years was to become a petulant dissatisfaction with literary London:

I have not come to the end of Ernest Fenollosa's notes by a long way, nor is it entirely perplexity which causes me to cease from translation . . . . But if I give them, with the necessary breaks for explanation, and a tedium of notes, it is quite certain that the personal hatred in which I am held by many, and the *invidia* which is directed against me because I have dared openly to declare my belief in certain young artists, will be brought to bear first on the flaws of such translation, and will then be merged into depreciation of the whole book of translations. Therefore I give only these unquestionable poems.

[10] "Status Rerum," *Poetry,* I (January, 1913) , 126.

Poems they unquestionably are; translations they are not. Sinologists have been making that clear for more than forty years. But when Eliot says "Pound is the inventor of Chinese poetry for our time," he means *"Cathay* will be a 'Windsor Translation' as Chapman and North are now 'Tudor Translations': it will be called (and justly) a 'magnificent specimen of XXth Century poetry' rather than a 'translation.' " [11] Critics other than Eliot, Yeats among them, have acknowledged that *Cathay* is even more than that. They see it as a major influence on all modern poetry and as a seminal volume in Pound's development, for *Cathay* leads directly into *Lustra,* 1916. His competence in Romance philology did not extend to the Oriental languages; but in his insistence that Fenollosa wanted his work treated as literature, not philology, Pound took liberties with the text, saturated himself with the philosophy behind the ideogram, learned how to assume new (Oriental) *personae,* investigated the Japanese *haiku* and *tanka,* and ultimately forged for himself an idiom through which he could mirror pre-war London. The Fenollosa manuscripts were catalysts in perfecting the "dry, hard, classical" style which Hulme had prophesied and Eliot so much admired.

Elkin Mathews published *Lustra* in London, Alfred Knopf in New York. Both editions included all of *Cathay,* "some new Chinese stuff," as Pound wrote Iris Barry, "and all of my own work since *Ripostes."* [12] His work "since *Ripostes"* revealed a new, sharp-tongued, sophisticated Pound. A *lustrum,* we are reminded on the title page, is "an offering for the sins of the whole people, made by the censors at the expiration of their five years of office." His skill in *vers libre* is everywhere evident in these seventy-six new poems, and it is not enough to say, as Eliot did in his anony-

[11] "Introduction: 1928," *Ezra Pound: Selected Poems,* ed. T. S. Eliot (London, 1928), pp. 14–15.
[12] *Letters,* p. 81.

mous *Ezra Pound: His Metric and Poetry* (1917), that skill such
as this "comes only after much work in rigid forms." Of course
the pre-*Ripostes* volumes demonstrate Pound's years of practice
with the sestina, the ballad, the conventional lyric. But *Lustra* is
also illustration in depth of Pound's 1913 prescription for modern poetry: direct treatment of the "thing"; accuracy and economy
of language; and rhythm "in sequence of the musical phrase, not
in sequence of the metronome." [13] His theory of verse-as-speech is
ably demonstrated here. When Eliot, in 1922, called Pound *il
miglior fabbro,* it is possible he had these poems in mind as well
as the first cantos. He had said as much, five years earlier, in his
anonymous essay: "When anyone has studied Mr. Pound's poems
in *chronological* order, and has mastered *Lustra* and *Cathay,* he is
prepared for the *Cantos*—but not till then." [14]

Three more volumes followed *Lustra* before Pound left London for Paris. *Quia Pauper Amavi,* published by the Egoist Press
in 1919, gave us eight more poems in the *Lustra* vein, six lyrics
labeled "Langue d'Oc," three cantos (some parts of which were
salvaged for the *Cantos*), and a version of certain passages in
Books II and III of the Elegies of Propertius which Pound carefully titled "Homage to Sextus Propertius." He wrote A. R.
Orage the next spring that "there was never any question of
translation [of Propertius], let alone literal translation. My job
was to bring a dead man to life, to present a living figure." [15] The
academicians ignored his title and misjudged his intentions. The
quarrel still continues. *Hugh Selwyn Mauberley,* published in
April, 1920, is Pound's climactic achievement, not only his fare-

[13] "Imagisme" and "A Few Don'ts by an Imagiste," *Poetry,* I (March, 1913), 198–
206.

[14] *Ezra Pound: His Metric and Poetry* (New York, 1917), p. 28.

[15] *Letters,* pp. 148–49. See also W. G. Hale, "Pegasus Impounded," *Poetry,* XIV
(April, 1919), 52–55, for violent disapproval of Pound's treatment of Propertius.

well to London but a reaffirmation of his role as midwife to modern poetry. *Umbra: The Early Poems of Ezra Pound,* dated June, 1920, is a gathering (and a most unsatisfactory one at that) of "all that [the poet] now wishes to keep in circulation from *Personae, Exultations, Ripostes,* etc., with translations from Guido Cavalcanti and Arnaut Daniel and poems by the late T. E. Hulme." It was the last of Pound's books to be printed by Elkin Mathews. In September, 1920, Pound unburdened himself to William Carlos Williams:

> AND now that there is no longer any intellectual *life* in England save what centres in this eight by ten pentagonal room; now that Remy [de Gourmont] and Henry [Henri Gaudier-Brzeska] are gone and Yeats faded, and NO literary publications whatever extant in England, save what "we" print (*Egoist* and Ovid Press), the question remains whether I have to give up every shred of comfort, every scrap of my personal life, and "gravitate" to a New York which wants me as little now as it did ten and fifteen years ago. Whether, from the medical point of view it is masochism for me even to stay here, instead of shifting to Paris. Whether self-inflicted torture ever has the slightest element of dignity in it?
>
> Or whether I am Omar.
>
> Have I a country at all . . . .[16]

By the end of the year he was ready to join the expatriate crowd in Paris, but he tired of them even more quickly and five years later left for Rapallo. Pound's country was everywhere and nowhere.

A mere recapitulation of publishing history, however impressive, will convince no one that these twelve years of Pound's life

---

[16] *Letters,* pp. 158–59.

may well be the apex of his genius. Students of poetry acquainted with the whole canon know the rest of the story, the feverish activity: Imagism, Amygism, Futurism, Vorticism; *Poetry, Blast,* the *Little Review,* the *Egoist,* the *Dial;* his months with Yeats at a turning point in their careers ("To talk over a poem with [Ezra] is like getting you to put a sentence into dialect. All becomes clear and natural.") ; his finding publishers for Joyce and Eliot and Wyndham Lewis; his letters to Chicago badgering Harriet Monroe ("Until 'we' accept what I've been insisting on for a decade, i.e., a universal standard which pays no attention to time or country—a Weltlitteratur standard—there is no hope."). Readers who come to Pound through the *Cantos,* alas, share none of this excitement, this growth of a bumptious young philologist, in love with Provence, into a perceptive critic and lyric poet. They see only the irascible old man who has turned his ideogrammic method into the logic of no logic and his ambitious epic into a deafening harangue. They say his ego has exploded; but his ego was always enormous and, if we believe Pound, it had to be.

He wrote to Alice Henderson in 1913:

> I wonder if *Poetry* really dares to devote a number to my *new* work. There'll be a *howl.* They won't like it. It's absolutely the *last* obsequies of the Victorian period. I won't permit any selection or editing. It stands now a series of 24 poems, most of them very short.

In the same letter he assured the editors:

> It's not futurism and it's not post-impressionism, but it's work contemporary with those schools and to my mind the most significant that I have yet brought off.
>
> BUTT they won't like it. They won't object as much as they did

to Whitman's outrages, because the stamina of stupidity is weaker. I guarantee you *one* thing. The reader will not be *bored.* He will say ahg, ahg, ahh, ahhh, but-bu-bu-bu-but this isn't Poetry.[17]

Yet these very poems are the breakthrough in modern poetry. If few readers were ready to recognize their quality, at least Pound knew what he had accomplished. They are what he meant when he wrote of Walt Whitman, "It was you that broke the new wood,/ Now is time for carving." He was determined his audience would come to like the "carving," and he nearly exhausted himself (and made enemies in the process) imposing this "new" poetry on them. That is not to discount Hulme or Flint or Ford Madox Ford, or even Harold Monro. They were in London before Pound arrived, setting the stage, founding the magazines, proclaiming the doctrine. Nor is it to deny that Yeats and Eliot ultimately surpassed Pound in the decade following the First World War. He was prepared for that; his letters leave no doubt.[18] What I fear, however, is the neglect of eleven volumes of verse— from *A Lume Spento* to *Umbra*—which so brilliantly illustrate, in a way that the *Cantos* do not, Pound's urbane lyricism, his bold metaphors and startling rhythms, his caustic wit, above all his contagious gusto. The individual volumes, of course, are out of print, but the poet's own selection of the best poems is readily available. In 1926, Horace Liveright asked Pound for a volume of collected poems. He chose two hundred, all pre-*Cantos,* and titled the book *Personae,* not with a perverse desire to confuse but for an obvious reason. They are the masks of his youth, reassembled. New Directions republished the collection in 1949, Faber and

---

[17] *Letters,* pp. 23–24.

[18] On receiving the manuscript of "Prufrock," he wrote Harriet Monroe that Eliot "is the only American I know of who has made what I can call an adequate preparation for writing. He has actually trained himself *and* modernized himself *on his own."* And with typical emphasis, he says of the poem: "PRAY GOD IT BE NOT A SINGLE AND UNIQUE SUCCESS" (*Letters,* p. 40) .

Faber in 1952. Both the student of poetry and the general reader will find it a textbook and a gallery.

To assume *personae* and translate other poets is to court the label "derivative." Pound took that risk; these were his apprentice pieces. His singing school in the London years ranged from the Provençal lyrics of Bertrans de Born and Arnaut Daniel to Guido Calvalcanti of thirteenth-century Florence, Swinburne and Browning, Dowson and Johnson and the Nineties crowd, some of Whitman, some of Kipling, especially Yeats. Before he left for Paris he had also absorbed Li Po through Fenollosa, Sappho through the Imagists, Catullus and Propertius, Gautier and Heine, Laforge and Corbière. The barrier of language was no deterrent. When he discovered the Chinese ideogram he was quick to see its similarity to the Anglo-Saxon kenning and to what Hulme was propounding in his emphasis on "the image." Being the eclectic humanist who never looked on "tradition" as mere conventionalism, Pound wanted to cut across the centuries and bring all Western poetry to life again. And so *Personae,* 1926, is among many things a gallery of adaptations. "The Ballad of the Goodly Fere" [19] takes a traditional verse form for an untraditional portrait: Jesus, "the goodliest fere o' all," no "capon priest" but a "man o' men" who "cried no cry when they drave the nails." The popular monologue, "Cino," laid in the Italian Campagna, 1309, opens with a Browning overtone:

> Bah! I have sung women in three cities,
> But it is all the same;
> And I will sing of the sun,

and descends into diction that was certain to set some teeth on edge. Cino's song is splendid mockery:

[19] "Fere" is a medieval word meaning "mate" or "companion."

> 'Pollo Phoibee, old tin pan, you
> Glory to Zeus' aegis-day,
> Shield o' steel-blue, th' heaven o'er us,
> Hath for boss thy lustre gay!

Pound was never one to treat his models gently. "You, Master Bob Browning," he shouts in the poem "Mesmerism": "Heart that was big as the bowels of Vesuvius . . . Here's to you, Old Hippety-Hop o' the accents." Of Whitman, he says, "I come to you as a grown child/ Who has had a pig-headed father." Heine he loved for his daring:

> O Harry Heine, curses be
> I live too late to sup with thee!
> Who can demolish at such polished ease
> Philistia's pomp and Art's pomposities!

The Troubadours he loved even more, particularly Bertrans de Born.[20] *Personae,* 1926, gives us his translation (i.e., adaptation) of Bertrans' plaint for Prince Henry Plantagenet, a noble lament turned into stately English in "Planh for the Young English King." He takes half of a stanza in Bertrans' "Dompna pois de me no us cal" and builds around it a haunting portrait, "Na Audiart," not wholly successful in rhyme and diction but an early exercise in rhythmic sweep. Bertrans' scorn of sloth and peace is occasion for Pound's most impressive demonstration of his powerful rhythmic control, "Sestina: Altaforte." Altaforte is Bertrans' castle; Papiols is his jongleur. "Dante Alighieri," Pound tells us in a headnote, "put this man in hell for that he was a stirrer up of

[20] See especially the first half of Pound's *The Spirit of Romance* (London, 1910). For more competent discussion than I can give of Pound's translations from Provençal originals, see Leonard Casper's informative article "Apprenticed in Provence," *Poetry,* LXXXI (December, 1952), 203–11.

strife. Eccovi! Judge ye! Have I dug him up again?" He has. With bold spondees, Bertrans bursts on the scene. We can hear Pound declaiming the lines in Bellotti's Soho restaurant, to the delight of the poets' club and the consternation of the other diners:

> Damn it all! all this our South stinks peace.
> You whoreson dog, Papiols, come! Let's to music!
> I have no life save when the swords clash.

Pound manipulates the demanding Provençal verse form with appropriate harshness ("There's no sound like to swords swords opposing") and shocking juxtaposition ("Hell grant soon we hear again the swords clash!" followed four stanzas later by "May God damn for ever all who cry 'Peace!' "). From the Troubadours he learned boldness in song and subject; from the Anglo-Saxons, exactness of image; from the English poets of the generation before him, a colloquial diction and late-Romantic themes. "The history of art," he tells us in *The Spirit of Romance*, "is the history of masterwork, not of failures, or mediocrity . . . . The study of literature is hero-worship." He said it another way in a letter to Margaret Anderson: "The strength of Picasso is largely in his having chewed through and chewed up a great mass of classicism: which, for example, the lesser cubists, and the flabby cubists have not." [21] But the jongleur must someday find his own voice, or he never becomes the troubadour. The apprentice, much as he learns by translation and adaptation, must make his own forms.

Personae, 1926, is replete with poems that show us Pound's individual talent. I shall be the first to admit that they are not profound poems. Pound's attempts at profundity are invariably falter-

[21] *Letters*, p. 113.

ing, and that, let us confess, is one of the troubles with the *Cantos*. But these short poems, in the conciseness of their notation, influenced twentieth-century poetry more than critics are willing to admit. Dated 1912–16, they set a tone and a style which in time was imitated just as Pound imitated his predecessors. The tone is alternately ecstatic, world-weary, caustic, fragile. The style is precise, strongly rhythmic, frequently colloquial, a style fitted for verse-as-speech, a style that never bores. "It is the business of the artist to prevent ennui," Pound believed, "to relieve, refresh, revive the mind of the reader—at reasonable intervals—with some form of ecstasy, by some splendor of thought, some presentation of sheer beauty, some lightning turn of phrase." [22] Ecstasy can be fragile. "The Encounter" has but five lines, yet the central image is remarkably supple and haunting:

> All the while they were talking the new morality
> Her eyes explored me.
> And when I arose to go
> Her fingers were like the tissue
> Of a Japanese paper napkin.

Almost as briefly, and with guileless understatement, he recalls past ecstasy in "Erat Hora":

> "Thank you, whatever comes." And then she turned
> And, as the ray of sun on hanging flowers
> Fades when the wind hath lifted them aside,
> Went swiftly from me. Nay, whatever comes
> One hour was sunlit and the most high gods
> May not make boast of any better thing
> Than to have watched that hour as it passed.

[22] *The Spirit of Romance*, p. 8.

Ecstasy can be visual. His familiar "L'Art, 1910" and "In a Station of the Metro" are too often reprinted in favor of the lesser-known but lovely "Gentildonna":

> She passed and left no quiver in the veins, who
>   now
> Moving among the trees, and clinging
>   in the air she severed,
> Fanning the grass she walked on then, endures:
> Grey olive leaves beneath a rain-cold sky.

The single image of "Alba" takes the severe economy of the Imagists as far as it can go:

> As cool as the pale wet leaves
>   of lily-of-the valley
> She lay beside me in the dawn.

Nor is Pound afraid of humor, though his humor is usually dry. "Laughter is no mean ecstasy," he tells us. In "Tame Cat" he says that it rests him to converse with beautiful women:

> Even though we talk nothing but nonsense,
>
> The purring of the invisible antennae
> Is both stimulating and delightful.

"Phyllidula," on the other hand, might have shocked in 1916:

> Phyllidula is scrawny but amorous,
> Thus have the gods awarded her,

That in pleasure she receives more than she can give;
If she does not count this blessed
Let her change her religion.

"The Temperaments" we know caused difficulties. Elkin Mathews marked it for deletion from *Lustra;* Alfred Knopf omitted it from the American trade edition but printed it privately in sixty copies not for sale:

Nine adulteries, 12 liaisons, 64 fornications and
    something approaching a rape
Rest nightly upon the soul of our delicate friend
    Florialis,
And yet the man is so quiet and reserved in demeanour
That he passes for both bloodless and sexless.
Bastidides, on the contrary, who both talks and writes
    of nothing save copulation,
Has become the father of twins,
But he accomplished this feat at some cost;
He had to be four times cuckold.

The reader unfamiliar with *Personae* may not be satisfied with these vignettes. He will want to read the more ambitious poems, reprinted in this 1926 volume, from *Ripostes, Lustra,* and *Cathay.* "Portrait d'une Femme" may have derived from Henry James; but in the opening lines we sense at once that Pound gives it his own spare diction and flat rhythm, the world-weary tone "Prufrock" made popular five years later:

Your mind and you are our Sargasso Sea,
London has swept about you this score years
And bright ships left you this or that in fee:

> Ideas, old gossip, oddments of all things,
> Strange spars of knowledge and dimmed wares of price.
> Great minds have sought you—lacking someone else.
> You have been second always. Tragical?
> No. You preferred it to the usual thing;
> One dull man, dulling and uxorious,
> One average mind—with one thought less, each year.

"Provincia Deserta" and "Near Perigord" are Pound in Provence, not mere borrowings from the Troubadours. "The River-Merchant's Wife: A Letter" and "Poem by the Bridge at Ten-Shin" derive from Fenollosa's notes on Li Po, but they are English syntax and idiom, dressing a universal subject. Pound has learned not only to assume the *persona* but to inhabit it. In "Moeurs Contemporaines," a group of eight sketches, there is no question of Pound's intentions: scathing satire, verse-as-speech, broken rhythms, colloquial diction. Conceivably they lead to Auden, Cummings, MacLeish, as well as to "The Wasteland."

Hugh Selwyn Mauberley is the major work, a sequence of dramatic lyrics. Pound keeps telling us that he is no more Mauberley than Eliot is Prufrock, and I suppose we must take his word. Back in 1908 he was telling Williams what the dramatic lyric meant to him:

> To me the short so-called dramatic lyric—at any rate the sort of thing I do—is the poetic part of a drama the rest of which (to me the prose part) is left to the reader's imagination or set in a short note. I catch the character I happen to be interested in at the moment he interests me, usually a moment of song, self-analysis, or sudden understanding or revelation. And the rest of the play would bore me and presumably the reader. I paint my man as I *conceive* him. Et voilà tout.[23]

[23] *Letters*, pp. 3–4.

Yet in preparing the poem for the New Directions reprinting, in 1949, of *Personae,* 1926, he added this note in small type at the foot of the title page: "The sequence is so distinctly a farewell to London that the reader who chooses to regard this as an exclusively American edition may as well omit it and turn at once to page 205." Let us read it then as a farewell, and whether Mauberley is Pound or another *persona* is irrelevant. He divides the poem into eighteen parts, speaking through his own voice in the first thirteen, admittedly the poet "out of key with his time," one who "strove to resuscitate the dead art of poetry," in vain. The last five parts, labeled "Mauberley 1920," can be read either as a five-part coda or as a "portrait d'un homme," that is, an imaginative projection of one facet of Pound or merely another picture in the gallery; but it is the poetry, not the identification, that is important.

It is impossible and unnecessary to rehearse this entire poem here, impossible because of its length, unnecessary because John J. Espey has done it so admirably in his study, *Ezra Pound's "Mauberley."* But I cannot end this essay without repeating, with alteration, Eliot's dictum of 1917. Not until we have read *Lustra* and *Cathay,* he felt, are we ready for the *Cantos.* Rather I should say, not until we have read *Personae,* 1926, are we ready for *Hugh Selwyn Mauberley.* But when we are ready, we will discover how extraordinarily subtle, precise, and evocative this sequence is, how much it is a collage of Pound's work from 1908 to 1920, neither obscure nor remote. Some parts of it are derivative. The thirteenth is patently Edmund Waller, reversed:

> Go, dumb-born book,
> Tell her that sang me once that song of Lawes:
> Hadst thou but song
> As thou hast subjects known,

> Then were there cause in thee that should condone
> Even my faults that heavy upon me lie,
> And build her glories their longevity.

Some parts are bitter satire. The ninth, "Mr. Nixon," could be a portrait of Arnold Bennett:

> In the cream gilded cabin of his steam yacht
> Mr. Nixon advised me kindly, to advance with fewer
> Dangers of delay. "Consider
>   "Carefully the reviewer.
>
> .   .   .   .
>
> "And no one knows, at sight, a masterpiece.
> "And give up verse, my boy,
> "There's nothing in it."

The fourth and fifth lament the loss of the best young men "for an old bitch gone in the teeth/ For a botched civilization." Pound felt that German guns had killed the best sculptor of his generation, Gaudier-Brzeska, a young critic, T. E. Hulme, a young poet, Rupert Brooke, and the liveliest mind in France, Remy de Gourmont. The second and third poems are bitter for equally personal reasons:

> The age demanded an image
> Of its accelerated grimace,
> Something for the modern stage,
> Not, at any rate, an Attic grace;
>
> Not, not certainly, the obscure reveries
> Of the inward gaze;
> Better mendacities
> Than the classics in paraphrase!

Other parts of the sequence are warm and sensitive portraits. Ford Madox Ford, an old friend back from the war, found London intolerable and retreated to Sussex:

> Beneath the sagging roof
> The stylist has taken shelter,
> Unpaid, uncelebrated,
> At last from the world's welter
>
> Nature receives him . . . .

From first to last line, in other words, Pound is in complete control, having tried out his forms, his rhythm, his diction for ten years and more. To his constant readers the sequence must have come, in 1920, as affirmation of his talent, not as baffling pastiche or willful obscurity. This talent for precise image and contrapuntal rhythms is spread in profusion over the pages of *Ripostes, Lustra,* and *Cathay. Mauberley* was his farewell; but it is, at the same time, his arrival.

Robert Frost

and

Man's "Royal Role"

Claude M. Simpson

IF IN the years since *Steeple Bush* (1947) Robert Frost has not seemed to produce much new poetry, we can scarcely be surprised. His public role has become onerous enough to tax a man half his age, and it is remarkable that his vitality has been equal to the demands of a heavy lecture schedule, a term as poetry consultant to the Library of Congress, trips to South America, Israel, England, and Ireland, and the exhausting attentions of an eager hero-worshiping public. There is no doubt that Frost has thrived amid all this stir, enjoying the role of seer and pundit, yet never forgetting that he speaks for poetry and poets. As a personality he has been an international success, but we may ask what has happened to his creativity during these years. The question is in some measure an impertinence, for after seventy a man should have the right to taper off as he pleases or to stop altogether if he sees his talents waning. Frost may have slowed down, but in the past decade or so he has given us enough glimpses of new work to let us sample his interests and discover the genuine quality of a poetical imagination that has scarcely flagged. I should like to consider a handful of recent poems, chiefly private issues presented to his friends at Christmas, some of them later published in magazines and all of them presumably destined for a new volume, *In the Clearing,* not yet in print as this is written.[1]

Unquestionably the localism characterizing so many of his familiar poems has lately become a minor and recessive note, as we can see from the blank verse dialogue, "A Cabin in the Clearing" (1951).[2] Although the sleepers in the cabin have

>   been here long enough
>   To push the woods back from around the house
>   And part them in the middle with a path,

Frost works at one remove from circumstantial realism; the dialogue is actually a *débat* on the human condition, carried on by Mist and Smoke—the former full of doubt, the latter capable of some optimism, but both considering themselves guardian spirits. Cabin and clearing are no more than symbols of man's scratching at civilization, and the poem is disembodied dialectic, not dramatic evocation. Mist doesn't believe the cabin people "Know where they are," and sees the path as leading only to "the equally bewildered." To find out where they are, they ask the "Red Man," the philosopher from the pulpit,

---

[1] All poems discussed here are from a new collection of poems by Robert Frost, copyright © 1962 by Robert Frost, and are reprinted with the permission of the poet and his publishers Holt, Rinehart and Winston, Inc.

Earlier working titles for the collection were *And All We Call American* and *The Great Misgiving.* On the latter, a phrase from "Kitty Hawk," see John Ciardi, "Robert Frost: Master Conversationalist at Work," *Saturday Review,* XLII (March 21, 1959) , 17–18.

[2] Dates are those of Frost's Christmas cards unless otherwise indicated.

anyone there is to ask—
In the fond faith accumulated fact
Will of itself take fire and light the world up.

But neither dogmatic theology nor pragmatic philosophy seems to serve the need of the human spirit. Smoke suggests that

when they know *who*
They are, they may know better where they are.

But even this sense of identity is not to be easily won: "They are too sudden to be credible." Mist, unwilling to "give them up for lost," proposes that the two of them eavesdrop on the talk in the darkened cabin, for "Putting the lamp out has not put their thought out"; but he expects little beyond perchance seeing "if we can tell the bass from the soprano." The poet, pondering the problem of man's self-knowledge, offers no apocalyptic light, but neither is he contemptuous of the almost pathetic groping for certitude. Far from being an example of Frost's unwillingness to grasp problems seriously, as Yvor Winters has charged of comparable contexts, the poem offers a symbolic statement of a situation as Frost sees it; his duty as poet does not require that he solve mankind's dilemmas (the obligation of a moralist is another question). The success of the poem is limited not by its epistemology but by its lack of dramatic tension; it partakes of the medieval morality play with none of the poignant flashes which occasionally illuminate *Everyman*.

Frost's later work, as even this example shows, has not been strongly grounded in concrete specification of New England life and lore. The other poems we shall examine are in no sense indigenous except for the continued Yankee "voice" which Frost never forsakes for long. His themes have kept pace with the times and reflect his increasingly conspicuous role as citizen of the world, as spokesman for humanity, as mediator between science and the humanities. His attitudes are not newly assumed but have been evident for a generation; the emphasis, however, has markedly shifted from the days when he was considered primarily a New England poet and his verse narratives were compared with the short stories of Sarah Orne Jewett, Mary Wilkins Freeman, and Alice Brown. Neither the "North of Boston" country nor its people can be said to have dominated his thought for the past twenty years. The world at large has forced itself in upon him, and it is a rare late poem—"Directive" is one such—which shows significant traces of the earlier regional specificity. His poetic strategies now more characteristically reflect America's concern with itself and with the past as it has unfolded on both sides of the ocean. This historical dimension in his work we can illustrate with two poems, both of them unmistakably American yet neither nationalistic.

The slighter of the two is top-heavy with one of Frost's longest titles: "Does No One But Me At All Ever Feel This Way in the Least." When it was belatedly mailed to his friends in the summer of 1953, it was accompanied by a note to explain the unseasonable gesture: "This Christmas poem, though not isolationist, is so dangerously near isolationist, it was thought better to send it out for Independence Day instead of Christmas." And the July 4 postmark was timely for a poem commenting on our ties to Europe and our problem of defining ourselves in some distinctive fashion. Frost apostrophizes the "ocean sea" as the great separator of the Old and New World, and reminds us that we would have been disappointed if our country hadn't developed at least "a single trait" of its own, despite a "homesickness" which could lead us to apply the old British word for wheat ("corn") to the Indian grain of maize. Nowadays, however, the sea is not the barrier of old:

> Our sailors ride a bullet for a boat.
> Our coverage of distance is so facile
> It makes us to have had a sea in vain.

Mock-seriously he orders the sea to "Do work for women"— grind shells "Into a lady's finger ring or thimble." He recognizes that the "ocean had been spoken to before" by such as King Canute and Lord Byron, but was no more likely now than then to pay heed. So the poet is left with the ego-salvaging device of betaking himself "So far inland the very name of ocean/ Goes mentionless except in baby-school." This is the near-isolationism of which Frost's note spoke, but what he seeks is really independence —the converse of colonialism, not mere xenophobia. The shrinkage of the world to the point that "Our moat around us is no more a moat,/ Our continent no more a moated castle" does not lead the poet to an explicit formulation of his discontent or sorrow or disillusionment. But one can surmise his temper from his title, and perhaps from such an earlier poem as "Triple Bronze" in which he seems glad to have layers of protection "between too much and me." Despite the fact that "Does No One" is a poem of the atomic age his retreat to an inland fastness is not imagined as physical self-preservation; only the survival of the spirit seems to concern him. But his primary attention is to the ocean, and he returns to it in the last stanza with a quip at the expense of the once mighty element: the "baby-school" is so far from salt water that the teacher, knowing nothing herself at first hand, calls the ocean "a pool" and tells her class "how Sinbad was a sailor." The poem is more diffuse and less certain in tone than "The Gift Outright," although the two share the common theme of "Our chance of being people newly born," and both express the difficulties (ever so differently conceived) of achieving independence.

"And All We Call American," [3] an engaging poem about Columbus, also develops the idea that the New World offered man a new opportunity. Queen Isabella, Frost says, backed Columbus for more than mere "scientific news," and when the Portuguese Da Gama about the same time brought back gold from India, it was embarrassing to the Spanish queen that Columbus' "reckoning was off a sea." He "might have boldly made the bluff" had he argued that his discovery of America meant "A fresh start for the human race." He would have deserved being celebrated "As a god who had given us/ A more than Moses' exodus." Columbus' explorations may have postponed trouble among men by giving us additional room, but eventually we would be "enacting out the doom/ Of being in each other's way," and we would have to face the problem of "how to crowd but still be kind." Because the significance of the voyages was not realized, Columbus was rewarded with imprisonment and "such small posthumous renown" as having a country, a town, a holiday named for him—nothing he would have found very gratifying.

Conjuring up a modern Flying Dutchman drama, Frost fancies that the "unlaid ghost" of Columbus' flagship still "probes and dents our rocky coast" looking for the Northwest Passage and cursing every inlet for not being a strait. "Some day," the poet predicts, "our navy"

> Will take in tow this derelict
> And lock him through Culebra Cut,
> His eyes as good (or bad) as shut

[3] Alone among the poems here discussed, "And All We Call American" was not used as a Christmas card. It appeared in the *Atlantic Monthly*, CLXXXVII (June, 1951), 28–29.

> To all the modern works of man
> And all we call American.

If Columbus finds himself in the Pacific he will not understand how he got past (or through) the continent, but will ascribe it "To naught but his own force of will/ Or at most some Andean quake," unmindful of "All he owes to the artifice/ Of tractor-plow and motor-drill." The Panama Canal serves Frost as an example of American technological genius, which he here holds in high esteem; but "all we call American" is endlessly subtle and complex.

> America is hard to see.
> Less partial witnesses than he
> In book on book have testified
> They could not see it from outside—
> Or inside either for that matter.
> We know the literary chatter.

The two concluding stanzas picture the ghostly Columbus as being too bent on his original quest to "stop for gratitude"; this hemisphere "was never his concern/ Except as it denied him way/ To fortune-hunting in Cathay." Getting such a late start, he will find that Asia

> Is about tired of being looted
> While having its beliefs disputed.
> His can be no such easy raid
> As Cortez on the Aztecs made.

Except for the vividly pictorial image of the derelict ship nuzzling the shoreline "from fifty north to fifty south," the force of the poem lies in its rhetorical cleverness, its good-natured, even playful dialectic. The fanciful machinery may be at times a bit heavy, but it serves Frost's purpose in contrasting the "promised land" of the New World with the chimeras of Asiatic fortune-hunting to which Columbus would forever be dedicated. The key line, "America is hard to see," is a native's protestation; the praise of our mechanized civilization is unusually chauvinistic for Frost; otherwise, however, the poet has an amused, somewhat detached point of view, alert to history and therefore able to maintain a wide-angle perspective here.

It is but a step from the internationalism of this pair of poems to an even more generalized sense of scene, and here we may instance those in which geographical setting is negligible or entirely absent, and an interesting group in which astronomical or cosmic associations are dominant. As an example of the first we may cite "Doom to Bloom," a modest poem of 1950 on the idea of progress, and "My Objection to Being Stepped On," an extended conceit. In the former a Roman speaker asks the Cumaean sibyl, "What are the simple facts of progress . . . ?" The answer of this "charming Ogress" is that if progress is "not a mere illusion," it is simply "diffusion—/ Of coats oats votes to all mankind." For whatever the political leanings of a state, its "one function is to give"; and the echoic series "coats oats votes" defines clearly enough a conception of the general welfare more liberal than Frost's social ideas are commonly held to be. Yet the poet seems committed to an egalitarian political philosophy rather than to a cradle-to-grave paternalism. Unlike many of his other political poems (e.g., "Build Soil," "Provide, Provide"), this one eschews an ironic or whimsical tone which could undercut our accepting the poetic statement at its face value. In the final stanza he re-phrases the idea of diffusion using a simple floral metaphor: "The bud must bloom till blowsy blown/ Its petals loosen and are strown"; this is "a fate it can't evade/ Unless 'twould rather wilt than fade." The alternatives in this closing line oppose an unnatural to a natural fulfillment of a life process. The wilted flower, starved of food or water, has not fulfilled its destiny, whereas the faded flower strews its petals as nature has ordained, symbolizing a seasonal completion. (Were the process not cyclic, the image could scarcely apply to a political state.) The sibyl cites as her authority the "Surviving Book," a name recalling by contrariety the familiar medieval Domesday Book, with which the poem's title "Doom to Bloom" resonates suggestively. The classical setting is incidental and the drama slight, for the sibyl's speech, comprising three of the four quatrains, lacks the tension of a thrust-and-parry exchange. The floral closing stanza, though crisply phrased, does not strengthen the central idea, perhaps because its function as reinforcement is too obvious.

In "My Objection to Being Stepped On" (1957), the poet has "stepped on the toe/ Of an unemployed hoe" and the handle has flown up and struck him "In the seat of my sense." The Biblical prophecy has been unaccountably reversed when "The first tool I step on" has "Turned into a weapon." Here again the setting of the verses is nothing. In his light, mirthful mood Frost plays with a figure that amuses him, and turns a formula around to watch it work. And it works well if we assume the persona to be a Thurberian man to whom things always happen and against whom the inanimate world is in conspiracy. This fine *jeu d'esprit* is marred only by a carelessly phrased title which encourages allegorical speculation at cross purposes with the simple matter-of-fact tone.

Some of Frost's most interesting poems have been at least enriched if not initially motivated by his knowledge of astronomy and his awareness of current scientific frontiers as they affect man's place in the physical universe. We shall look first at "One More Brevity" and "A-Wishing Well," which are nominally concerned with star and satellite (old style). And finally we shall examine "Accidentally On Purpose" and "Kitty Hawk," in which biological or physical science becomes an avenue to Frost's resounding affirmation of man and his "royal role" in the cosmic scheme.

The astronomical pieces are to be put beside "Choose Something Like a Star," "Desert Places," "The Star-Splitter," "Fireflies in the Garden," and others in which lore of the heavens is easily and familiarly exploited even when it is not dominant in the argument of the poem. Central in "One More Brevity" (1953) [4] is the simple fact that Sirius, brightest star in the firmament, is called the Dog Star. The multilevel verbal possibilities engage Frost's wit as well as his metaphysical interest. A Dalmatian dog wanders into the poet's house late one night and the poet immediately sets out water and food, preparing to adapt his life to his new companion. Next morning, however, the dog leaves as precipitately as he had come. This is the framework about which the poem is built. In setting the stage for the episode Frost has his narrator step outside before going to bed:

> Before I gave up seeing and slept
> I said I would see how Sirius kept
> His watch dog eye on what remained
> To be gone into if not explained.

It is this stellar contemplation that prepares us for the appearance of what is "Not a heavenly dog made manifest,/ But an earthly

---

[4] Reprinted in *Atlantic Monthly*, CXCIII (June, 1954), 34.

dog of the carriage breed." And after the Dalmatian has left next day the narrator speculates on whether there was something supernatural about the experience. The dog "might have been the dream of a ghost/ In spite of the way his tail had smacked/ My floor so hard and matter-of-fact." He could even persuade himself that the dog was an incarnation of Sirius, come down to earth —and here Frost shifts from the all-round countryman to the rather self-conscious bard—

> To show by deeds he didn't resent
> My profiting by his virtue so long,
> Yet doing so little about it in song.[5]

What does the poet make of the brief experience? It may have been intended to convey a symbolic meaning—"A meaning I was supposed to seek,/ And finding, was indisposed to speak." He is content to leave it thus unresolved.

Most engaging to the reader is the lively account of the Dalmatian's entrance and reception. Here Frost is at his best, happy in his language and vivid in every characterizing image.

> He dumped himself like a bag of bones,
> He sighed himself a couple of groans,
> And head to tail then firmly curled
> Like swearing off on the traffic world.

In the presence of water and food set for him,

---

[5] Frost appended a footnote naming two poems to show that he had not been wholly neglectful. One is "Canis Major," a fine short piece describing the "great Overdog" romping across the southern sky and himself as "a poor underdog" who tonight will bark with his great companion. The other is "Choose Something Like a Star," a poem on steadfastness which addresses the "fairest" star in sight, evidently Sirius.

> He rolled an eye with gratitude
> (Or merely manners it may have been),
> But never so much as lifted chin.

The poet, half-understanding the dog's reluctance, speaks to him "in tones of adoption":

> "Gustie, old boy, Dalmatian Gus
> You're right, there's nothing to discuss.
> Don't try to tell me what's on your mind,
> The sorrow of having been left behind,
> Or the sorrow of having run away.
> All that can wait for the light of day.
> Meanwhile feel obligation-free.
> Nobody has to confide in me."

But this one-sided conversation is unsatisfactory even to the poet, and he says, "I wasn't sure I was talking dog."
    The brief encounter leaves him

> to taste in little the grief
> That comes of dogs' lives being so brief,
> Only a fraction of ours at most.

Thus without emotional excess he hints at the immediate and literal significance of the episode. If its ulterior meaning shreds away in the closing lines, the reason may lie partially in Frost's dislike of the stock response. Moreover, when he suggests "An intimation, a shot of ray," he will not be committed to the task of trying to express the inexpressible. He has hinted at supernatural and metaphysical implications of the overnight drama; this is enough for the poem.

"A-Wishing Well" (note the unexpected hyphenation) is another piece of amiable make-believe in which Frost plays a puckish role of celestial mythmaker. He begins this poem of 1959 [6] by picturing a poet who, in framing some conventional wishes, concludes with "one thing more that may not be." Assuming that the notion expresses "Some quaint dissatisfaction" of the poet's which cannot be unriddled, Frost proceeds to develop what his own wish would be in the circumstance, and this gives us the body of the poem. His desire is "for a better sky," and in an expansive mood, "Like splashing phosphorescent paint," he'd like to "fill the sky as full of moons/ As circus day of toy balloons." But realizing that a tradition of restraint has been built into his make-up from childhood, he revises his wish:

> Some planets, the unblinking four,
> Are seen to juggle moons galore.
> A lot would be a lot of fun.
> But all I ask's an extra one.
> Let's get my incantation right:
> "I wish I may I wish I might"
> Give earth another satellite.[7]

This poem may not have been conceived before the Sputniks and Discoverers began to orbit the earth in 1958, but it did antedate the August, 1960, launching of Echo I, the first artificial satellite visible to the naked eye, shining with substantially the brightness of Sirius. Frost surely took great delight in these scientific accomplishments, but he would not have put too much stock in the clairvoyance of these lines, for his own thought was moving in a somewhat different direction.

[6] Reprinted in *Atlantic Monthly,* CCV (April, 1960) , 63.

[7] I suppose the "unblinking four" to be Mars, Earth, Jupiter, and Saturn, which have two dozen satellites among them.

Since our one moon was "torn" from Earth's "Pacific side," he thinks that

> It needn't be quite so terrific
> To get another from the Atlantic.
> It needn't be quite so gigantic
> As coming from a lesser ocean.

He describes what Arcadians recalled of the event "When unto Earth her first was born" in the dawn of history.

> All the sea water in one tide
> And all the air rushed to the spot,

and people "saved themselves by hanging on/ To a plant called the silphion," which "can't be pulled up by the root." The concussion produced a grotesque effect: "Men's legs and bodies in the gale/ Streamed out like pennants swallow-tail." Continuing a mythical account worthy of Pliny, Frost pays tribute to the intrepid who held on to the silphion so fiercely that "Some of them gave way at the wrist/ Before they gave way at the fist"—their grip tenacious even when the wind's force sundered them from their extremities.

Although "Good liberals" would think Frost's wish for a new and lesser satellite "too hard on the human race," he holds that "Man's practically inexterminate," and concludes the poem with an allusion to the Flood as symbolic of the periodic cataclysms that have threatened our extinction:

> There's always been an Ararat
> Where someone else begat
> To start the world all over at.

The cap-and-bells treatment of rhyme here is in keeping with Frost's indulgent whimsy, which is neither too egocentric nor too ponderous. His humor is dexterous and his control of fantasy skillful. From the long perspective of historical time he pictures man as indomitable, although the subject of the poem is ostensibly the creation of earth's moons. "And All We Call American" spoke of Columbus' discovery as offering mankind a fresh start; "A-Wishing Well" celebrates the principle of repeated renascence as the reason for believing that man will continue to prevail. Without heroics the poet shows himself stouthearted in the face of paralyzing threats to life on this planet. He is the well-wisher.

When he contemplates the place of humanity in a mechanistic universe his optimism is centered on man's intellectual prowess. This is partially true in "Kitty Hawk," as we shall see, but the balance of intellect and emotion is more evident in "Accidentally On Purpose" (1960).[8] This brief poem on design in the universe begins with the most simplistic definition one can easily conceive: "The Universe is but the Thing of things,/ The things but balls all going round in rings." Two following stanzas develop a hypothesis that "all was rolling blind/ Till accidentally it hit on mind," and thus through mankind the universe developed purpose, with Darwin at hand "To show the evolution how to steer." But in the middle of the poem he brings us up short: "Don't you believe it." There must have been "purpose from the first"; "We were just purpose coming to a head." Whether the ordering hand was "His or Hers or Its," the existence of a divinity is clear if one grant "intention, purpose, and design." The poem might well have ended here, but a final stanza moves from the question of design and the designer to the poet's very personal and no longer detached attitude toward scientific truth.

---

[8] Reprinted in *Atlantic Monthly,* CCVII (March, 1961), 50.

> And yet for all this help of head and brain
> How happily instinctive we remain,
> Our best guide upward further to the light,
> Passionate preference such as love at sight.

Frost appears to be rejoicing in instinct as if it were free will, as if through its exercise man transcended the purposive ordering of materialistic phenomena. "Love," "preference," and, of course, "passionate" are here the key words, words which help to define man's humanity as a harmonious combination of head and heart. If instinct is in one sense design, it is also an individuating response, never quite identical in any two people. Teleologically Frost has his cake and eats it; at least he has gone beyond Thomas Huxley and has stopped this side of Sartre.

Vivian C. Hopkins observed of *Steeple Bush* that most of the volume is "weighed down by the threat of extinction hovering over the world since Hiroshima." [9] In more recent work, however, Frost's buoyancy seems to have been restored by man's challenge of space and by an implicit faith in humanity's ability to survive the nuclear threats to life on this planet. A generation ago he was prophetically expressing an expansive view of the future in the poem "On a Tree Fallen Across the Road"; there he pictured the human race, not limited to "aimless circling in one place," steering "straight off after something into space." His language is primarily figurative, but the space metaphor suggests a limitless view of man's aspirations to which Frost can again subscribe. During the past decade, as fantasies have been transformed into current events, he has refined his views in the complex poem "Kitty Hawk," which can almost stand alone as *the* representative work of the 1950's. Except for his two masques, it is the longest

---

[9] "Robert Frost: Out Far and In Deep," *Western Humanities Review*, XIV (Summer, 1960), 259.

poem he has written since "New Hampshire." As the most ambitious work of our group it will repay a detailed examination, and is not the less interesting for having grown under Frost's hand after he had begun to release it for publication.

Its original form, called "Kitty Hawk, 1894," was issued as Frost's Christmas card for 1956. The centenary issue of the *Atlantic Monthly* in 1957 contained "Kitty Hawk," a revised and expanded version of the original poem plus a new second part of approximately equal length, bringing the whole to almost 450 lines.[10] In 1959 an excerpt from the second part, with textual alterations and twenty-five new lines, appeared in the *Saturday Review*.[11] The final text of the poem may reveal further changes.

"Kitty Hawk" is an outgrowth of an event of 1894 which the poet recalls sixty years after. The twenty-year-old Frost was trying to make a favorable impression on his former schoolmate Elinor White, who after graduation had gone to St. Lawrence College in Canton, New York. As a very personal tribute to the young woman who soon afterward became his wife, he had a little pamphlet of five of his poems locally printed in an edition of two copies; in October of 1894, he presented *Twilight* to her. For reasons which Mrs. Sergeant's biography does not really explain, Frost's gesture seems to have been coolly received, so much so that he tore up his own copy of *Twilight* and wandered away into the South for a month. That December he wrote that he had been "out of time a little while," and more specifically, "Four weeks ago and until Friday last I was in Virginia, North Carolina, and Maryland, very literally and without address." [12] "Kitty Hawk" makes it clear that he touched at Elizabeth City and accompanied

[10] CC (November, 1957), 52–56.

[11] XLII (March 21, 1959), 18.

[12] Elizabeth Shepley Sergeant, *Robert Frost: The Trial by Existence* (New York, 1960), p. 44.

some hospitable North Carolinians on a duck hunt in Currituck Sound and along the adjacent "banks." The complex perspective from which he writes also takes account of the historic flight of the Wright brothers in 1903—not actually described, but clearly the stimulus to much of his thought in Part II—and of a conversation he had years later with Orville Wright.

At the outset Frost says that when he first visited Kitty Hawk he might have written "A prophetic ditty"—a "flight" of his own, prophetic of the exploits of the Wright brothers on the same sands. Pursuing the metaphor as it applied to himself, he recalls that "It was then as though/ I could hardly wait/ To degravitate," and he goes on:

> I might well have soared,
> I might well have sung,
> Though my bent was toward
> Little more, alas,
> Than Cape Hatteras . . . .

The reason for his mood, concisely phrased in his 1956 text, was his feeling "Out of sorts with fate,"

> Wandering to and fro
> In the earth alone,
> You might say too poor
> Spirited to care
> Who I was or where.

The effect is intensified by a passage that begins the 1957 interpolation of almost a hundred lines. Here he comes closest to revealing the extent of his emotional disturbance, but not its cause:

> I was being blown
> Down along the coast
> Like a crumpled better-
> Left-unwritten letter
> I to waste had thrown—
> Given up for dead.

But after an interval at nearby Nag's Head he felt less dispirited, and the urge came upon him to poetize his new knowledge of "what/ Love is all about." Had he carried out his intention, he

> might well have sung
> The initial flight
> That was to be flown
> Into the sublime
> Off these sands of Time.

Continuing his fancy—we are still speaking of the long 1957 interpolation—he recounts jesting with one of the Wright brothers that the earliest flight from Kitty Hawk might have been his own. Would Wright have minded? "Could he tell me why/ Be original?/ Why was it so very,/ Very necessary/ To be first of all?" But this was no jesting matter; there had been conflicting claims which

> Money and maneuver
> Fostered overlong
> Until Herbert Hoover
> Raised this tower shaft
> To undo the wrong.[13]

---

[13] The National Kitty Hawk Memorial was erected by the United States government and dedicated November 19, 1932. President Hoover was not present, but his letter was read at the ceremonies.

Because America neglected the Wrights for so long, their pioneer plane—"this craft/ Man was first to waft/ Like a kiss to God"—reposed abroad where it was appreciated. "The theft of glory," he says, is worse than grave-robbing, but, fortunately, "All has been redressed." [14]

Even had his own soaring in 1894 laid "one claim/ To the Runway's fame," he couldn't (in 1957)

> make it seem
> More than that my theme
> Might have been a dream
> Of Cape Hatteras,
> Or else Roanoke,
> One more fond alas
> For the seed of folk
> Sowed in vain by Raleigh . . . .

His self-centered malaise had been displaced by a sense of the locale—the historical reality of Roanoke Island and its ill-fated colony settled in 1584, the evocation of Cape Hatteras as a grave-yard of the western Atlantic.

If these stimuli produced no poetry at the time, the reason was, he says, that

> Getting too befriended,
> As so often, ended
> Any melancholy
> I was to have sung.

Here the interpolation ends and the rest of the section is almost identical in both versions. He describes the kindness and solici-

---

[14] For some twenty years the plane was on display at the Science Museum in London. It was returned to the United States and installed in the Smithsonian Institution on December 17, 1948, the forty-fifth anniversary of the flight.

tude of the Southerners ("Some kind of committee/ From Elizabeth City") who set out with guns and liquor on a duck hunt and
included him "Like a little brother," taking care that his "in-
nocence/ Should at all events/ Tenderly be kept." But their
need "To make someone glad" could not minister to him, and he
broke away for a solitary walk along the ocean sands at Kitty
Hawk. Here he "fell in/ With a lone coast guard/ On midnight
patrol" who "Asked about my soul/ And where-all I'd been,"
and recalled to him the legend that the ship of Theodosia Burr
was wrecked off Hatteras—she was sailing from South Carolina to
New York to visit her father Aaron Burr and the ship disappeared.
The patrolman interpreted the episode as punishment for her
and even more for her father: "We don't know what for;/ There
was no confession." But Burr seemed to be "too devoted" to his
daughter.[15]

Twice in one day the poet, "at odds with men," observed "their
pity:/ For a daughter drowned,/ For a son astray." [16] In the final
lines of this section the mood is generalized when the poet
admonishes Kitty Hawk not to be dismayed:

> some time in some
> Mood akin to pity
> You would weep no less
> For mankind's success
> Than for their distress.

[15] Burr had returned in May, 1812, from a protracted exile in Europe, and
Theodosia left Georgetown, S. C., on December 30 of that year. Among the legends
concerning the ill-fated vessel was the persistent story that pirates waylaid it and
forced passengers to walk the plank. The boat was said to have drifted ashore at
Kitty Hawk, and persons going aboard found everything in place, including silk
dresses in the cabin. Thus the basis for the coast guard's reference to "Things they
think she wore . . . / In someone's possession/ Here at Kitty Hawk."

[16] The 1957 revision, reversing the last two lines, gives greater emphasis to the sea
tragedy than to the poet's inner disturbances, while defining pity toward the two as
"Equally profound."

The last pair of lines was sharpened to "For man's small success/ Than his unsuccess"—not an unqualified improvement. The important 1957 change was the addition of a line immediately before those just quoted: Kitty Hawk is not to be dismayed, for "Men will get away." This idea gives more point to the final verses of Part I:

> You'd be overcome
> In the deathless scene
> When that common scoff,
> Poor Darius Green,
> And his fool machine
> Finally took off.

The reference is to the familiar humorous poem of John T. Trowbridge, written a generation before the Wrights' plane "Finally took off." Until they succeeded, the Wrights were in little higher esteem than the awkward barnyard experimenter Darius Green, and the linking of the two efforts is skillful in its control of tone—note the ambiguity of "overcome" and the irony of "deathless scene." What has been gathering to a focus in the last stretches of this section is the idea of indulgence, of sympathy for either tragedy or triumph. Frost treats the theme personally in his remarks on the kind North Carolinians, then moves a step away to record the attitude of the coast guardsman; finally, he applies the notion to Kitty Hawk, invoking its spirit as presiding over the scene. Genuine emotion is in order, whether for congratulation or pity.

Part II is a meditation on man's challenge of nature, his place in the universe, and the humanistic use of science. Briefly summarized, the argument is that although we couldn't have foreseen that man would fly, man did. The triumph was one of mind;

we men are the only "thinking race/ Anywhere in space," and our insatiable curiosity led us to organize the known and explore the unknown. We named everything (a process he describes as mastery "By . . . nomenclature"), including bodies in space— and once we had named them we wished to "touch/ Not to mention clutch." He scorns those who hold that mere "reaching toward" is divinely sanctioned as "its own reward." What we have done in conquering space may not yet be very impressive, but one should not sell man short: "We have made a pass/ At the infinite,/ Made it as it were/ Rationally ours," and we aim at "More or less control" of the universe. If this seems like undue glorification of man, there are limits:

> It will not be his
> Ever to create
> One least germ or coal.

He will not, that is, confuse himself with God. But Frost wants us to "keep starring man/ In the royal role." And, writing in 1953, he calmly foresees man's rocketing through space as a natural consequence of viewing the universe as dynamic:

> this flight we wave
> At the stars and moon
> Means that we approve
> Of things on the move.

And he uses a kitchen simile to compare our behavior to that of a "Titanic . . . spoon" which keeps "all things stirred."

> Matter mustn't curd
> Separate and settle.
> Motion is the word.

While Frost's "we" is usually mankind in general, he shows on occasion that he is thinking of Western civilization or specifically of Hebraic-Christian tradition. One important verse paragraph, which oscillates between the universal and the more limited of these significations, defends the materialism of the West. Although the theologian would "censure"

> Our godless adventure
> Since we took that fall
> From the apple tree
> Into what they call
> The Material,

Frost interprets "God's own descent/ Into flesh" as showing

> That the supreme merit
> Lay in risking spirit
> In substantiation.

What he calls "the science zest" to penetrate the secrets of matter has been progressing "West Northwest," and the Orient, shaking off its meditative mood, is now perhaps paying us the compliment of imitation. God's symbolic gesture toward mankind in incarnating Himself in Christ he interprets as giving sanction to man's preoccupation with material phenomena.

Materialism, for all the celebration of it in this part of the poem, is means, not end. "There creation is," he says, using the noun to signify the universe as well as the abstract concept of that creativity reserved to God. But he goes on:

> More or less control
> Of it is the whole
> Business of the soul.

These lines were expanded in the *Saturday Review* excerpt of 1959, which appeared with a title resembling a sermon text: "The Great Event Is Science. The Great Misgiving, the Fear of God, Is That the Meaning of It Shall Be Lost." The import of "more or less control" he now defines in greater detail, saying that if we can't create "germ or coal," we can take comfort

> In the covenant
> We may get control
> If not of the whole
> Of at least some part
> Where not too immense,
> So by craft and art
> We can give the part
> Wholeness in a sense.

The "business of the soul," then, is to give significance—some sort of wholeness—to the fragments which man's experience allows him to comprehend. And the words "craft" and "art" are key Frostian terms for those creative powers properly man's. The remainder of this expanded passage is new, and represents a fleshing out of what he had originally called, without explaining it, "the soul's misgiving." The 1959 title indicates his hope that while accepting science as "the Great Event," we will not fail to recognize it as but part of the whole.

> The becoming fear
> That becomes us best

> Is lest habit ridden
> In the kitchen midden
> Of our dump of earning
> And our dump of learning
> We come nowhere near
> Getting this expressed.

In this poem Frost speaks for the humanity of man, and though treating the "science shop" respectfully, finds in an event such as the Kitty Hawk flight more than a triumph of technology. The movement of the whole poem is from personal, self-centered melancholy to a mood of reassurance; in ever-widening circles of attention Frost moves from one man to all men, from the single incident to a general view of thought and behavior, from a kind of Byronic self-dramatization to a celebration of the indomitable glory of mind. Adopting a desert metaphor, he speaks of our reclaiming space, which had been simply waste in fact and in name. If our relatively insignificant Earth has become "Capital/ Of the universe," Frost twits us that we cast only reflected light— but the reflection is

> From our rocks, and yes,
> From our brains no less.
> And the better part
> Is the ray we dart
> From the head and heart,
> The *mens animi.*

The mind he respects is that of the quester—and the scientist is in the forefront of his thought here—but he is far more concerned with the frontiers of knowledge as a challenge and spur to mankind than he is with the accomplishments of an industrial civilization. The "ray . . . from the head and heart" is the sign of man's ultimate creativity, his nearest approach to the divine. And it is with touching confidence in man's "royal role" that Frost can even at his age fix his eye steadily upon a spacious future. One hopes some of us shall live to see it.

Sherwood Anderson's
"Mid-American Chants"

Walter B. Rideout

ROBERT FROST once remarked in comparing Sherwood Anderson to Edgar Lee Masters that the former "was more of a poet." [1] What Frost seems to have been thinking of was Anderson's peculiar ability as a storyteller, in talk and print, suddenly to live within an imagined mood or human relationship and to speak from its heart with a quiet, lyric intensity. Anderson of course did write some actual poems. His third book, which appeared in the spring of 1918, was a verse collection entitled *Mid-American Chants,* and nine years later he published *A New Testament,* fragments of a poetic "autobiography of the fanciful life." Neither volume has ever received much critical approval, and justly, for Anderson was a better poet in prose than in verse, despite his feeling that the poems were among the most intimate expressions of his inner life. It is the very fact of this intimateness, however,

---

[1] Robert Frost in a letter to the writer, December 30, 1958.

that justifies the biographer's attention to Anderson's poetry. An examination even of *Mid-American Chants* by itself provides insights into both man and writer, and demonstrates that his life and his work are reciprocally illuminating.

Characteristic of the lack of critical interest in the poems that make up *Mid-American Chants* has been the usual casual ascription of their composition to periods anywhere from 1913 onward. From a study of Anderson's correspondence, however, it is now possible to date the composition of the "chants" fairly precisely; and even more important, from the location of them in time it is possible to understand more clearly Anderson's motivation and his intention in breaking into what he habitually called "song."

To give the conclusion before the necessarily detailed proof, it can be stated that the poems later collected as *Mid-American Chants* were written entirely, or almost entirely, in one short period of sudden creative impulse lasting some two or three months, from the final week or so of February, 1917, to mid-April and possibly into May of that year. Just prior to this period Anderson, by his own account, had been working solely in prose. In a letter dated January 15, 1917, and addressed to Waldo Frank, who with Van Wyck Brooks was then helping James Oppenheim to edit in New York the literary monthly *The Seven Arts*,[2] Anderson mentions having begun "a new book that I shall call 'Immaturity' "—from his brief description of it a first version of *Poor White*—and then asserts that up to now in "this winter" he has been writing stories.[3] No suggestion is made in this letter, or in any other previous letter by Anderson which I have seen, of any

---

[2] Oppenheim was editor and Frank and Brooks the associate editors of *The Seven Arts*. Robert Frost was on the Advisory Board.

[3] All letters referred to in this essay are in the Sherwood Anderson Collection in the Newberry Library, Chicago. For permission to print excerpts from them I make grateful acknowledgment here to the Library and to Mrs. Sherwood Anderson, donor of the Collection.

attempts at poetry.[4] Then in a letter almost certainly to be dated late February or early March of 1917, only some six weeks after the January communication, he writes Waldo Frank that "a madness has seized me. I do nothing but write songs." The first definitely dated reference to his having begun to write poems is in another letter to Frank of March 2, 1917, in which Anderson praises his own verses with exaggerated humor but insists that "you can't see them yet." [5] If we consider the intense interest of each man in the other's work at this time, the implication is fairly definite that the writing of poems was a new occupation with Anderson.

Evidently Anderson could not long withhold his experiments from his New York friend, for in a letter to Frank of March 5 he writes: "I cannot resist sending you two of my songs. There are about twenty of them now." A postscript states that the poems were not being submitted for consideration in *The Seven Arts,* but this reservation too broke down shortly. A month later, on April 5, Anderson writes Frank that he has already sent him several of the "songs," is sending two or three more, and wants to know soon whether *The Seven Arts* will print any of them. "The impulse towards these things continues," he comments, "and I have now about 40 of them." If, as the available evidence implies, most of these "40" were to appear in the collected volume, which contains forty-nine poems in all, Anderson had already completed drafts of a large majority of the chants by early April of 1917. Furthermore, the speed with which the poems were being written— about twenty by March 5 and about forty by April 5—suggests

---

[4] Neither do manuscripts exist to indicate prior attempts at anything but prose. A majority of the *Winesburg* tales were written in the winter of 1915–16, and before then Anderson appears to have been engaged with revisions of his first two published novels and at least one other unpublished one, *Talbot Whittingham.*

[5] Reprinted in Howard Mumford Jones, in association with Walter B. Rideout (eds.), *Letters of Sherwood Anderson* (Boston, 1953), Letter No. 9, pp. 9–10. In subsequent notes, this volume will be referred to as *LSA.*

that they were rushing forth in response to some current sharp imaginative stimulus.

Just how much longer the "impulse towards these things" did continue is not known. Three of five poems directly concerned with World War I appear to have been written after the United States joined the Allies on April 6, the title of one of the three being flatly, "We Enter In." Another of these war poems, moreover, is the only poem in the collected volume that can be placed with exactness in the stream of time. In a dictated letter, typed on the stationery of the advertising firm where he worked, and hence carefully dated "Thursday, April 19, 1917," Anderson again writes to Waldo Frank to say:

> I am sending you enclosed in this letter a thing I just wrote this morning, called *Mid-American Prayer*. This I believe strikes the note that I have been reaching for in this war matter.
>
> I didn't take time to digest the thing after writing it but am sending it hot to you.

This, one of the three longest poems in *Mid-American Chants*—consider Anderson's speed of composition here—was published in the June issue of *The Seven Arts,* a fact that is consistent with the April 19 date. But here in mid-April the definite record ends. Two more letters to Frank that refer to the chants have tentatively been dated as written in May,[6] but early in June Anderson was off for the summer to a camp colony at Lake Chateaugay in the upper Adirondacks, where Frank joined him for a week in mid-month. According to a neighboring cottager, Sue de Lorenzi, the conversations between the two men were lengthy and literary;[7] but when

---

[6] Reprinted in *LSA*, Letters No. 13 and 14, pp. 12–14. The seventh paragraph of Letter No. 13 is a prose version of "Song of the Middle World" (*Mid-American Chants*, p. 35), particularly of the poem's last two sections.

[7] Interview with Miss Sue de Lorenzi by the writer, August 15, 1960.

Anderson did start to write again during the summer, he went back to the prose of *Immaturity*. His season of poetry was over for a while.

To return to the implied question: Why should Anderson have been suddenly and overwhelmingly "seized" with "song" in the mid-winter and spring of 1917? The response presupposes a commensurate stimulus, and such a stimulus can in fact be found in the visit Anderson paid to the *Seven Arts* editors in New York during, as he wrote Waldo Frank in anticipation, "the week beginning February 12th." [8] Anderson's subsequent correspondence with Frank and Van Wyck Brooks reveals the very great impact the visit had on him. After several days crammed with conversations, impressions, and ideas, Anderson came home from New York, as he shortly thereafter wrote Frank, with gratitude for his willingness and that of Brooks and Oppenheim "to listen to my provincial, Western point of view" and "with an odd feeling of reverence and humbleness." [9]

The reasons for Anderson's rather apologetic tone in this letter need to be considered. It was not that he had never met literary people before, for he was already acquainted with the leading ones in Chicago. He had known and been encouraged by Floyd Dell before the latter had left Chicago's 57th Street for Greenwich Village, and he frequently saw Ben Hecht, Carl Sandburg, and other figures, many of them grouped around the Chicago *Daily News* while Henry Justin Smith was news editor. But for one thing, as Dell's departure had already indicated, New York exercised a very strong pull on the literary mind, and, to paraphrase the Boston lady, the editors of *The Seven Arts* were in the East already. Again, Dell, Hecht, and Sandburg, quick-witted or

---

[8] Anderson to Frank, February 2, 1917.

[9] *LSA,* Letter No. 6, p. 7.

ruminative as they might be, were not trained thinkers. On the other hand, although Frank was passionately, where Brooks was coolly, intense, both had had university educations and were men of considerable intellectual sophistication.[10] Then, too, though Frank, Brooks, and Oppenheim were articulately striving to break the dead grip of the past on American life, all three were closely aware of three viable sources of cultural energy. They had a stronger sense than did the Chicagoans of the centuries-thick impaction of cultural tradition in Europe always open to the selective mind; they felt the fresh winds of change blowing across that continent just over the water from the "port of New York"; they had all begun to rediscover what they believed to be the true soul of America in the Ungenteel Tradition of Whitman, Twain, and Lincoln.

Anderson's response to the men of *The Seven Arts* was characteristically complicated. On the one hand, he did feel reverent and humble before the Easterners with their intellectual subtlety, their awareness of Europe, their at-homeness in the great world of ideas. He still felt that way more than a year later when he confessed to Frank: "But both you and Brooks are more civilized than myself. Much that is in me wavering and uncertain is in you fixed and real." And in the same letter, though in a somewhat different context, he admits: "I have a feeling sometime[s], in view of the affections that have been given me, that I am like a crude woodsman that has been received into the affection of princes." [11] The terms of comparison are revealing. Toward his

[10] Frank had received both his A.B. and M.A. from Yale in 1911, and Brooks had received his A.B. from Harvard in 1907 after three years of residence. Oppenheim, with whom Anderson corresponded only infrequently and whom he seems to have known less well, had spent two years at Columbia and had been a teacher for four years thereafter. Both Frank and Brooks, it may be noted, had already experienced Europe directly. Frank had had a year of schooling in Switzerland; Brooks had lived for several years in England with visits to the Continent.

[11] *LSA,* Letter No. 31, pp. 35–36.

"dear brothers of the East" Anderson felt himself in part to be the coarse-grained provincial, the unsophisticate, even the child "suckled face downward in the black earth of my western cornland," as he wrote in "Mid-American Prayer."

But in another part of himself Anderson did not feel reverent and humble at all. With an ambivalence that a biographer of Anderson comes to expect, he at the same time felt big-brotherly and even superior toward the Easterners. Strongly attracted to these intellectuals as he was and recognizing in them qualities that he admittedly lacked himself, he felt a correlative need to assert his independence and worth. If a woodsman was not a prince, a prince was not a woodsman. Even before the New York visit he saw the relationship between Frank and himself as one leading to mutual growth: "I want to know many little subtle things you know and that I do not know, and I want to tell you things, make you feel things concerning life and writing that I have felt and that you have not felt." [12] In the actual situation, of course, Anderson had reason for feeling proud as well as humble. The first issue of *The Seven Arts,* in November, 1916, had contained an enthusiastic review by Frank of *Windy McPherson's Son* entitled "Emerging Greatness"; the magazine had printed a *Winesburg* story in its December, 1916, issue and another in that for January, 1917; and Frank was openly and joyfully impressed to find in Anderson an image of what he in turn was seeking. As Frank was to write years later after Anderson's death, "To me, the young New Yorker who knew his Europe well and had scarce seen his own land beyond the Eastern seaboard, Sherwood Anderson was America; the discovery of him was an exhilarating part of my discovery of my own country." Frank goes on in this same memoir to record his own conviction of Anderson's ambivalent response

[12] *LSA,* Letter No. 5, p. 6.

to the East: "And to him, his New York friends . . . represented *le grand monde* of intellect and culture. Nevertheless, although respectful, he was reserved; although impressed, he was suspicious. I recall walking up Fifth Avenue with him, one sunny day; as the throngs of shoppers tided over us, he suddenly broke his silence: 'All these people,' he said, 'simply *do not count.*' He was comparing them, unfavorably, in his mind with the lost and fumbling men, the frantic girls, the inarticulate mothers, of his stories." [13]

If we assume, as I think we must, that the New York visit precipitated Anderson's sudden turn to verse as a means of self-expression, then the verse itself should record this double attitude on the part of its creator. As we shall shortly see, this is indeed what it does. Again and again, in statement, theme, image, and symbol, sometimes separately in different poems and sometimes together in the same poem, Anderson announces his twin attitude of humbleness and pride. Admitting the crudeness, the provinciality, the immaturity of himself and of "Mid-America," the terrible ugliness of the industrial cities, the lack in both poet and region of a sure art and a clear purpose, he constantly counterbalances his anger and despair with the joyous affirmation of his own and his region's contribution to American culture, a contribution which he asserts to be different in kind from that of the more learned, more sophisticated Easterners, yet potentially of even greater value.

When the *Chants* are looked at in this way, as expressions of Anderson's complicated, even paradoxical, response to a concrete confrontation of the East, the poet's bardic language and prophetic posture are not surprising. Quite evidently the poems were an attempt by Anderson to define a public image both of the poet and of the Midwest. But the suddenness and near uncontrollability of

[13] Waldo Frank, "Sherwood Anderson: A Personal Note," *Newberry Library Bulletin*, Second Series, No. 2 (December, 1948), p. 41.

this rush of poetry still seem to require behind it a greater psychological pressure, a more intense necessity. What that pressure and necessity were will become clearer after an examination of the poems themselves.

II

Mid-American Chants was published by the John Lane Company on or close to April 12, 1918, approximately a year after the poetic seizure that produced the individual poems.[14] One of the minor questions about this first book of Anderson's poetry is why the noun in the title should be *"Chants."* Whenever the author refers to his poems in his correspondence before their publication as a volume, he calls them "songs"; and despite the book's title, "song" is the word almost invariably used in the titles of the separate poems, if any such word is used at all, both in the Table of Contents listing and in prior magazine publication. When, for example, in July, 1917, Harriet Monroe selected six of the poems for the September issue of *Poetry,* Anderson himself asked that the group be called "Mid-American Songs." The only answer to the question seems to be that implied by Anderson in his Foreword to *Mid-American Chants,* dated February, 1918. The most beautiful songs, he argues in this two-page statement, are written only when a people have for generations walked the cities and the countryside of their land; but "we" Midwesterners, "hurried and harried through life by the terrible engine—industrialism," are

[14] Eleven of the *Chants* had been published in periodicals prior to book publication: two in *The Seven Arts* (May and June, 1917), three in *Others* (June, 1917, "A Chicago Number"), and six in *Poetry* (September, 1917). With the publication of *Mid-American Chants* in 1918 the John Lane Company completed its contract for Anderson's first three books. After B. W. Huebsch became Anderson's publisher, *Mid-American Chants* was reissued in 1923 with a new title page bearing the Huebsch imprint.

just beginning to turn toward maturity and can only "feel our way toward the promise of song." Since "beauty . . . is not yet native to our cities and fields," the poems of *Mid-American Chants* are merely attempts like others now being made secretly by "a million men and women . . . to express the hunger within . . . . " His poems, Anderson appears to be suggesting, should therefore rightly be called "chants" because they do not, and because of their time cannot, have the finished beauty of "song." We may suspect here a covert peace offering to critics and reviewers, but Anderson's final assertion combines both modesty and self-confidence: " . . . I have dared to put these chants forth only because I hope and believe they may find an answering and clearer call in the hearts of other Mid-Americans."

Though the modesty in these concluding remarks might throw us off, the sense of them should sound familiar. The assumption that by speaking his own feelings Anderson would become a spokesman for others is not unlike that of Walt Whitman's in *Leaves of Grass;* and in fact, one of the obvious influences on *Mid-American Chants* is this same poet, whom Anderson had long considered as belonging "among the two or three really great American artists." [15] The indebtedness to Whitman appears frequently and variously in the *Chants:* the long, unrhymed lines; the rhetorical rhythms with their balanced elements and repetitions; even brief catalogues of states, cities, rivers ("Keokuk, Tennessee, Michigan, Chicago, Kalamazoo—don't the names in this country make you fairly drunk?"). Like Whitman's, Anderson's diction mixes the declamatory, the colloquial, and the lyrical, though it is noteworthy that Anderson lacks Whitman's love of nouns and verbs that freshly and exactly describe sense impressions. Like Whitman's too, is Anderson's desire for honesty and

[15] *LSA*, Letter No. 1, p. 3.

"perfect personal candor," but his inclusiveness is admittedly not that of Whitman. He will sing the ugly and the common, but only the latter gladly, for he hates the ugliness of factories too much to see optimistically any ultimate good in hideous sound and black smoke. Most importantly, Anderson is a latter-day, lesser Whitman in concealing a multiple personality behind the pervasive pronoun "I," the actual personality of the poet fusing with that of a mystically representative American through whose voice other Americans may be heard.

Since Anderson knew Whitman's poems directly, there is no need to interpose the influence of Carl Sandburg, concerning whom Anderson once remarked, "Most of his verses do not sing, but he does." [16] Very few of the Chants—"Song of the Soul of Chicago" and "Little Song to a Western Statesman" are notable exceptions—have the wry, slangy tone of many Sandburg poems, and one seldom finds anything resembling Sandburg's impressionistic color pictures. A basic difference in temperament between the two men is clear from a comparison of the poem each wrote entitled "Chicago." Sandburg's city is "a tall bold slugger . . . laughing as a young man laughs"; Anderson's is "a confused child in a confused world." Although there is no sure evidence for it, one might more profitably speculate instead on the influence of James Oppenheim's free-verse poetry. Anderson may never have read *Songs for the New Age* (1914) —one notes the first word of the title—and *War and Laughter* (1916) , the two books of rather foggy "polyrhythmical poetry" that Oppenheim had already published before Anderson met him in New York; but Oppenheim, also a devotee of Whitman, was publishing poems in *The Seven Arts* which have a passionate vagueness similar to that which too frequently envelops the *Chants,* and his forsaking of fiction for

[16] *LSA,* Letter No. 12, p. 12.

verse about the year 1915 might conceivably have helped to turn Anderson temporarily in the same direction.

One other influence is not conjectural at all, however. The second major influence on the *Chants*, besides Whitman, is the Bible. Anderson's quite nonsectarian love for the prose of the King James Version is well documented, and its rhythms often sound in his stories. Echoes of Genesis and the Song of Songs can be heard in the *Chants*. Thus the poet in "Song of Stephen the Westerner" says, "My children are as the dust of city streets for numbers," a statement that recalls God's promise to Jacob in Genesis 28:14 that "thy seed shall be as the dust of the earth"; and in at least eight of the Chants the poet addresses some un-named, generalized person as "my beloved," while the abrupt transitions, the sensuous imagery, and the calculated ambiguous-ness in parts of the Song of Songs are often imitated in Ander-son's poems. But Anderson's echoing of Biblical tone and rhythm can best be seen in quotation. Here is the fifth section or "stanza" —perhaps the best word in this context is "verse"—from "The Cornfields," the opening poem in the book.

> On my knees I crawled before my people. I debased myself. The excretions of their bodies I took for my food. Into the ground I went and my body died. I emerged in the corn, in the long cornfields. My head arose and was touched by the west wind. The light of old things, of beautiful old things, awoke in me. In the cornfields the sacred vessel is set up.

Anderson of course did not put off writing his poems until he had first conscientiously studied the prosodic techniques of Whit-man and the Bible; so disciplined an approach would have been quite alien to his nature. Instead, probably like many another who burst into "polyrhythmical poetry" during the free-verse excite-ment of the 1910's, he adapted by ear, as it were, from both major sources because poetry to him was direct self-expression, and formal metrics, about which he knew little, seemed a barrier erected by schoolmen to restrict that expression. More positively, the Bible's cadenced prose and Whitman's relatively loose line were both vehicles for certain religious or quasi-religious beliefs, to some of which, particularly Whitman's, he was much attracted. Here was a vital tradition of which he had been long aware, a prophetic idiom ready shaped for what he was feeling and what he wanted, needed, to say.

What did he have to say? A number of the Chants are slight in content, attempts to fix evanescent moods or to recall memories. But very many of them, so many that they reveal a basic pre-occupation on Anderson's part, relate in some way to his conception of the development of American life, a development most fully and effectively to be embodied in *Poor White* and toward which he was already working when his poetic seizure interrupted his first attempts at the uncompleted *Immaturity*. It is a familiar conception that may here be pieced together from different poems. The farm and small-town society of the past was a golden age. "Our fathers in the village streets/ Had flowing beards and they believed," Anderson writes in "Industrialism." In "Song of Stephen the Westerner," he nostalgically recalls the time when, as in pre-industrial Bidwell in *Poor White,* everyone lived under an invisible roof of secure, unconscious community. "In the long house at evening the old things were sweet"; and "On the straw in the stables sat Enid the maker of harness," at whose side were old men who "talked of old gods" while "Long we lay listening and listening." In these lost times of the nation "When I was a boy in my village here in the West," as Anderson writes in "Song of Industrial America,"

I always knew all the old men. How sweet they were—quite Biblical too—makers of wagons and harness and plows—sailors and soldiers and pioneers. We got Walt and Abraham out of that lot.

But this craftsman age with its patriarchal American heroes has vanished before the "terrible engine" of industrialism. Now, Anderson continues in "Song of Industrial America,"

You know my city—Chicago triumphant—factories and marts and the roar of machines—horrible, terrible, ugly and brutal.

The Machine Age has broken the old ties of community, herded people like animals into the great, grim cities, where, in the roar and smoke, they either starve or grow fat on lies and the telling of lies. As in *Poor White,* industrialism is the destroyer—of the land, of beauty, of the ancient simplicity and dignity, of human community, of all order. Significantly, in both "Song of Industrial America" and Hugh McVey's dream in Chapter II of *Poor White,* modern machine civilization is imaged in terms of storm and flood, of "disorder and darkness."

Just as Anderson's revulsion against his present time issues from him in extreme images, so he hints at the coming of a new age in highly charged but vague terms that show how remote the *Chants* are from the verse of programmatic social protest. In some of the "anti-industrial" poems the poet breaks his own bonds—or "bands," as Anderson prefers to call them—of emotional numbness and spiritual blindness; for to Anderson the worst enslavement produced by industrialism is psychological rather than economic. In other poems, as in "Song of Industrial America," the poet metaphorically seeks community with his "brothers":

We have to find each other. Have you courage to-night for a song? Lift your voices. Come.

A more positive, though no more specific, way of imaging the approach of the new age involves Anderson's conception of the

"I" in the *Chants,* a conception that clearly is indebted to *Leaves of Grass.* Very much as in Whitman's poems, the multiple personalities of the "I" may at any one time include Anderson himself, Anderson as representative American, and Anderson the inspired bard and prophet who speaks to America and articulates its hidden dream. Thus "Song of Cedric the Silent" becomes a fragmentary "Song of Myself" in which, at first, literal biography is joined to figurative statement: "The Son of Irwin and Emma I am, here in America, come into a kingship." Cedric (Sherwood) prophesies that "Into the land of my fathers, from Huron to Keokuk, beauty shall come—out of the black ground, out of the deep black ground." He, the poet, will "hurl" his songs "into the mighty wheels of the engine"; and the poem concludes with a self-adjuration:

> Cedric, the son of Irwin and Emma, stand up. Give your life, give
> your soul to America now. Cedric, be strong.

Often directly linked with this many-personed "I" is a theme that recurs again and again through these poems, and is indeed one of the chief devices for intimating the coming of a new American age—the theme of death and rebirth. Sometimes, as in three of the poems on the war, this theme is asserted in terms of creation proceeding out of destruction. So "Mid-American Prayer" concludes:

> May we get to gods and the greater brotherhood through
> growth springing out of the destruction of men.
> For all of Mid-America the greater prayer and the birth of
> humbleness.[17]

[17] That Anderson literally could see himself in at least a semiprophetic role is indicated by the remainder of his letter to Waldo Frank of April 19, 1917, enclosing the copy of "Mid-American Prayer": "It strikes me that this is the sort of thing

More often death and rebirth are expressed in fertility images of human procreation and nurture or of the planting and growth of seeds in soil. "Song of Stephen the Westerner" illustrates Anderson's typical reliance on the death-rebirth pattern to suggest a cycle of eternal return, from the acknowledgment of which the poet and his listeners may derive hope that some ineffable future will come out of the wasteland of the industrial present.

> Deep in the corn I lay—ages and ages—folded and broken—old and benumbed. My mother the black ground suckled me. When I was strong I builded a house facing the east. The hair on my arm was like the long grass by the edge of the forests.

This passage, with its Whitmanesque fusing of the poet and his Midwest land, reveals the very close connection between the death-rebirth theme and yet another element in the poems—the symbolic use of corn and cornfields. That corn symbolism is of peculiar importance in the *Chants* is implied even by so mechanical a piece of evidence as a count of the poems in which it significantly appears. Of the forty-nine poems in the book, twelve, or about a quarter of them, make central use of corn as symbol. In addition, corn or cornfields are specifically mentioned in fourteen more "songs," while in several others corn may presumably be referred to within the general class of growing crops. Considering Anderson's usual fondness for the symbolisms of both hands

---

that we need have spread over the country. If you like it I would like to have you publish it in Seven Arts and I wish it were possible to publish it all over the country.

"I don't care anything at all about whether you pay me anything at all for it or not, but would it not be a splendid thing for your magazine in the Middle West and for the Middle West also, to run this off in a phamplet [*sic*] as coming from Seven Arts and send it to your mailing list as you sometime [*sic*] ago sent out the discussion on Art by Dreiser. Also send it to the newspapers—then put it in the June number of Seven Arts."

and doors, it is remarkable that neither of these appears more than occasionally in the poems; and no other symbols, not even those drawn from industrialism or war, occur anywhere nearly so frequently as that of corn. Quite fittingly, the copies of the John Lane edition of *Mid-American Chants* bore the design of a partly husked ear of corn stamped in gold on a green panel on their yellow front covers. Corn is the master symbol of the book.

This symbol was an appropriate one for use by the poet who could tell his Eastern friend, Van Wyck Brooks: "The place between mountain and mountain I call Mid-America is my land. Good or bad, it's all I'll ever have." [18] At the simplest level, the cornfields, so much a part of the Midwest landscape, were for Anderson a means of distinguishing his own physical setting from that of his new friends in the East, but the corn theme could dramatically state a contrast in cultural background as well. The poem "Manhattan," almost certainly written soon after Anderson's return from New York, records his visit in such terms of contrast.

> From the place of the cornfields I went into the new places. I went into the city. How men laughed and put their hands into mine.

Out of an emotional contact with the city crowds he achieved, the poet says, a sense of himself; and he proudly asserts his identity in one of the finest passages in the book, a passage directly recalling both Whitman and the Bible:

> I am of the West, the long West of the sunsets. I am of the deep fields where the corn grows. The sweat of apples is in me. I am the beginning of things and the end of things.

[18] *LSA*, Letter No. 37, p. 43.

To the poet, thus represented as a kind of culture-hero, came the men of the city, old men full of pain. And the poem concludes:

> In the morning I arose from my bed and was healed. To the corn-fields I went laughing and singing. The men who are old have entered into me. As I stood on the high place above the city they kissed me. The caress of those who are weary has come into the cornfields.

The full complexity of Anderson's emotional response to his New York visit is pointedly lacking here; for, while the poet admits to having been emotionally modified by his experience, Anderson's real though partial sense of inferiority has been minimized. Instead, we observe, through the insistence on the cornfields the worth of Anderson and of Mid-America have become symbolically enlarged.[19]

As "Manhattan" further suggests, the symbol of corn is for Anderson much more than a geographical or even a cultural index; it assumes, in fact, a quasi-religious meaning, to which is closely joined the Whitmanesque conception of the poet as prophet and priest. "I am come"—he writes in "Song of the Beginning of Courage"—"to the face of the gods through the corn-fields." Again, in "The Cornfields," the poet proclaims that by virtue of his songs he broke the "bands" that bound him and that still bind the people of his time because "They had forgotten the long fields and the standing corn":

---

[19] The insistence of the poet on his vigorous youth in this poem, a positive reversal of the theme of immaturity, shows Anderson's preference for projecting emotional states rather than stating literal facts. Anderson, born in 1876, was older by six years than Oppenheim, by ten years than Brooks, and by thirteen years than Frank. Age here would seem to refer to the Easterners' relation to and greater awareness of an older cultural history.

. . . I was determined to bring old things into the land of the new. A sacred vessel I found and ran with it into the fields, into the long fields where the corn rustles.

Dying into the ground, as the seed which is the soul in the New Testament parable, the poet is reborn in the cornfields and "will renew in my people the worship of gods," will "bring love" into their hearts. Where Whitman found both death and new life in his master symbols of the sea and the grass, Anderson finds them in the corn, which dies and is reborn in an endless circle of renewal. What Anderson calls for, of course, is not at all a simple, literal "return to the land" or "return to the village"; rather, he urges a change of heart. As "The Cornfields" makes clear despite the intentional vagueness of its prophetic utterance, the poet seeks to re-establish in each person, man or woman, the love of his fellows so that instead of living as now their fragmented, isolated, and emotionally impoverished lives, all may dwell once again, as in America's golden age, under the invisible roof of community, but now a roof extended to cover the world.

This sub-rational, highly intuitive "message" is reinforced by two other attributes of the corn, though it is useful first to observe the ways in which corn is *not* described. It is never referred to by any color word, such as "yellow" or "golden," or by any word suggesting shape. (It is said in one poem to be "fat" and in another to be "rich, milky," but these are generalized words mostly suggesting fullness of growth.) It is characterized by smell only once (again "rich, milky") and by movement only twice ("sways" and "nods"). Somewhat more frequently the sound of the corn ("rustling" or "whispering") is mentioned, but even this attribute seems to have little significance. Anderson simply is not interested in creating hard, clear, descriptive images.

What *is* significant is his tendency, as it appears in several Chants, to refer to corn within the context of sexuality, a sexuality far more diffuse than that of Whitman's songs but like it in transcending the merely physical. Not once in *Mid-American Chants* does Anderson make the obvious, even expected, link between corn ear or cornstalk and phallus. Instead, as in most of Anderson's writing in either prose or verse, sex and the sexual act are primarily metaphors for the intuitive union of one personality with another. So in "Spring Song" the poet begins by stating that the rhythm of death and rebirth manifests itself again in forest and field. "Now, America," he continues in Whitmanesque idiom, "you press your lips to mine,/ Feel on your lips the throbbing of my blood." And the poem reaches its climax by asserting a union of the physical with the spiritual, of a people with its prophet.

> Spring. God in the air above old fields.
> Farmers marking fields for the planting of the corn.
> Fields marked for corn to stand in long straight aisles.
>
> In the spring I press your body down on wet cold new-
>   plowed ground.
> Men, give your souls to me.
> I would have my sacred way with you.

The poem ends with men singing in unison, while "Everywhere in the fields now the orderly planting of corn."

Given Anderson's acquaintance with Whitman, it is not at all surprising that in "Spring Song" an explicit sexual context should be furnished for the dual planting, of corn seeds in the earth and of prophetic revelations in the consciousness of mankind; but the poem also assigns to the corn an unexpected final attribute, the extraordinary importance of which to Anderson is established by the frequency of its appearance in the *Chants*. Again and again it is the spatial arrangement of the corn in the field, not its color or odor or shape, but its "orderly planting" and growth that the poet emphasizes. In poem after poem the corn is described as standing in long, deep, or endless rows; and, as in "Spring Song," the endless symmetry of the lines of corn is always to be understood as far more than an aesthetic matter. Again the meaning is quasi-religious. In "Song of the Middle World" the poet has "been to the Dakotas when the fields were plowed" and "stood by the Ohio when the dawn broke forth," and he has seen the "Promise of corn,/ Long aisles running into the dawn and beyond/ To the throne of gods." The physical order of the corn on the land, in short, symbolizes the metaphysical order of "the gods," who represent the essentially religious harmony of brotherhood toward which the poet hopes to guide Mid- and all America, indeed the whole of mankind.

The reiteration of the image of the cornfields and their symmetry suggests that order had an obsessive value for Anderson, and there is evidence external to the poems to confirm this suggestion into something more definite. Writing to Van Wyck Brooks only a few weeks after the publication of *Mid-American Chants,* in a letter that ambivalently mingles praise and censure, self-assertion and self-effacement, Anderson plaintively asks his Eastern friend why he does not "sympathize with me in such expressions as my essay 'An Apology for Crudity' or my *Chants?*"

> In the chants I reached into my own personal muttering, half insane and disordered, and tried to take out of them a little something ordered. You should see how I clutched at the ordered cornfield[s], insisted on them to myself, took them as about the only thing I could see.[20]

[20] *LSA,* Letter No. 32, p. 37.

Here is the missing final figure in the pattern of desire and need that lay behind Anderson's sudden outpouring of song in the late winter and early spring of 1917. Through the poems Anderson hoped to define not only a public image but a private one as well. For him they would be new steps in an old journey toward self-discovery, toward self-identification. They would be attempts to find order, not only within the confusion of a particular time, but also within the confusion of the poet still seeking his way from businessman to artist.

The need to find an order was a compelling one for Anderson, who in the spring of 1917 had already written and was soon to publish his novel, *Marching Men,* which told of Beaut Mc-Gregor's revolt against the disorder of contemporary society and his vision of achieving order through the striding of men in wordless unison. Like the symbol of the marching men, the symbol of the corn rows in *Mid-American Chants* was another in a series of efforts by Anderson to integrate his world, both external and internal.[21] What made him return from his excursion into prophetic verse almost as abruptly as he set off on it must ultimately have been his realization that he could express his meaning and his need more fully and exactly in the "other harmony" of prose. *Poor White,* his best novel, exists to show that he was right.

----

[21] Corn as a symbol of purposeful order had already been used specifically, though sporadically, by Anderson in Book I of *Windy McPherson's Son* (see p. 73 particularly) and in *Marching Men.* In the essay-sketch of Chicago with which Book IV of *Marching Men* opens, he writes, in phraseology similar to that of the *Chants:* "Chicago is one vast gulf of disorder. Here is the passion for gain, the very spirit of the bourgeoisie gone drunk with desire. The result is something terrible. Chicago is leaderless, purposeless, slovenly, down at the heels.

"And back of Chicago lie the long corn fields that are not disorderly. There is hope in the corn. Spring comes and the corn is green. It shoots up out of the black land and stands up in orderly rows. The corn grows and thinks of nothing but growth. Fruition comes to the corn and it is cut down and disappears. Barns are filled to bursting with the yellow fruit of the corn.

"And Chicago has forgotten the lesson of the corn. All men have forgotten. It has never been told to the young men who come out of the corn fields to live in the city."

"The Bridge" and Hart Crane's "Span of Consciousness"

Albert Van Nostrand

To ALL INTENTS, *The Bridge* was the end, both the aim and the termination, of Hart Crane's short, violent career as a poet. It took him seven years to render it, from what he first called a "new longish poem" based on the tendencies of "Faustus and Helen" to the final structure of some eighteen hundred lines. Crane composed its parts during brief, intense periods which were separated by long intervals, often many months, of obsessive inactivity. He finally achieved a sequence of fifteen poems in eight sections, which he stoutly believed to be a single, organic structure.

Whether apologetic or derogatory, critics of *The Bridge* have been both ingenious and unusually dedicated. The majority opinion holds, however, that Crane, a legatee of Walt Whitman, failed to render his intended "American synthesis" because the concept itself was faulty. Moreover, "Cape Hatteras" is usually offered as a symptom of *The*

Bridge as a whole—or rather of its failure to be whole: merely a striking series of uneven lyrics, uneasily shuttling back and forth between high hope and despair.

This majority opinion reflects the truth, but not the whole truth. For one thing, the terms in which *The Bridge* was conceived denied at the beginning any chance of its succeeding in a rational or ideological way. Understanding Crane's attempt to render a doctrine is of course crucial to understanding the poem, but the subject of *The Bridge* lies as much in the poet's attempt as it does in the doctrine itself. Moreover, the way in which the poem ideologically fails marks a continuous and prominent strain in American writing: the attempt to achieve a peculiar contradiction one might call practical idealism, which has accounted for the most vital works of fiction in our literary history.

Crane attempted to render continent, community, and individual man into a divine, organic entity simply by subsuming these elements to his own vision. For a long while he believed that he had only to find metaphors for this ideal in order to realize it. He explained at the outset that his poem would concern "a mystical synthesis of 'America.' History and fact, location, etc., all have to be transfigured into abstract form that would almost function independently of its subject matter." [1] This oneness of America was his deliberative subject. It was the subject to be pondered. But Crane himself believed that a poem renders more than merely a doctrinal or deliberative subject, that its special kind of knowledge must come from something else. "Poetry," he said, "is simply the concrete *evidence* of the *experience* of a recognition (*knowledge* if you like)." The poem offers a ratio of experience and fact, he insisted: "It is both perception and thing perceived." [2] The

[1] Hart Crane to Gorham Munson (February 18, 1923), in Brom Weber, ed., *The Letters of Hart Crane: 1916–1932* (New York, 1952), p. 124. All of my citations of Crane's correspondence refer to this collection.

[2] To Gorham Munson (March 17, 1926), *Letters*, p. 237.

dramatic quality of the act of perceiving must inhere in any poem.

Crane insisted on this subjective reality as the vital principle of his art. He understood what Emerson and Santayana had defined as the process of unfixing and rearranging empirical data— the need first to "decreate," as Wallace Stevens put it. More precisely, the process of perceiving is reality. Crane once celebrated, for example, the fact that Alfred Stieglitz made the camera into an "instrument of something more specially vital—apprehension." [3] The process of Crane's own apprehending is the vital principle of *The Bridge*. The point is not that it makes the poem succeed; rather, it *makes* the poem.

The Bridge represents Crane's struggle with his own material. It dramatizes his attempts to deputize voices to explain and rationalize the vision of Brooklyn Bridge which he had in the first place. These voices reveal Crane's search for evidence to justify the organic unity of the world which the Bridge first symbolized to him and which he stated in "Proem" and "Atlantis." Between these two lyrics addressed to the Bridge itself, at either end of the whole poem, a restless consciousness presides. In the printed sequence the lyrics reveal an apparent order in this search for the one-world: excursions into the past followed by inspections of the present experience for evidence to support the conviction of unity. But the sequence of their composition is something else again. This sequence is the really convincing fact of Crane's own participation. The tortuous record of it lies in his correspondence.

Crane began at the end, with his vision of the Bridge as the apotheosis of human experience, and then in fits and starts he constructed the seven preceding parts and a proem, working backwards and forwards toward the physical and dramatic center of the

[3] To Alfred Stieglitz (April 15, 1923) , *Letters,* p. 132.

poem. As he explained to Otto Kahn, the poem's inception was his midnight vision of Brooklyn Bridge:

> Strangely enough that final section of the poem has been the first to be completed,—yet there's a logic to it, after all; it is the mystic consummation toward which all the other sections of the poem converge. Their contents are implicit in its summary.[4]

The problem was to make these implicit "contents" explicit. The great burden of the poem for Crane was the necessity of having to specify the circumstances that might have comprised this "mystic consummation," and to recreate a convincing illusion of them.

Crane had substantially finished "Atlantis" by July of 1923, yet two and a half years later, newly revised, it was still the only completed section of *The Bridge*. The bulk of *The Bridge* was written during the spring and summer of 1926. During this period of intense writing he set to work on the "Ave Maria" section; he sketched out a sequence for all the lyrics, then composed the Proem and "Cutty Sark"; he worked on three parts of "Powhatan's Daughter" and completed "The Tunnel." In the order of composition Crane skipped from Section VIII to Section I, to the Proem, to Section II, to Section VII—always working toward a center of some sort which might finally define the poem's dialectic. But it was more than another year—in the autumn of 1927—before he could finally specify what the center sections of the poem would be; and it was nearly two years after that, in the summer of 1929, that he was finally and feverishly working on these interior parts: "Cape Hatteras," "Quaker Hill," and the last section of "Powhatan's Daughter."

So far, it appears that two related conditions have marked the

---

[4] To Otto H. Kahn (March 18, 1926) , *Letters,* p. 240.

history of *The Bridge:* Crane's explicit attempts to make the poem work in terms of some doctrine, and a general tendency among critics to take him at his word. Accordingly, spokesmen have viewed the poem as a fragmented failure, or they have defended it by explaining sources and analogies of the doctrine. In Crane's theory, however, a poem is as much about the experiencing as about the experience. It is this fact which makes the poem a whole. That its deliberative subject—its doctrine—can and should be viewed in terms of this poet-poem relationship Crane's letters clearly indicate; and the poem bears him out.

These are the conclusions which the record of his work supports, not only the poem as statement but also the traumas of its composition which this correspondence reveals. This record is already familiar, but as evidence of Crane's consuming need to build a new New World, indeed as part of his struggle to do so, it will bear more scrutiny. These letters show how Hart Crane conceived a highly subjective proposition about a monistic world, and declared it to be the subject of *The Bridge;* and how he found himself overwhelmed by the burden of simultaneously defining both the concept and the idiom by which to convey it. He had to correlate his own perceiving, or what (in "Cape Hatteras") he called "the span of consciousness." Although his struggle to make this correlation was not his declared intention, it became his preoccupation.

I propose that Hart Crane's involvement in his poem was such that his struggle to form it became in fact the subject of the poem, and that when the poem is read in this way it is a whole document whose parts are organic. To illustrate this I will discuss, in the following order, these elements of Crane's poetic program (even though, as problems, they beset him more or less simultaneously) : his attempt to form a precept based on some kind of mysticism; his search for a dramatic form which would define his declared subject; and his organization of the poem around him-self—culminating in "Cape Hatteras." Finally, on this evidence, I propose that Crane's inability to extricate himself from his own poem—even assuming that he might have wanted to—helps to explain its historical significance in the literature.

II

Even Crane's first letter to Otto Kahn about *The Bridge* im-plies the poet's unusual involvement by the way he states its doc-trine: "aiming as it does to enunciate a new cultural synthesis of values in terms of our America." [5] Insofar as he specified an emblematic America the poem went according to plan. This par-ticular America has no geographical finitude: it extends from the origins of Columbus in the east to an indefinite west described as Cathay; it has no boundaries at the north or south. It is not a con-tinent but a condition. This America has no political or economic ideology, no concept of the United States, for example. It has virtually no population. Although it is the locus of a great many dramatic situations, they represent merely fragments of persons. The only sustained personage in this America is the speaker of the poem, the voice in its various guises, the consciousness which generates this spiritual New World and then tries to evangelize it.

The poet's sense of mission regarding this idealized world ani-mated his letters, for example, whenever he was thinking about T. S. Eliot, which was often. Eliot's poetry had a peculiar impor-tance in helping Crane to define his own attitude about the pos-sibilities of mankind. In his own words, Crane wished to affirm where Eliot negated. He decried "the fashionable pessimism of

---

[5] To Otto H. Kahn (December 3, 1925), *Letters,* p. 223.

the hour so well established by T. S. Eliot" [6] and blamed Eliot for "the poetic determinism of our age." [7] As Crane explained to Allen Tate, "In his own realm Eliot presents us with an absolute *impasse* . . . . I, for instance, would like to leave a few of his 'negations' behind me, risk the realm of the obvious more, in quest of new sensations, *humeurs*." [8] He wrote this in 1922, before he conceived of *The Bridge*. In this letter he was already working out a strategy with reference to Eliot's poetry, "a safe tangent to strike which, if I can possibly explain the position,— goes *through* him toward a *different goal*."

Crane elaborated on this strategy and clarified his own dogma a few months later in a letter to Gorham Munson:

> There is no one writing in English who can command so much respect, to my mind, as Eliot. However, I take Eliot as a point of departure toward an almost complete reverse of direction. His pessimism is amply justified, in his own case. But I would apply as much of his erudition and technique as I can absorb and assemble toward a more positive, or (if [I] must put it so in a sceptical age) ecstatic goal. I should not think of this if a kind of rhythm and ecstasy were not (at odd moments, and rare!) a very real thing to me. I feel that Eliot ignores certain spiritual events and possibilities as real and powerful now as, say, in the time of Blake.[9]

One month after this testament to the reality of "a kind of rhythm and ecstasy," Crane announced to Munson, "I am ruminating on a new longish poem under the title of *The Bridge* . . . . " [10]

[6] To Seldon Rodman (May 22, 1930) , *Letters,* p. 351.

[7] To Gorham Munson (March 5, 1926) , *Letters,* p. 236.

[8] To Allen Tate (June 12, 1922) , *Letters,* p. 90.

[9] To Gorham Munson (January 5, 1923) , *Letters,* pp. 114–15.

[10] To Gorham Munson (February 6, 1923) , *Letters,* p. 118.

The letters about Eliot consistently indicate Crane's belief in a certain editorial affirmation which he thought his own poem must have. He not only anticipated its criticism on these grounds, he invited it. And the criticism inevitably came. The two major biographies of Crane differently summarize the contemporary judgment, but with substantially the same conclusion. Philip Horton remarked on Crane's anguished agreement with some of his critics: "even the most enthusiastic with one or two exceptions gave voice to qualifications and doubts which sounded in Crane's ears like echoes of his own fearful conscience." [11] Somehow his doctrine had failed him. Brom Weber observed that Crane had dissociated himself from any organized, theoretical system of knowledge: "Crane tried to perform the function of scientist and philosopher when he set himself up as a modern myth-maker." [12] Crane came to realize it. The reviewers made it difficult for him to do otherwise.

Throughout the long years of its composition, Crane had confided his plans for *The Bridge* to a few literary colleagues whose approbation he very much wanted. When *The Bridge* was first published two of these colleagues, Gorham Munson and Waldo Frank, were silent; three others wrote reviews—Malcolm Cowley, Allen Tate, and Yvor Winters—which in sum ranged from equivocal praise to outright deprecation. The crux of each review was the allegedly faulty doctrine of the poem. Together they make a useful summary; they anticipate the range of attitudes in the criticism of *The Bridge* ever since.

Cowley acknowledged Crane's "attempt to create the myth of America" with all the tact he could: "We might well conclude

[11] Philip Horton, *Hart Crane: The Life of an American Poet* (New York, 1937), p. 265.

[12] Brom Weber, *Hart Crane: A Biographical and Critical Study* (New York, 1948), p. 276.

that such an attempt was foredoomed to failure." [13] Then having raised the question he diplomatically begged it. The poem had succeeded "to an impressive degree," he said, "in its presumptuous effort"—not wholly, of course, "for its faults are obvious." Cowley pointedly declined to specify these faults, but Allen Tate and Yvor Winters were both explicit about the poem's doctrinal failure.

Tate perceived that the poem "lacks an objective pattern of ideas elaborate enough to carry it through an epic or heroic work." [14] It lacked a coherent plot, symbolic or narrative; instead, "the coherence of the work consists in the personal quality of the writing—in mood, feeling, and tone."

> If we subtract from Crane's idea what he has to say about it, we have left only the static abstraction, "the grandeur of America," which is not only incapable of further elucidation on the logical plane, but actually obstructs it.

Yvor Winters also acknowledged Crane's "endeavor to create and embody a national myth," and he agreed that Whitman had been an accessory before the fact. But in Winters' singular judgment this amounted to a moral indictment. It was long after Crane's death, however, before Winters finally completed his prosecution. On the grounds that a poem is a technique of contemplation and comprehension, and therefore necessarily a moral discipline, he later argued (*In Defense of Reason*, 1947) that poetic morality and poetic feeling are inseparable. Moreover, since the tradition of *The Bridge*—dating back to Whitman and Emer-

---

[13] Malcolm Cowley, "A Preface to Hart Crane," *New Republic*, LXII (April 23, 1930), 276.

[14] Allen Tate, "A Distinguished Poet," *Hound and Horn*, III (July–September, 1930), 581.

son—countenanced a moral relativism, then it was downright dangerous. This explains the satisfaction with which Winters concluded his review of *The Bridge,* triumphantly offering "Crane's wreckage" as evidence of the end of the "Whitmanian tradition."

Between his earlier review and his later prosecution Winters changed his indictment of this "Whitmanian tradition." His review charged that "The Whitmanian basis of Mr. Crane's book makes a hero . . . impossible." [15] Why this is so Winters did not make at all clear, but of its effect on *The Bridge* he was certain. The "destiny" of a nation is hard enough to get at, he said, but to abstract this concept without any control is to make it even more remote.

> It reduces itself, when one comes to describe it—without a hero— to the most elementary and least interesting aspects of the general landscape, aspects which cannot possibly be imbued with any definite significance, no matter how excited one may get, for the simple reason that no definite significance is available.

Although Tate and Winters both identified an unfortunate separation between Crane's vision and his doctrine, there is a distinction between their arguments which should become more evident. It is certainly important. Winters asserted that there is no hero, no consciousness in the poem that might rescue the abstract doctrine from itself. What Tate said was something else again: "the coherence of the work consists in the personal quality of the writing—in mood, feeling, and tone." To subtract Crane's idea from what he has to say about it "would leave only the static abstraction." The distinction is significant in that Tate did rec-

[15] Yvor Winters, "The Progress of Hart Crane," *Poetry,* XXXVI (June, 1930), 157.

ognize Crane's participation, on stage as it were, in his own poem. That Crane did not sufficiently preside over his own materials, to the detriment of the poem—as Tate argued—is subsequent to his premise that Crane did participate.

Crane was unable to discover precisely what it was he wanted to correlate. Allen Tate precisely diagnosed the symptom when he said, "The poet has not observed the distinction between a metaphor and a philosophical idea." [16] Fundamentally, Crane's difficulty was that neither metaphor nor philosophical idea could adequately represent the consciousness which he felt compelled to express. He could approximately fix his concept, "the mystical synthesis of America," in metaphor, but he could not define it. In fact, he found himself in the curious position of proselytizing others in order to explain to himself the concept in the first place.

"Crane seriously considered himself a mystic," [17] Brom Weber reminds us, and the poet's letters confirm it. This mystical bent partly explains Crane's whole problem of artistic representation. William James pointed out that one certain characteristic of the mystical experience is its ineffability. Its essence is non-transferable; it cannot even be accurately described, since words are derived from the sensory-intellectual consciousness whose range the mystical experience escapes. But this does not deny the validity of the experience itself. The efficacy of such an experience in most cases, James said, was "to add a supersensitive meaning to the outward data of consciousness." [18] As a rule mystical states are excitements, "gifts to our spirit by means of which facts already objectively before us fall into a new expressiveness and make a new connection with our active life."

[16] Tate, "A Distinguished Poet," p. 581.

[17] Weber, *Hart Crane*, p. 215.

[18] William James, *The Varieties of Religious Experience: A Study in Human Nature* (New York, 1902), p. 427.

Such was apparently Crane's case. It was also his artistic problem, for he was trying to convey the ineffable. The project he had set for himself was impossible. The feeling he wanted to formalize was beyond the sense of what discursive language could convey. By testimony of mystics for centuries, the essence of the mystical experience is apparently its transport beyond any concept whatever. It is the achievement of a supersensuous, super-rational consciousness, by its nature devoid of idea. The received opinion in this regard has been restated by Walter Stace, who infers from the testimony of mystics that "the essence of the experience is the undifferentiated unity."

> When it is not interfered with by theologians and ecclesiastical hierarchies it is interpreted nondualistically as transcending the distinction between subject and object, between the individual self and the Infinite.[19]

This transcendent state, of the self absorbed into the Infinite, was beyond Crane's power to convey. The next best thing would be an approximation of some sort, such as the *idea* of mysticism, some extrapolation from the mystical experience itself. His "mystical synthesis of America" was just such a derivative. But Crane also had an acute awareness of his own identity. His excitement with himself was what he really could be sure of. The "supersensitive meaning," to use James's term, which Crane derived from mystical experience was evidently and peculiarly a new self-consciousness. This is what really engaged him. His famous letter to Gorham Munson, describing his ecstatic experience while under anesthesia in the dentist's chair, for example, emphasizes a distinct self in a dramatic situation. Although his mind "spiraled

---

[19] Walter T. Stace, *The Teachings of the Mystics* (New York: Mentor Books, 1960), p. 221.

to a kind of seventh heaven of consciousness," Crane could still recall performing an "egoistic dance among the seven spheres" and listening to the words of another, discrete presence: " . . . something like an objective voice kept saying to me—'You have the higher consciousness—you have the higher consciousness. This is something that very few have. This is what is called genius.' " Crane went on to say, "I felt the two worlds. And at once." [20] On another occasion Crane explained to Waldo Frank the ecstasy of walking hand-in-hand with a lover across the Brooklyn Bridge—"the cables enclosing us and pulling us upwards in such a dance as I have never walked and never can walk with another"—in terms which came closer to the undifferentiated oneness of mystical experience—"I have seen the Word made Flesh" —yet his description still emphasized the sublimation of the discrete self.[21]

By whatever sequence Crane derived a concept of the mystical experience, his distinctive self seems always to have been at the center of it. Although this present self—and self-awareness— contradicted the mystical experience, it nevertheless provided the only continuity Crane had from the experience to the world of images and sensuous associations by which every poet communicates. Tate's review of *The Bridge* pointed out that Crane indiscriminately perceived "bridges" wherever he looked. "The poet has not observed the distinction between a metaphor and a philosophical idea." Moreover, this syndrome reveals how Crane imposed himself on his material. He employed himself—or rather some version of himself—as a kind of continuous bridge between two planes of consciousness. This self generates the intensity of the whole poem.

[20] To Gorham Munson (*ca.* June 18, 1922), *Letters,* pp. 91–92.
[21] To Waldo Frank (March 21, 1924), *Letters,* p. 181.

Crane searched long and hard for some relevant form, some way of controlling the images he visualized. The subject continually recurs in his letters. Although he was not always aware of it, this search for a form was the means by which Crane was really organizing the poem around his own presence. He explored various possibilities, always looking for that organizing metaphor and remarking excitedly whenever one seemed to present itself, such as he did with the musical analogies. He wanted to devise a language in which sound might escape verbal limitations to a kind of music, in the manner of the Symbolists, whose legacy he readily acknowledged. "Observe the water-swell rhythm that persists until the Palos reference," he wrote of the "Ave Maria" lyric, "then the more absolute and marked intimation of the great *Te Deum* of the court, later held,—here in terms of C[olumbus]'s own cosmography." [22] He was enthusiastic about the jazz rhythm at the beginning of "The River," and of its modulation to a slow regularity approximating the gait of the hobos along the railroad track. "Cutty Sark" was a fugue. But "Atlantis" in particular was to be the great "symphonic" composition.

He was ever searching for a form that would somehow control a fluid, escaping language. "Let us invent an idiom for the proper transposition of jazz into words! Something clean, sparkling, elusive!" [23] unconstrained by any rhyme scheme. He wanted what he called "an 'interior' form, a form that is so thorough and intense as to dye the words themselves with a peculiarity of meaning, slightly different maybe from the ordering definition of them separate from the poem." [24]

Crane's later theorizing about the aims and obligations of the

[22] To Waldo Frank (July 26, 1926) , *Letters,* p. 268.

[23] To Allen Tate (May 16, 1922) , *Letters,* p. 89.

[24] To Sherwood Anderson (January 10, 1922) , *Letters,* p. 77.

poet helps to explain his urgent search for an "interior form," and to specify how personally he intended his own phrase, "peculiarity of meaning." In his essay "Modern Poetry," he insisted that the poet's concern "must be, as always, self-discipline toward a formal integration of experience," and that modern poetry must now "absorb the machine, i.e., *acclimatize* it," as it has done with "all other human associations of the past." [25]

This task would impose a singular responsibility on the poet. In order to assimilate all dogma—of the "Machine Age," in this case—the modern poet must develop "an extraordinary capacity for surrender, at least temporarily, to the sensations of urban life." This opinion he had already stated earlier. "What I am after is an assimilation of this experience," Crane explained in his first synopsis of *The Bridge,* "a more organic panorama, showing the continuous and living evidence of the past in the inmost vital substance of the present." [26]

The principle of assimilation through surrender, analogous as it is to Keats's theory of "negative capability," meant in Crane's case, however, a special kind of participation in the poem. With his insistence on the poet's "immersion" in his material, the "interior form" he was searching for was some way of making his subjective presence dramatically possible. Crane's letters reveal the intense frustration and excitement of his struggle to find an organizing principle that would make his fiction persuasive. Whatever part of *The Bridge* happened to engage him at the moment, he tended to consider the "real center" of the poem—ironically, since the poem had no center at all for many years, other than his search for it.

---

[25] Hart Crane, "Modern Poetry," in Waldo Frank, ed., *The Collected Poems of Hart Crane* (New York, 1933), p. 175 ff. The essay first appeared in Oliver Saylor, ed., *Revolt in the Arts* (New York, 1929).

[26] To Otto H. Kahn (September 12, 1927), *Letters,* p. 305.

After all, the first and principal metaphor of his monism was the "bridge," which had its own sufficiency and denied development. The connotation of "Atlantis," his paean to the Bridge, is the poet's sense of its fullness; no further change or development seemed possible. Rhetorically, this apostrophe to the Bridge is one long, suspended period. Although grammatically there are many verbs in its ninety-six lines, the only verb that governs the rhetorical apostrophe ("O arching strands of song . . . hold thy floating singer late") occurs nearly seventy lines after its subject. There is no motion in this state of sufficiency. "Atlantis" is all noun.

The syntax of "Atlantis" really does correlate the "mystic consummation" which Crane intended to dramatize. This was his point of departure; how could he possibly get beyond it? His despair over his repeated failure to do so is recorded in the letter to Waldo Frank, during the summer of 1926, which virtually every commentary on *The Bridge* acknowledges. Crane confessed that he was trying to write shorthand about an endless subject. "Emotionally I should like to write *The Bridge;* intellectually judged the whole theme and project seems more and more absurd." The metaphors of past and present, by which he had hoped to represent an organic world, suddenly would not work. "By which I mean that however great their subjective significance to me . . . these forms, materials, dynamics are simply non-existent in the world." However Crane might delight himself in thinking that his material was valid, he said, "I am only evading a recognition and playing Don Quixote in an immorally conscious way." [27]

It is all familiar, but still it does not by itself document the crisis in this poet-poem relationship. Barely more than a month after Crane had posted this letter, he wrote again to Frank, ecstatically celebrating his reunion with the whole project. He

[27] To Waldo Frank (June 20, 1926), *Letters*, p. 261.

had just finished "Proem: To Brooklyn Bridge," and was ready to take on the whole monistic world again.

> Hail Brother! I feel an absolute music in the air again, and some tremendous rondure floating somewhere—perhaps my little dedication ["To Brooklyn Bridge"] is going to swing me back to San Cristobal again . . . . That little prelude, by the way, I think to be almost the best thing I've ever written, something steady and uncompromising about it.[28]

The irony of Crane's regeneration is unmistakable. For all it renewed his faith, his new proem represented no advance whatever into the dialectic of *The Bridge*. It is an exciting invocation, but it merely calls upon the Bridge to "lend a myth to God," that is, to become the symbol which Crane had already made of it three years before. He had merely recalled the Bridge to mind and literally invoked its presence again. And so it went for years. He had already begun at that "real center" for which he was still looking.

At some point during Crane's struggle to order his material, the struggle itself became the subject of the poem. Not the doctrine, not even the symbol of the Bridge, presides over the poem, but instead, the illusion of a wild and restless consciousness. It is a lyric voice, scantily disguised, by turns, in other voices. The whole poem, in fact, in all its parts, is an organization of voices. In "Atlantis" the voice which deifies the Bridge is scarcely aware of itself, but in the interior sections, "Indiana," "Cape Hatteras," and "Quaker Hill," precisely the ones he put off writing, the voice becomes self-conscious, public, and editorial. The dramatic difference between the concluding lyric which Crane wrote first and

[28] To Waldo Frank (July 24, 1926), *Letters*, p. 267.

those interior sections which Crane wrote last marks the extent of his struggle to idealize a world.

III

As Crane's self was the subject of *The Bridge,* how then was he to organize within it those voices which would echo him? This was the great technical problem; and he could solve it only to the degree to which he might realize that he was indeed the subject. He approached this realization by fits and starts, tentatively and obliquely. He had defined a poem as "the concrete *evidence* of the *experience* of a recognition." A poem's organization would presumably follow from this premise, but just *how* is not certain. This is what Crane was trying to work out.

Given the fact that "the *experience* of a recognition" is a subjective event, and that Crane's "synthesis of America" involved a number of such events, *The Bridge* is a fiction. More precisely, Crane's commitment to representing this fiction is really the subject of the fiction. Although he was far from reaching this realization, his remarks about technique in general show that he was groping toward it. The materials of a poem, he said, must reveal an "emotional dynamics" by virtue of their "associational meanings."

As to technical considerations: the motivation of the poem must be derived from the implicit emotional dynamics of the materials used, and the terms of the expression employed are often selected less for their logical (literal) significance than for their associational meanings.[29]

[29] Hart Crane, "General Aims and Theories," in Horton, *Hart Crane,* p. 327.

These "associational meanings" should theoretically reveal some presiding consciousness. But the problem of rendering fiction, certainly a fiction as thoroughly autobiographical as *The Bridge,* is that of sufficiently displacing oneself from it to make it dramatically persuasive. The problem is to objectify one's own personality through some scheme or pattern (of "associational meanings," if that is what the author chooses). But what made it so difficult for Crane to diffuse or displace the poet within his poem was the fact that in the saga of composing it he himself had become personally and actually the hero.

His letters make this clear. Crane dramatized himself as a voice in the wilderness with an urgent need to explain, to confess it all. He was set apart from his community and painfully aware of this fact. He was at odds with his parents; he could make love to no woman; and he compulsively put off his friends when he most needed them. Crane railed at his poverty, at having to take jobs which prostituted him; yet when some benefactor paid his debts, he would suffer in abject luxury, awed by his obligation to write poetry in return for the subsidy. Always tending toward extremes, he wanted to confess and yet to justify himself at the same time. He wanted to assimilate, to devour whole experiences; and he despaired because he could not. He wanted to settle down; but he was rarely at home wherever he was, always moving from city to town and back again, always looking for an exit. No wonder his fascination—in *The Bridge*—with the notion of journeying, the restlessness, and the sense of urgency. The voice in *The Bridge* speaks for a questing, hungering evangelist.

But although Crane's intensely autobiographical letters offer symptoms of the lyric voice in *The Bridge,* this voice was not to be mistaken for the actual poet if Crane could help it. He was intrigued with a more deliberate fiction. He characteristically used the voice of the poet as a symbolic presence in the poem. In his early poem "Chaplinesque," for example, the speaking voice identifies itself as "we," which, Crane explained, refers to all the poets of the world, including Charlie Chaplin, who are in danger of being annihilated in the eroding contemporary experience.[30]

The involvement of this persona of the poet in a poem could become very intricate. Such was the case with "Recitative," about the apparent separation of human beings and yet the possibility of their common identity—or so Crane's explanation implies. He explained the poem in terms of his human epitome, the poet, as an onstage presence within the poem. Notice how involved it becomes.

> Imagine the poet, say, on a platform speaking it. The audience is one-half of Humanity, Man . . . and the poet the other. ALSO, the poet sees himself in the audience as in a mirror. ALSO, the audience sees itself, in part, in the poet. Against this paradoxical DUALITY is opposed the UNITY, or the conception of it . . . in the last verse.

But this was only the half of it. "In another sense the poet is *talking to himself* all the way through the poem . . . ."[31]

The persona of the poet was also intended to be the cohering factor in the three lyrics of "Faustus and Helen." Crane explained that the poems were to form a "bridge" between the past and the present, "between so-called classic experience and many divergent realities of our seething, confused cosmos of today . . . ."

> So I found "Helen" sitting in a street car; the Dionysian revels of her court and her seduction were transferred to a Metropolitan

---

[30] To William Wright (October 17, 1921), *Letters,* p. 68.

[31] To Allen Tate (March 1, 1924), *Letters,* p. 176.

roof garden with a jazz orchestra; and the *katharsis* of the fall of Troy I saw approximated in the recent World War.

"The importance of this scaffolding," Crane explained, was that it gave him "a series of correspondences between two widely separated worlds on which to sound some major themes of human speculation—love, beauty, death, renascence." [32] In order to dramatize these "correspondences," Crane epitomized the figures of Helen and Faustus: "Helen, the symbol of this abstract 'sense of beauty,' Faustus the symbol of myself, the poetic or imaginative man of all times." [33] What makes the poem is the recognition of correspondence between past and present by the emblematic poet within the poem.

In such terms Crane regarded "Faustus and Helen" as a point of departure for *The Bridge:* "I am ruminating on a new longish poem under the title of *The Bridge* which carries on further the tendencies manifest in 'F and H.' " [34] In both works he dramatized the poet-figure's assimilation of things seen. It was not the mere naming of parts that interested Crane, not the retinal images, but their assimilation. Crane argued for more than impressionism. He wanted to evoke a state of consciousness, the singular presence of a mind assimilating sensations and recollections. Hence, the theory of his technique: "the motivation of the poem must be derived from the implicit emotional dynamics of the materials used, and the terms of expression employed are often selected less for their logical (literal) significance than for their associational meanings."

What Crane called the "organic substances" of *The Bridge* are so by means of the lyric voice which names them. The scenery

[32] Crane, "General Aims and Theories," in Horton, *Hart Crane*, p. 324.

[33] To Waldo Frank (February 7, 1923) , *Letters*, p. 120.

[34] To Gorham Munson (February 6, 1923) , *Letters*, p. 118.

and the situations in *The Bridge* are dramatically organic, part and parcel of the speaker's awareness. In this way the fifteen lyrics do become a whole poem. The organizing technique of the poem is the speaker's repeated questing for unity. This repetition occurs through a series of apostrophes: monologues addressed to real or imagined listeners, called up or recalled for each occasion. These apostrophes invoke the presence of things, of legends, and of poets and explorers and pioneers.

What the apostrophes repeat is the idealizing of a subject, for none of the invoked presences is alive or—except for the Bridge—actual at the time of invocation. Columbus calls upon two faithful peers who become a third partisan in the speaker's mind; then, dehumanized, they represent the spirit of exploration and search. A speaker addresses an emblematic lover and then Rip Van Winkle, who becomes a metaphor of the bewildering orientation of oneself to everything else. A speaker invokes Pocahontas as the fertile earth incarnate, but interrupts the incantation with an address to the Indian chief who first possessed the symbolic Pocahontas. Later, Walt Whitman becomes the apocalyptic singer; and Poe, an emblem of disembodied horror. Finally, the Bridge becomes the revelation of God.

The lyric voice idealizes each time, generating what it names into some iconic significance. The Tunnel becomes a sort of anti-Bridge—however illogically—and Quaker Hill is the desecrated "Promised Land." "Three Songs" variously epitomize womankind: the Southern Cross, disappearing over the horizon, incarnates a "nameless" ideal; the stripteaser becomes the definitive "burlesque of our lust—and faith"; and "Virginia" palely idealizes the playmate and companion. With every new lyric the voice summons up a world which is literally immaterial; it bespeaks a consciousness that has its own sufficiency.

This consciousness repeatedly embarks on metaphorical journeys. In the printed order of its parts, as I have mentioned, *The Bridge* is a sequence of explorations: first, into the historical or legendary past, to discover some grand holistic scheme; then, into a various present, searching for evidence to test it. In these excursions the seeking consciousness conjoins the most various co-ordinates, exchanging metaphors of space and time: voyaging at once westward and into the past, or along city streets to pluperfect recollections, or up the Hudson to primal spring. Time and space become relative to the observer, and this witness sings of plenitude, which absorbs all movement into a continuum. These are all subjective journeys. But Crane also attempted to say all this editorially. Midway in the whole sequence, in "Cape Hatteras," the lyric voice invokes both past and present in order to establish—by assertion—the organic unity of all experience. But, we recall, this was virtually the last journey in *The Bridge.* Viewed in the order of their composition, which was so different from their printed sequence, these journeys bespeak a kind of therapeutic itinerary of Crane's, to arrive—in "Cape Hatteras" —at some definition of his visionary idea.

This is the part of *The Bridge,* according to most commentary, where Crane's "doctrinal failure" damages the poetry. Brom Weber summed up the critical consensus in an unequivocal statement, with which I cannot agree. "This section is a failure, both as complete poem and as a contributory part of *The Bridge*": except for scattered lines and stanzas, an abysmal descent from Crane's usual level of writing.[35] The symbolism of the earlier sections, Weber wrote, has been dissipated in mere virtuosity. Karl Shapiro's extended analysis of the "Cape Hatteras" manuscript makes the point that the fault in the poetry is precisely that failure to assimilate the machine images which Crane had discussed in his

[35] Weber, *Hart Crane,* p. 365.

essay "Modern Poetry." The fault, said Shapiro—echoing Winters
—lies in the false image of life Crane appropriated from Whitman, although he indicted on a different charge, saying that this
devalues the poetry as poetry.[36]

To insist on such a reading of "Cape Hatteras" is to make a
small point by missing the large one, since the subject of this
poem *is* the struggle—as Shapiro so well put it—of "a demonic
poet who has lost his way." Working backwards and forwards
through his material, Crane finally arrived at the point where
empirical knowledge obviously contradicted his visionary order,
at the point where the contradiction must somehow be resolved
into a state of belief, into a commitment of some sort. At this
point Crane had to make a stand. This was the denouement of
his drama.

IV

Crane himself signaled the importance of "Cape Hatteras" to
The Bridge. In the first synopsis which he sent to Otto Kahn a
projected episode about Whitman was to be one of the center sections of the poem; and more than four years later, even with an
entirely new version of his homage to Whitman, he reminded
Caresse Crosby, " . . . according to *my* ideas of *The Bridge*
this edition wouldn't be complete or even representative without it." [37]

The function of "Cape Hatteras" was to reveal Whitman's visionary monism, by which the human epoch with its shallow past
might be joined to the ages of geological time.

[36] Karl Shapiro, "The Meaning of the Discarded Poem," *Poets at Work* (New
York, 1948), pp. 111 ff.

[37] To Caresse Crosby (September 6, 1929), *Letters*, p. 345.

> Those continental folded aeons, surcharged
> With sweetness below derricks, chimneys, tunnels—

is one of many metaphorical assertions of the human imposition
on the natural world.[38] But it is a transient imposition; thus "that
star-glistered salver of infinity . . . Is sluiced by motion,—sub-
jugated never." Whitman's precept that divinity inheres in continuously involving forms is relevant to this present condition of
the world insofar as it carries a promise of imminent beatitude,
to be had simply for the realization of it. "Cape Hatteras" begins
as though it might test this precept against the uncongenial evidence of discrepancy between fact and vision. Thus:

> . . . We know the strident rule
> Of wings imperious . . . Space, instantaneous,
> Flickers a moment, consumes us in a smile:
> A flash over the horizon—shifting gears—
> And we have laughter, or more sudden tears.

But after citing the technological evidence with its negative con-
notations, the lyric becomes an impassioned defense of Whitman's
precept in spite of the evidence.

The argument is as elliptical as any essay of Emerson's or any
Puritan sermon, and with cause. Its premise is that truth already
exists; it is not to be reasoned out but simply discovered. Long
before he wrote "Cape Hatteras," Crane had decided that Whitman, better than any other, had been able to order the world into
a personal vision. But "Cape Hatteras" follows more than just the
inherited premise about the pre-existence of truth. Its sequence
stylizes the whole doctrine-reasons-uses-order-of-sermon argument. The poem begins with a statement of the doctrine—in

---

[38] Crane, *Collected Poems*, pp. 31 ff.

four stanzas—of the futility of mankind's tenancy on earth without monistic revelation. Six more stanzas amplify the "reasons" of this doctrine, imaging first the bright, brainless speed of mechanical parts, and then the short, fatal flight of a warplane.

In this elaboration of the "reasons," fourteen lines of metaphors —in stanza five—reduce the energy of dynamos ("The nasal whine of power") to a drunken parody of parts in motion. The dizzy, gyrating hardware, on bearings confined "in oilrinsed circles of blind ecstasy," relentlessly and ridiculously transforms energy to no consequence.

> Power's script,—wound, bobbin-bound, refined—
> Is stropped to the slap of belts on booming spools, spurred
> Into the bulging bouillon, harnessed jelly of the stars.
> Towards what?

Then five more stanzas launch a warplane and shoot it down— "down whizzing/ Zodiacs . . . into mashed and shapeless débris . . . . "

After these two caricatures of mankind's futility, the dynamos and the plane, the poet apostrophizes Whitman, and the tone of this sermonlike lyric changes. These last seven stanzas present the program, the "uses" of the doctrine. This is the longest part of the poem's argument, beginning with

> The stars have grooved our eyes with old persuasions
> Of love and hatred, birth,—surcease of nations . . .
> But who has held the heights more sure than thou,
> O Walt!

It is also the most programmatic. Herein the poet declares that he will reinstate the "span of consciousness" which Whitman celebrated; and herein lies the "use" of Whitman's vision and its beatific consequence. The engines return, but now their images connote rebirth, vitality.

> And now, as launched in abysmal cupolas of space,
> Toward endless terminals, Easters of speeding light—
> Vast engines outward veering with seraphic grace
> On clarion cylinders pass out of sight
> To course that span of consciousness thou'st named
> The Open Road—thy vision is reclaimed!
> What heritage thou'st signalled to our hands!

This is a prospectus for a better world, which depends on the realization that creates it. "The Open Road" is one of two allusions in "Cape Hatteras" to poems of Whitman which assume this premise. The other, quoted in the epigram ("The seas all cross'd, weathered the capes, the voyage done . . . "), acknowledges "Passage to India." Each of Whitman's poems anticipates the programmatic "Cape Hatteras"; each defines subjective realization as the life-giving process and then attempts to put it to work. In "Song of the Open Road," the poet travels by an unchartered route to meet the essence, within himself, of things previously seen ("Here is realization!"; "Here is the efflux of the soul . . . . here is happiness."). Then the program follows: "Allons!" whoever will; "Allons, we must not stop here"; "Allons!" sufficiency is in the great companionship of "superior journeys."

"Passage to India" dramatizes the same self-realization and prescribes the same agenda. What evolves in "Passage to India" is the poet's realization that his own consciousness will accomplish the final assimilation of all experience. In the course of celebrating "the vast rondure of the world," Whitman perceives—in Section 5—that it is his own consciousness which encompasses it. "Now first it seems my thought begins to span thee." The essence of this vast rondure is his own realization of it, and immediately thereafter he commits the redundance of setting out to accomplish what he has already achieved. God's purpose, he says, is about to be completed. The pact in "Cape Hatteras" commits this same redundance.

Somehow Whitman's subjective reality is not so until he proclaims it so, even though it has already been experienced. Edited from several stanzas, this is his program:

> After the great captains and engineers have accomplished their work . . . the poet . . . the true son of God shall come singing his songs . . . . Then . . . all these separations and gaps shall be taken up and hook'd and link'd together. The whole earth, this cold impassive voiceless earth shall be completely justified . . . gloriously accomplished by the true son of God, the poet.

The poet's utterance "shall absolutely fuse" all the created parts. The few remaining sections of the poem then lead to the poet's final "passage . . . to primal thought," a destination at which, ironically, he has already arrived.

This is the contradiction that besets "Cape Hatteras" and, in fact, the whole saga of *The Bridge*. The subjective vision has its own efficacy; beyond this it is ineffable. The attempt to convey it causes a dramatic crisis, which becomes a subject in itself. In this sense of the struggling consciousness *The Bridge* is indeed a whole and single drama.

The subject of every fiction sooner or later is one's relation to the world, and to some extent all fiction subsumes the actual world to one's personal vision of it. In the extreme, when the personal vision becomes, or is assumed to be, authoritative, then the fiction takes on an extra dramatic value, concerning the writer's struggle to order his material and make it serve his vision. In this regard, *The Bridge* belongs to a whole canon of writings in the Whitman legacy. The crisis of this evangelistic literature is in the poet's inability to tolerate the contradiction of the empirically knowable world which he means to transform. Instead of conscious irony there is tortured self-consciousness.

V

Hart Crane's prodigious attempt to write a "synthesis of America" is a matter of great importance in literary history. He produced a major work of art, and one which is beyond the capacity of any single theory of literature to explain. *The Bridge* transcends Yvor Winters' ethical insistence. Most obviously in our time, however, it transcends the confines of the New Criticism. The assumptions that a work of art is itself the experience and the subject for analysis, and that a poem's meaning inheres exclusively in the relationships between its parts can only partly explain *The Bridge,* much less appraise it. The whole poem records the struggle to render into a moral awareness the perception of certain social, historical, and legendary circumstances which a militantly aesthetic critic is bound to call extrinsic and therefore irrelevant, and about which he really has nothing to say.

Of course, Crane committed the indiscretion which is known in the glossary of the New Criticism as the "intentional fallacy." He announced ahead of time, even shouted, what his poem was about, thus depriving everyone else of the privilege. But his trespass, or rather his attack, was more than a matter of forthright candor. Crane's particular dissatisfaction with Eliot's poetry testifies to this. In order to contradict Eliot's doctrine he also waived the concept of an impersonal poem. Crane's concept of a poem as "the record of the *experience* of a recognition" contradicted

Eliot's theory of the poet's need to annihilate himself in some pattern which becomes the new experience.

It is curious that the New Critical methods, deriving as they do from Coleridge's philosophy of composition, should be so incapable of appraising a poem which ultimately derived from the same source. The form of a poem Coleridge considered to be the physical correlation of the soul within it. Accordingly, the poem is not a cunning construction of parts but a growth from a central, vital principle. Crane's letters made it abundantly clear that the central, living principle in *The Bridge* is the on-stage consciousness, contemplating the Bridge and trying to generate a new significance about it. Without this vital presence the Bridge would have no nature apart from its mere actuality as a magnificent engineering structure.

But Crane had to make this generating presence dramatically convincing. In organizing the various voices that would speak the poem, Crane was limited by the fact that he was really the subject of his own fiction. He must displace himself; yet to what extent? His editorializing in "Quaker Hill" is too obviously arbitrary to allow the reader to collaborate in any illusion beyond that of Crane speaking. But this man also lacked that sense of humor, the ironic awareness, which is apparently necessary in creating a deliberately different speaker, an on-stage character. The mother who intones in "Indiana" is utterly unconvincing. Given her past and her present circumstance, she simply would not speak the way Crane made her speak. His intellectualizing overwhelmed the disguise he contrived for it.

The Bridge is compelling, however, when the speaking voice remains personal yet without insistent personification. Thus: in "Ave Maria" Columbus becomes less the human figure and more the spirit of search; in "Cutty Sark"—and to a degree in "The Tunnel"—the fugue of disembodied voices registers upon a present consciousness, as does the speaker in "The River" and "The Dance"—and especially in "Cape Hatteras." These all accomplish illusions of a consciousness becoming charged by the impressions it receives, to a point almost beyond endurance.

By this extremity, by its desperate excitement, *The Bridge* is an overstatement of what has always been a preoccupation in this national literature. It is an emphatic document in the American domestication of romanticism. It presumes to correct an inherited assumption about the human condition, namely, that the glory of the past and the hope for the future are at odds with the dreary present. The author of course appropriates a subjective reordering of the world; but more than that, he does so on the singular assumption of his ability to do something about it. The "ideal" is more than a condition; it is a great power to be harnessed and put to work for mankind's well-being—but through the alembic of the poet.

Emerson, of course, and Whitman; but they were scarcely the first evangelists. Joel Barlow's *Columbiad* had already conducted a search for a hero who could properly represent the New World—and take responsibility for it. (For that matter, under other auspices, so had Cotton Mather.) Ever since the eighteenth century the constitutional guarantee of the pursuit of happiness has had a continuing literary response, in this New Republic, but a response always tending toward the didactic, as though the happiness itself were categorically obtainable in some national sense. The literary program of William Cullen Bryant, for example, and of James Russell Lowell, Hamlin Garland, and Frank Norris all assume the same extended coverage of this guarantee. All of these programs for a literature reveal a determination to teach, as though the individual's perception might be reduced to a program.

The romantic search for the limitless achievement—or rather

the assumption of its success—has caused certain continuing characteristics in our literature. There is a voracity which begets a corresponding despair: a despair of ever accomplishing the urge to "acclimatize," as Crane put it, to absorb all human experience into a subjective yet effable system.

Often the dilemma of a subjective reality that is empirically contradicted—voracity and despair—involves the author in his own subject in spite of himself, as in Jack London's *Martin Eden,* Frank Norris' *The Octopus,* all of Thomas Wolfe's novels, and *The Bridge.* Occasionally a writer deliberately objectifies the individual's struggle to reconcile these two realizations—of the inability to attain and yet the need to try—in terms of a character, such as Ahab or Gatsby or Quentin Compson, or in Henry Adams' persona of himself. But this becomes another subject involving the conventions of fiction.

What usually happens is that the questing consciousness is so immersed in the actuality from which it is trying to abstract a new world, that the author fails to achieve any ideological definitiveness. But as a consequence a new and dramatic subject emerges. It is the struggle and failure of the fiction's point of view, a moving, endless struggle to inform actuality with oneself. It is doomed to irresolution, yet this irresolution defines one's relation to the world that one sought in fiction in the first place. Hart Crane's version of this irresolvable struggle is one of the high points in the expression of the American mind.

Crane himself believed that Whitman had uttered the last word on this subject. Very possibly he had, although not in terms of any ideology. In his valedictory "So Long!" ("To conclude, I announce what comes after me"), Whitman said,

> Camerado, this is no book,
> Who touches this touches a man . . . .

Wallace Stevens'
Ice-Cream [1]

Richard Ellmann

IN CONTEMPLATING the poetry written by executives of large insurance companies, it is hard not to be curious about their treatment of the great fact of death upon which their ample livelihood depends. Lugubrious as the subject is, it offers a way into the obliquities of Wallace Stevens. Death appears importunately several times in Stevens' first volume, *Harmonium,* and less frequently thereafter, but a better beginning is his early play, "Three Travellers Watch a Sunrise," because in it the principal bit of stage property is a corpse. It is the corpse of a dead lover, murdered by his girl's father; and the question in the play is how the three Chinese travelers, who have come out to watch the sunrise and not to look at corpses, will take the discovery of the body. It soon becomes apparent that they do not mind it a bit;

[1] Reprinted from the *Kenyon Review,* 1957, by permission of the editors and the author.

they sympathize with the grief-stricken girl, but the corpse itself they treat as one more matter to be included in their surveyal of the scene. The sun, they say, will shine on the corpse as on another new thing:

> Red is not only
> The color of blood,
> Or
>
> > [*indicating the body*]
>
> Of a man's eyes,
> Or
>
> > [*pointedly*]
>
> Of a girl's.
> And as the red of the sun
> Is one thing to me
> And one thing to another,
> So it is the green of one tree
>
> > [*indicating*]
>
> And the green of another,
> Without which it would all be black.
> Sunrise is multiplied,
> Like the earth on which it shines,
> By the eyes that open on it,
> Even dead eyes,
> As red is multiplied by the leaves of trees.

They have no horror of death and no fear of it; but rather they take it as part of some larger order which they have long since learned to accept as essential. The green of life and the red of grief or death are both preferable to blackness. The sun shines not indifferently but intimately upon death as upon life. A corpse contributes to the variety of the landscape. Probably Stevens put this point of view, which is his own, into the mouths of three Chinese because it seemed to him vaguely oriental. But his setting is not China but eastern Pennsylvania, his Chinese are Chinese Americans, and we would be wrong to follow his equivocal hint in assuming that he advocates that the West accept the acceptance of the East.

If we look at his poems about death, we will find that he has decisive personal views about it. The early poems are even a little truculent. In "The Death of a Soldier," he tells us that the soldier "does not become a three-days personage,/ Imposing his separation,/ Calling for pomp," and in "Cortège for Rosenbloom," a more difficult poem, he defends the view of death which he has labeled Chinese by challenging its opposite, by challenging, that is, the notion that death is something apart and isolated. The ceremony of conventional mourning, its stilted decorum, its withdrawal of the dead man from the natural world, its figmental afterlife, are all satirized here. *Que faites-vous dans ce galère,* what are *you* doing in this mortician's heaven? the poet seems to be asking "the wry Rosenbloom" whose body is so absurdly apotheosized. The name of Rosenbloom suggests both an ordinary man and someone who springs like a flower out of nature and should not be separated from it.

> Now, the wry Rosenbloom is dead
> And his finical carriers tread,
> On a hundred legs, the tread
> Of the dead.
> Rosenbloom is dead.

The finical mourners are made buglike.

> They carry the wizened one
> Of the color of horn
> To the sullen hill,
> Treading a tread
> In unison for the dead.

(Horn is death's color in Stevens' verse.)

> Rosenbloom is dead.
> The tread of the carriers does not halt
> On the hill, but turns
> Up the sky.
> They are bearing his body into the sky.

The next stanza makes quite clear what the poet thinks of this extraordinary ascent from the *ground,* from the solidity of the real, toward nothingness and nebulousness:

> It is the infants of misanthropes
> And the infants of nothingness
> That tread
> The wooden ascents
> Of the ascending of the dead.

The mourners are infants because their concepts of man are undeveloped and founded on a dislike of man's real nature; hence they love their extrahuman illusions.

> It is turbans they wear
> And boots of fur
> As they tread the boards
> In a region of frost,
> Viewing the frost;

These are the tripsters of mourning; here they come with their conventional accoutrements, viewing death as an isolated, frigid country.

> To a chirr of gongs
> And a chitter of cries
> And the heavy thrum
> Of the endless tread
> That they tread;

Again they are insectlike, antlike, their absurd noises adding to their general absurdity.

> To a jangle of doom
> And a jumble of words
> Of the intense poem
> Of the strictest prose
> Of Rosenbloom.
>
> And they bury him there,
> Body and soul,
> In a place in the sky.
> The lamentable tread!
> Rosenbloom is dead.

The real nature of man, Stevens is suggesting to us, is comprehended only in terms of an adult, human culture; Rosenbloom himself is an intense poem, is strictest prose, and prose and poetry are set against infants and insects. No wonder the mourners jumble the essence of Rosenbloom. This cortège, then, in the simplest terms, is the wrong way to conduct a funeral. What is the right way? "The Emperor of Ice-Cream" is the right way. Here the poet is hortatory, not descriptive, and his tone is buoyant and defiant. It defies the mourners of Rosenbloom, who would like to treat this corpse with the usual ceremony, but the poet will have none of their services. Instead he summons the living, and, to emphasize his point, he makes clear that everyone living is welcome, and especially those who proceed by nature with scant ceremony; this time the season is summer, as favored in Stevens' verse as winter is disfavored.

> Call the roller of big cigars,
> The muscular one, and bid him whip
> In kitchen cups concupiscent curds.
> Let the wenches dawdle in such dress
> As they are used to wear, and let the boys
> Bring flowers in last month's newspapers.
> Let be be finale of seem.
> The only emperor is the emperor of ice-cream.
>
> Take from the dresser of deal,
> Lacking the three glass knobs, that sheet
> On which she embroidered fantails once
> And spread it so as to cover her face.
> If her horny feet protrude, they come
> To show how cold she is, and dumb.
> Let the lamp affix its beam.
> The only emperor is the emperor of ice-cream.

The way to treat death is to wear ordinary clothes, not turbans or boots of fur. It is to whip up some ice-cream in the kitchen, not to be finical; it is to spread flowers, not to toll the bell or ululate. Death, as we learned from the Chinese, is not horrible. The horny feet may protrude, and if they do, it is just as well. Do not call the embalmers. "Let be be finale of seem"—that is, away with the panoply of empty conventional mourning and empty conventional myths of death and afterlife. Let us accept being, which like the sun's rays comprehends death with life.

The last battlement before us is the line, "The only emperor is the emperor of ice-cream." There are two going interpretations of this line, one that the emperor is life, the other that he is death. When Stevens was informed of this difference of critical opinion, he said, in effect, "So much the better!" and refused to judge between them. If we take the emperor to be life, and the poet's whole sympathy to be with the living, then why does the poem deal so precisely and deliberately with the corpse in the second stanza? Why not push it out of the way instead of displaying it? And can a wake, even an ice-cream wake, be completely detached from death? On the other hand, if the emperor is to be identified with death, why bring in the cigar-rolling, ice-cream–mixing muscular man? Is concupiscence desirable at funerals?

I think we may reach a little nearer if we remember that the characteristics of ice-cream are that it is tasty, transitory, and cold. Life may be tasty and perishable, but it is not cold. Death may be cold but scarcely transitory, unless we assume that Stevens believes in an afterlife, which he doesn't, or tasty, unless we assume he has a death-wish, which he doesn't. Whoever the emperor is, he is realer than the run-of-the-mill emperors, the kaisers and Erlkönige, and his domain seems to include both life and death. The coldness of ice-cream suggests the corpse, as its sweetness suggests life's concupiscence. Stevens has said that his only daughter had a superlative liking for ice-cream, and is reported to have said also that she asked him to write a poem about it. Whether she did or not, there is a childlike quality about the poem—its absence of taboo, its complete, simultaneous, unruffled acceptance of conventional contraries—party food and horny feet. The child examines both without distaste. Both are included in the imperial domain. Ice-cream, then, is death and life.

But we must not think of death and life as a dual monarchy loosely joined by an indifferent ruler. The emperor is more than his ice-cream empire; he is the force that inspires and makes it one. Here again I call Stevens for my rather uncommunicative witness. He commented of the poem that it contained something of the essential gaudiness of poetry; this gaudiness must affect our estimate of the emperor. It is the more appropriate when we remember that in the poem "Metaphor as Degeneration," Stevens asserts that *being* includes death and the imagination. My candidate for the emperor of ice-cream, then, is the force of being, understood as including life, death, and the imagination which plays in this poem so gustily upon both. The emperor creates ice-cream, expresses himself through death and life, conceives of them as a unity, and is immanent in both of them.

If the volume *Harmonium* has an integrating theme, it is this deliberate acceptance of death with life. Stevens will have none of heaven or immortality; these fictions, always of questionable value, are worn through. In both "Sunday Morning" and "Le Monocle de Mon Oncle" Stevens endeavors to show just what place death has in being. The first is an argument with a woman who, on Sunday morning, is prompted to think of Christ's sacrificial death and of the heaven which Christ opened to man by dying for him. The poet asks, "Why should she give her bounty to the dead?" and calls to her mind the beauty of the landscape. But when she continues to long for some imperishable bliss as contrasted with the cyclical, seasonal landscape, he advises her:

> Death is the mother of beauty; hence from her,
> Alone, shall come fulfillment to our dreams
> And our desires. Although she strews the leaves
> Of sure obliteration on our paths,
> The path sick sorrow took, the many paths

> Where triumph rang its brassy phrase, or love
> Whispered a little out of tenderness,
> She makes the willow shiver in the sun
> For maidens who were wont to sit and gaze
> Upon the grass, relinquished to their feet.
> She causes boys to pile new plums and pears
> On disregarded plate. The maidens taste
> And stray impassioned in the littering leaves.

The threat of something contrary to love, of obliteration, is what gives love its force. If there were no door there would be no room, but we are interested in the room, not the door. Then the poet mocks heaven and its attempt to abstract life from being and leave death behind:

> Is there no change of death in paradise?
> Does ripe fruit never fall? Or do the boughs
> Hang always heavy in that perfect sky,
> Unchanging, yet so like our perishing earth,
> With rivers like our own that seek for seas
> They never find, the same receding shores
> That never touch with inarticulate pang?
> Why set the pear upon those river-banks
> Or spice the shores with odors of the plum?
> Alas, that they should wear our colors there,
> The silken weavings of our afternoons,
> And pick the strings of our insipid lutes!
> Death is the mother of beauty, mystical,
> Within whose burning bosom we devise
> Our earthly mothers waiting, sleeplessly.

It is in the context of death that we see our earthly mothers of beauty—our loves, who are waiting sleeplessly because, like the heroine, they are anxious with the problem of perishability.

Supple and turbulent, a ring of men
Shall chant in orgy on a summer morn
Their boisterous devotion to the sun,
Not as a god, but as a god might be,
Naked among them, like a savage source.
Their chant shall be a chant of paradise,
Out of their blood, returning to the sky;
And in their chant shall enter, voice by voice,
The windy lake wherein their lord delights,
The trees, like serafin, and echoing hills,
That choir among themselves long afterward.
They shall know well the heavenly fellowship
Of men that perish and of summer morn.
And whence they came and whither they shall go
The dew upon their feet shall manifest.

Here, in more mellifluous phrases, are the same elements as in
"The Emperor of Ice-Cream"; the men are supple, in the other
poem muscular; here they are turbulent, boisterous, in orgy, there
they are eaters of concupiscent curds. The sun to which they
chant cannot be taken only as the power which creates life, for
Stevens emphasizes that the singers are men who perish like dew;
it has to be also the power that moves in death. Let us say tentatively that it is what Dylan Thomas calls the force that through
the green fuse drives the flower and blasts the roots of trees. Here
we not only accept being, we worship it. And because life is such
a good thing, death, upon which it depends, must be a good thing
too. But death is only a small part of being; instead of speaking
of life and death as if they were equals, we might speak of a god
whose death is no more than a cue for his instant rebirth.

Stevens returns to the problem of death in another fine poem
in *Harmonium,* "Le Monocle de Mon Oncle." It is characteristic
of this poet, who wrote English as if it were French (just as Carlyle

wrote English as if it were German), that he puts his most serious thoughts into a courtly dialogue between a man and a woman.
The poem begins in a willfully pretentious style:

> "Mother of heaven, regina of the clouds,
> O sceptre of the sun, crown of the moon,
> There is not nothing, no, no, never nothing,
> Like the clashed edges of two words that kill."

The first two lines, which echo the litany, are pseudo-religious,
in violent contrast with the next two. The lethal quality of two
words is itself illustrated by the jarring double negatives of the
third line. But there is more to the third line than that. It has
been suggested that this is just one of Stevens' playful linguistic
tricks, but the real reason will become clear as we proceed:

> And so I mocked her in magnificent measure.
> Or was it that I mocked myself alone?
> I wish that I might be a thinking stone.
> The sea of spuming thought foists up again
> The radiant bubble that she was. And then
> A deep up-pouring from some saltier well
> Within me, bursts its watery syllable.

> A red bird flies across the golden floor.
> It is a red bird that seeks out his choir
> Among the choirs of wind and wet and wing.
> A torrent will fall from him when he finds.
> Shall I uncrumple this much-crumpled thing?
> I am a man of fortune greeting heirs;
> For it has come that thus I greet the spring.
> These choirs of welcome choir for me farewell.
> No spring can follow past meridian.
> Yet you persist with anecdotal bliss
> To make believe a starry *connaissance*.

> Is it for nothing, then, that old Chinese
> Sat tittivating by their mountain pools
> Or in the Yangtse studied out their beards?
> I shall not play the flat historic scale.
> You know how Utamaro's beauties sought
> The end of love in their all-speaking braids.
> You know the mountainous coiffures of Bath.
> Alas! Have all the barbers lived in vain
> That not one curl in naure has survived?
> Why, without pity on these studious ghosts,
> Do you come dripping in your hair from sleep?

The repetition of *nothing* in the third stanza makes clear that the word *nothing* is one which he has borrowed from her and therefore repeated so mockingly in the first stanza. We have to imagine the dialogue as beginning before the poem starts, when the woman, having left her bed with her hair in disarray, says to the poet that now that she is middle-aged there is *nothing* left for her but old age and death and after that, she hopes, heaven— that starry *connaissance* for lovers once young. The problem of the poem then is to win her over to accepting death and denying an afterlife. The speaker begins by associating himself with her feeling of age and regret, but ends by insisting that we should concern ourselves, even in old age, with life rather than with death.

> This luscious and impeccable fruit of life
> Falls, it appears, of its own weight to earth.
> When you were Eve, its acrid juice was sweet,
> Untasted, in its heavenly, orchard air.

So long as we remain immortal in Eden, we long for life, and pluck its apple even if death comes with it:

An apple serves as well as any skull
To be the book in which to read a round,
And is as excellent, in that it is composed
Of what, like skulls, comes rotting back to ground.

The poet then offers a series of parabolic instances, the first of
which proves that

The honey of heaven may or may not come,
But that of earth both comes and goes at once.

For earth's honey, like ice-cream, is vested in perishability. He
next establishes that life and love continue even though individuals depart, and finally demonstrates that life, which has offered
strong passions to the young, offers to the aged the power to
value its ephemeral, perishing moments.

In his later poetry Stevens continues his efforts to make death
subordinate to life. His attitude does not alter, but his emphasis
in later poems falls less on rebuking others for erroneous ideas
of death than on attempting to portray his own idea. He endeavors to find a picture of death which will not terrify us and
will not separate it from life. Some of these treatments of death,
such as "The Owl in the Sarcophagus," where he finds death to
be made up of three modern mythological personages—peace,
sleep, and memory; "The Airman's Death," where the airman
sinks into a profound emptiness which yet is somehow made
close and a part of us; and "Burghers of Petty Death," where actual death seems a little thing beside the feeling of death that
sometimes pervades the mind, are not so seductive as his early
arguments. In "Esthétique du Mal," Stevens tries in the seventh
section to come to grips with the problem entirely in pictorial

form, and this poem is more winning. Like "Cortège for Rosen-bloom," it begins by anchoring the hero in nature like a rose:

> How red the rose that is the soldier's wound,
> The wounds of many soldiers, the wounds of all
> The soldiers that have fallen, red in blood,
> The soldier of time grown deathless in great size.
>
> A mountain in which no ease is ever found,
> Unless indifference to deeper death
> Is ease, stands in the dark, a shadows' hill,
> And there the soldier of time has deathless rest.
>
> Concentric circles of shadows, motionless
> Of their own part, yet moving on the wind,
> Form mystical convolutions in the sleep
> Of time's red soldier deathless on his bed.
>
> The shadows of his fellows ring him round
> In the high night, the summer breathes for them
> Its fragrance, a heavy somnolence, and for him,
> For the soldier of time, it breathes a summer sleep,
>
> In which his wound is good because life was.
> No part of him was ever part of death.
> A woman smoothes her forehead with her hand
> And the soldier of time lies calm beneath that stroke.

This death is deathless in the sense that it is close to nature, close to life, close to the community of men living and men dead. It has nothing to do with the great looming abstraction of capital-ized Death. The woman smoothing her hair might seem alto-gether detached from the soldier, but the soldier has never left the living and her gesture is a part of his being. This conception begins with the physical nearness of living and dead, but implies a metaphysical bond as well.

In Stevens' later verse there are many suggestions that death is what we make of it. "Madame la Fleurie" is a poem about a man who read horror into nature, and instead of seeing her as a lady with flowers conceived of her as a bearded queen, wicked in her dead light. He died in this falsification, and the result is that there are no blue jays for him to remember, now that he is dead; he is not like the soldier whose death is merely an extension, in a different tempo, of his life.

I suggested earlier that to Stevens the sun is the primal force which, as in Dylan Thomas, creates and destroys. I think we should correct this now to indicate that the destructive force is much less important for Stevens than for Thomas, that they are nearly opposites. For in Thomas, who sees the body as a shroud, and life as either a rapturous ignorance of death or a knowing horror of it, the main revelation is that death pervades life, while in Stevens it is that life pervades death. In Thomas the glory of life is stolen from death. Stevens' vision, for it is almost that, is of living and unliving—a term which seems closer to his ideas than dead—men joined together in admiration, whether vocal or mute, of being. Being is the great poem, and all our lesser poems only approximate its intensity and power.

The sun is this primal force of being, reflected alike by living and unliving, by people and by things. Our dualisms disguise their single origin. It can be called God or the Imagination ("Final Soliloquy of the Interior Paramour"), though these terms are also only metaphors for what is ultimately a mystery to be worshiped rather than fathomed. The beauty that the sun creates antedates human life; long before we came on the earth the sun was covering the rock of reality with leaves, but once arrived here, we too participate in it. The sun is the Ulysses to which we and the world are the faithful Penelope. Its force is constant, and anchors in repetition all the changes which occur in the world, as the ever-changing gleams of sunshine stem always from the same burning source. It is bodiless, unreal in that sense, yet it fills bodies with light and inspirits them. "It is the ever-never-changing-same," Stevens writes in "Adult Epigram," and elsewhere he says it is the will to change which underlies all changes. We are, he writes in "An Ordinary Evening in New Haven," in a permanence composed of impermanence.

Many of Stevens' poems can be read as accounts of the interaction of imagination and reality, but they have a theme which underlies that. "Peter Quince at the Clavier," for instance, seems to be about an Abt Vogler building up a mountain of music from a few hints in experience, but the theme which was, I think, even more important to Stevens, is summarized in the lines,

> The body dies; the body's beauty lives.
> So gardens die, in their green going,
> A wave, interminably flowing.

The wave is a frequent metaphor for the force elsewhere saluted as the sun. As Stevens says in one of his essays, "A wave is a force and not the water of which it is composed, which is never the same." Sometimes he epitomizes this force as a river called Swatara, or simply as an unnamed river in Connecticut that flows nowhere like the sea; sometimes it is a changing giant ("Things of August"), sometimes a bodiless serpent ("St. John and the Back-Ache," "The Auroras of Autumn"). But the force can also be found in a creature like the blackbird in "Thirteen Ways of Looking at a Blackbird," a poem which we would be well advised to read not as a declaration that there are thirteen ways of looking at a blackbird but that there is a blackbird behind all these impressions. I do not think it has been remarked that Stevens is unsympathetic to only one of the thirteen ways, Number XI, in which the protagonist is not "I" but "He."

> He rode over Connecticut
> In a glass coach.
> Once, a fear pierced him,
> In that he mistook
> The shadow of his equipage
> For blackbirds.

The error of the man in the glass coach—and glass is almost always a bar to sight in Stevens' poems—is that he sees the blackbird merely as death; the further proof of his error is that he has *not* seen the blackbird, has seen only his own dark mind, the shadow of his equipage. And so, like the man in "Madame la Fleurie," he abstracts the blackbird from nature and sees only fear in it.

Most of Stevens' poems are based upon images which somehow participate in this primal force of being, and it is the existence of the force in them that he is concerned to demonstrate. The sense of "The Worms at Heaven's Gate" is almost destroyed by its isolation in anthologies, where it seems to mean that the sardonic worms are handing up bits of a corpse with ironic comments on their deterioration. For Stevens the beauty does continue, it survives corruption, and the worms, not sardonic at all, can only talk of beauty, not of death.

In the individual person, the self, as Stevens says in "The Plant on the Table," is the sun. This self should be dominated by the imagination, a solar light within the mind. In expressing our imagination we express the force of being. But in the individual man the light may be deflected. The imagination may look not upon the rest of being, but only upon itself; so, like Chieftain If-fucan, it may disparage the world of nature, or, like the other bantam in pine woods, solipsistically fail to recognize that we are all parts of a common world and bound together by the shared light of the sun. The danger of such narcissism is that it leads to empty hallucinations, such as that denial of being which is heaven, that denial of beauty which is modern religion, that denial of the imagination which is reason, that denial of life which is nostalgia. The trouble with all these is that they are petrifying, they produce bad statues instead of men, the creative fire is thwarted in them. The imagination should queen it over the mind, with reason as her obsequious butler and memory as her underpaid maid-of-all-work. But she must always see the teeming earth, not the empty sky, as her domain. If she doesn't, the world becomes fixed and inert instead of malleable and suffusable. The imagination is constantly reshaping and reforming reality; it is not the poet's exclusive preserve—everyone has it—but the poet uses it more steadily and powerfully and with more recognition of its value. It is the imagination, like the sun, which keeps the world from being black. Memory and reason can aid instead of impeding it, by confirming the imagination's felt bond with all existence.

We can see why Stevens' poetry is so different from that of Eliot. Although Stevens occasionally takes note of our age as a leaden time, this is not at all a principal theme. In no sense does Stevens sigh for lost beliefs; rather he is elated that old hallucinations are over now so that the imagination can get a fresh start. They have prevented us from living in the physical world, and the great poverty for man is not to live there. The major man—Stevens' modest version of the superman—is the man who brings most sunlight to most rock, most imagination to most reality, and is closest to the primal force.

Although there is an obvious similarity between Stevens and Yeats in that they both worship in the church of the imagination, Stevens conceives of the primal force as existing independent of man and prior to him, while Yeats often suggests that it begins with man and is altogether human. In Stevens the imagination is impersonal and anonymous; it reminds us of Ortega y Gasset's contention that much modern art is dehumanized; but for Yeats the imagination works always through proper names. I find, more brashly, a second imperfect parallel in Stevens and his fellow American, the muscular one, Ernest Hemingway. When we think of Hemingway's stories about death, and particularly of "The Snows of Kilimanjaro," what strikes us is that the rather ignoble hero is given in the end a noble hero's death, and for a moment we may be baffled and ask why this man who has made such a mess of his talents and of his marriages should be treated by his creator so well. It is because, with all his defects, he has remained true to his eye; the great virtue in Hemingway is not to live the good life, but to see, as the great virtue in Stevens is to imagine. Even if the hero of "The Snows" has not done anything else, he has seen, and so mastered reality. In Wallace Stevens, the soldier, wounded also by life, is also saved by what he has found in it. Death, in both Stevens and Hemingway, comes beneficently to those who have expressed the primal force of vision, who have lived in the sun.

Most of Stevens' poetry is an essay in the intricacies of contentment, the mind and nature conspiring to render more lovely and awesome the force of being. There are sensual poems about plums, and philosophical poems about the mind's embrace of the plum, and a few, but only a few, poems about plumlessness, a state which depends upon plums for recognition. Stevens objects to those poets who make their pleas to the night bird, who dwell upon discontent. His interest in grief, anger, and other unpleasant emotions is cursory. He does not evade tragedy, but he does not regard it as very important. An atmosphere of elation pervades his work as he surveys the marvels of the world; he insures us against death by assigning it so minor and integral a place in being. He is too fascinated by the endless procession of beauties to pay much mind to the retirements of particular individuals. He confronts us with a table of fragrancies and succulencies, solemnly reminds us that all of these, like us, are islanded between the nothingness that precedes form and the rot that ends it, and then urges us to fall to.

"The Situation of Our Time":
Auden in His American Phase

Frederick P. W. McDowell

Now THAT we have perspective, Auden's poems written before and during the first years of his American career, which began in 1939, seem the most significant. Some reviewers of *Another Time* (1940) expressed regret that Auden had begun to write in a looser style than that found in *Poems* (1930) or *Poems* (1933).[1] The direction of Auden's development in *Another Time* had become apparent in *On This Island* (1937), and some commentators upon that volume had noted the beginnings of a different stance, style, and diction.[2] The earlier poems were more sensuous and more concrete; for the present-day reader, however, many of these poems reveal an exuberant, sometimes frivolous display of energy which lacks

[1] David Daiches, *Poetry*, LVI (April, 1940), 40–43; Michael Roberts, *Spectator*, CLXV (July 26, 1940), 100; Peter Monro Jack, *New York Times Book Review* (February 18, 1940), 2.

[2] G. W. Stonier, *New Statesman and Nation*, XII (November 14, 1936), 776; Edwin Muir, *Spectator*, CLVII (December 4, 1936), 1008; Randall Jarrell, "Changes of Attitude and Rhetoric in Auden's Poetry," *Southern Review*, VII (1941), 326–49.

direction and focus. Furthermore, the style, though individual and effective within its limits, seems more mannered than it did to Auden's earlier audience who saw in it a possible revitalizing of the language. This energizing of poetry was to derive in part from the rhythms and patterns of Anglo-Saxon and fourteenth-century alliterative verse, in part from the parallel structure of Biblical sentences and free verse, in part from distortions of syntax and sentence structure, and in part from a calculated use of the spoken language.[3] By the application of these techniques, Auden often produced an impression more of artifice than of spontaneity.

When, beginning with *On This Island,* Auden became more abstract and less dependent for his effects upon sensuous imagery and the exploitation of the techniques mentioned above, there was gain as well as loss. Auden's increasing subtlety of thought demanded a more flexible medium. The telegraphic style with its ellipses and disjunctions no longer sufficed to communicate the complexities of his vision. The result is that "September 1, 1939," with its well-developed periods, seems more important— and a better poem—to us nowadays than it did to most of the reviewers of *Another Time,* since we are not perplexed—as these critics were—by the beginnings of a new method.

Even the best early work retained in *The Collected Poetry* (1945) now seems stylistically elaborate and intellectually pretentious: "As Well as Can Be Expected," "We All Make Mistakes," and "Let History Be My Judge" (all from *Poems,* 1930). The most famous early poem, "Something Is Bound to Happen" (*Poems,* 1933), is the finest precisely because it is the most lucidly expressed, and is the least tied to Auden's overt social and intellectual program during this period. His "revolt" in the 1930's now

---

[3] For a detailed discussion of Auden's earlier style, see Jarrell, *op. cit.*

seems parochial and rootless, characterized more by donnish superiority than by depth of indignation, and by obscurities in style
which are not justified by oversimplified views of life and society.
A mature seriousness is present to some degree in *On This Island,*
however, and is unmistakably evident in *Journey to a War* (1939).
The well-known "Paysage Moralisé" (*On This Island*) and "Law
Like Love" (*Another Time*) in part depend upon the elliptical
and concentrated rhythms which Auden used in his early volumes. These rhythms are now at the service of an expanded content, and the terseness of the style underscores at all points the
strength of a deepened consciousness of reality.

In *On This Island, Letters from Iceland, Journey to a War,*
and *Another Time,* Auden evolved the technique best suited to
convey his increasingly intricate thought. Predominantly, he made
use of the relaxed line derived from, and accommodated to, the
rhythms of speech. The result is a poetry which registers in the
mind with the authority of the spoken word at its most idiomatic
and forceful. This line also derives in part from nineteenth- and
twentieth-century blank verse and free verse. Poets as different
as Whitman, Browning, and T. S. Eliot (all of them are in Auden's background) had abandoned, to a greater or lesser extent,
rhyme and elaborate stanzaic forms and had made increasing use
of conversational rhythms in their blank verse and free verse. In
many of his poems Auden has, of course, done much the same
thing, but his facility with language is so great that he has been
able to accommodate, more often perhaps than his forebears,
these same freer meters to varying rhyme and stanzaic patterns.
Thereby he has secured body, strength, and resilience for the
colloquial rhythms he has exploited, and his lines have for the
most part escaped the flaccid.

The resources of the spoken language allow him, moreover, to
achieve effects of complication beyond those possible for a poetry

based on artifice like the poetry of his first volumes. Since the middle 1930's Auden has used the relaxed inflections and patterns of oral English when he is being the most deliberate. The involuted ironies underlying his interpretation of experience are defined through his manipulations of the spoken word. Even a medium responsive to the modulations of Auden's thought is not sensitive enough to record them all; the result is a poetry which suggests more than is ever said. The exaggeration and understatement inseparable from a colloquial diction also convey some sense of the fracture Auden felt between the nightmarish present and his vision of an ideal order.

Auden's language became less sensuous and decorative, more sparse, bare, and "flat" in the late 1930's and after. This was a studied effort in a writer who was distrustful from the first of the effusive generality and who tried instead to achieve "the wry, the sotto-voce,/ Ironic and monochrome." [4] His subdued and neutral tone provides an effective foil for the lines of sensuous beauty or crystalline purity to be found in all of his best work. In Auden the lyric impulse is never far below a prosaic surface. Upon a cursory reading, his verse often seems to read like prose, to make excessive use, that is, of discursive thought directly presented. The intensity of his intellectual passion and the plasticity of his language usually convince us, in the end, that we are reading poetry.[5] Auden noted in the work of Robert Frost effects similar to those which we discern in his own poetry: "Only a mature and disciplined poet could keep every line so deliberately flat, and yet

---

[4] "To Reinhold and Ursula Niebuhr," *Nones* (New York, 1950), p. 7. See also Robert Roth, "The Sophistication of W. H. Auden: A Sketch in Longinian Method," *Modern Philology,* XLVIII (February, 1951), 192–204.

[5] This aspect of Auden is favorably presented in John Peale Bishop, "The Unconstraining Voice," *Nation,* CL (April 6, 1940), 452–54, and unfavorably in Joseph Warren Beach, "The Poems of Auden and the Prose Diathesis," *Virginia Quarterly Review,* XXV (Summer, 1949), 365–83.

achieve a poetic effect." [6] Through the precision of their rhythms, Auden's direct statements in verse likewise achieve strength and an intensive identity, even when the brilliantly appointed image may be in abeyance:

> By mourning tongues
> The death of the poet was kept from his poems.
>
> .   .   .
>
> And the poor have the sufferings to which they are
>   fairly accustomed,
>
> .   .   .
>
> A few thousand will think of this day
> As one thinks of a day when one did something
>   slightly unusual.

Edmund Wilson once said that Auden is a poet like Browning who should be read in bulk.[7] Wilson's comment implies what is indeed so, that there are more indispensable titles in Auden than in any other recent poet of his stature. Anthologists have made current some of his most distinctive work like "Musée des Beaux Arts," "Voltaire at Ferney," "September 1, 1939," "In Memory of W. B. Yeats," "Something Is Bound to Happen," "Law Like Love," "Mundus et Infans," "In Memory of Sigmund Freud," and "Lay your sleeping head, my love." There are, however, many poems which the anthologist has not been able to find room for but which deserve greater currency than they now have. For myself, in addition to the titles just mentioned, I would include the

---

[6] "Four Prefaces to a Book: I," *Recognition of Robert Frost: Twenty-fifth Anniversary,* ed. Richard Thornton (New York, 1937), p. 296.

[7] "W. H. Auden in America," *New Statesman and Nation,* LI (June 9, 1956), 659.

following as vintage Auden (I list them in the order in which they appear in *The Collected Poetry*) : "The Composer," "Journey to Iceland," "The Labyrinth," "Who's Who," "Are You There," "The Climbers," "To E. M. Forster," "Pascal," "Perhaps," "Casino," "In Father's Footsteps," "Aera sub Lege," "Our Bias," "Rimbaud," "Leap Before You Look," "In Memory of Ernst Toller," "The Ship," "What Do You Think," "The Unknown Citizen," "The Walking Tour," "Herman Melville," "Canzone," "The Voyage," "Crisis," "As He Is," "Spain, 1937," "As I walked out one evening," "Fish in the unruffled lakes," "Song for St. Cecilia's Day," "Lady, weeping at the crossroads," "Look, stranger, on this island now," "Now the leaves are falling fast," "O who can ever gaze his fill," "Oh who can ever praise enough," and "Stop all the clocks." My list does not include the fine sonnets in "The Quest" and "In Time of War," "Commentary" from "In Time of War" (at least the last lines beginning with "Night falls on China" reveal impassioned conviction) , and the exuberant *tour de force* not included in *The Collected Poetry,* "Letter to Lord Byron."

More than three-fourths of these poems come from the volumes published after *On This Island* (1937) . Thus Auden's best and most characteristic work is that written in the informal and conversational yet intellectually vigorous mode illustrated by these poems. Of course, he has developed this vein still further in the work of the 1940's and 1950's. It would be profitable to discuss in detail the intimate relationships between idea and technique in some of the poems I have listed above; but I have chosen to limit my detailed discourse to two longer poems published in the 1940's, "New Year Letter" (1941) and "The Sea and the Mirror" (1944) , which have been surprisingly neglected. Two other long poems from this decade, "For the Time Being" (1944) and "The Age of Anxiety" (1947) , I shall discuss more briefly. Since I wish

to consider the poetry somewhat apart from Auden's development, which has been treated exhaustively in the books by Richard Hoggart and Joseph Warren Beach,[8] I feel justified in confining most of my discussion to the first two, which are aesthetically,
I believe, the most successful. All four of them are united, however, by a concern with "the real problem" for modern man, "the
relation of . . . the Word to the flesh, the universal to the individual, the eternal to the historical."[9]

II

In "For the Time Being: A Christmas Oratorio," Auden not
only expounds the tenets of his recently acquired faith (see especially "The Meditation of Simeon"), but exposes the illness of
the modern era. Sometimes condemnation is direct as in the
narrator's meditative comments; sometimes the modern is seen
only by implication in Auden's picture of Roman decadence;
sometimes it is present by implied contrast when Auden emphasizes the sanctity of his biblical characters. The work is uneven,
more impressive in certain parts than as a whole. In the best sections of the poem Auden's use of the vernacular reminds us effectively of the contemporary aspects of his materials, whereas
the most explicitly satirical passages ("Fugal-Chorus" from "The
Summons," "The Massacre of the Innocents," and the "Voices of
the Desert" speeches from "Flight into Egypt") fail because they
are overemphatic. Auden's use of anachronism is, on the whole,
excessively direct, contrived, violent, and indecorous. Through

---

[8] *Auden: An Introductory Essay* (New Haven, 1951); *The Making of the Auden Canon* (Minneapolis, 1957).

[9] "Some Notes on D. H. Lawrence," *Nation*, CLXIV (April 26, 1947), 482.

linking the brassily modern to characters and incidents from the Bible, Auden produces discords often to no purpose. In his off-hand, flippant treatment (Joseph, for example, is presented as a swain with his shoes shined and his "pants . . . cleaned and pressed"), he achieves for his materials vulgarity rather than earthiness. The strength which Auden sought for Christian legend by contrasting it with the trivial remains unachieved. The poem has less serenity than we might expect from Auden's efforts to resolve the conflict between opposites and to reconcile them in the Word. Though Herod's section of the poem has often been praised, there is paranoid violence rather than just indignation in the analysis of Herod's deficiencies as a "liberal," when Auden, as it were, vicariously flays his own former self.

Still, in the portrayals of the wise men, the shepherds, Simeon, and the Virgin Mary, the note of "reverent frivolity" is present, as Auden no doubt intended it to be in the whole poem. There are graphic presentations of the modern chaos, particularly in "Advent":

> Darkness and snow descend . . .
> On all personality . . .
> Outside the civil garden
> Of every day of love there
> Crouches a wild passion
>   To destroy and be destroyed . . .
> We are afraid
> Of pain but more afraid of silence; for no nightmare
> Of hostile objects could be as terrible as this Void.

There is serene beauty in Mary's lullaby over Christ, when she fears that her very love for Him may be corrupting; and there is starkness and urgency in Joseph and Mary's last refrain:

> Safe in Egypt we shall sigh
> For lost insecurity;
> Only when her terrors come
> Does our flesh feel quite at home.

The last lines reveal Auden's flair for the epigram, as does his description of faith: "To choose what is difficult all one's days/ As if it were easy, that is faith."

"The Age of Anxiety" displays Auden's virtuosity, his use of accentual verse to good effect, and his ability to establish (except for a few lapses) a tone at once grimly gay and grimly serious. However, Auden's handling of the Old English line is occasionally labored. Thus the arch humor intended in these lines, as Rosetta nostalgically recalls her past in England, is self-conscious and over-emphatic: "Long-legged ladies with little-legged dogs/ Lolled with their lovers by lapsing brooks." The alliterative requirements in such verse sometimes result in excessively "literary" expression, for example, when Emble describes what he sees in the Hermetic Gardens: "A miniature railroad with mossy halts/ Wambles through wanton groves." At times, Auden's attempts at humor are embarrassing, as in Quant's evocation of the "local spirits" in Rosetta's apartment when he thinks that she and Emble may become lovers:

> Ye little larvae, lords of the household,
> Potty, P-P, Peppermill, Lampshade,
> Funnybone, Faucet, Face-in-the-wall,
> Head-over-heels and Upsy-daisy
> And Collywobbles and Cupboard-Love
> Be good, little gods, and guard these lives . . . .

The absence of strong feeling in the characters, who ostensibly illustrate "the temptation to sin . . . what the psychologist calls anxiety, and the Christian calls lack of faith," [10] is a more serious blemish. This is partly the result of their mental fatigue which is in excess of their situation; they lack the energy, as Auden has conceived them, to translate their disordered emotions into poignant poetry. The characters, moreover, analyze themselves excessively for the insights they achieve, and as "displaced persons and paralyzed Hamlets," [11] they seem less "engaged" with the horrors of the modern age than apathetic before them. They take pleasure in seeing themselves drift: they relish their despair rather than attempt to penetrate its meaning. They thus exist at the periphery of "the age of anxiety," not at its center. Neither are they incisive individuals, since they have been stylized to serve as philosophers. They are all, except Malin, too intellectual for their limited interests, their vapid personalities, and their narrow experience.

Auden's failure in the "Seven Stages" is especially serious, for much of the poem's meaning inheres in this section. The characters are too nebulous for their spiritual meanderings to convey urgency or to arouse interest. As description, the stages of the dream journey are vivid; as interfusion of landscape with psychology, they are pallid and superficial. Since the characters are only imperfectly merged with their dream, the external pattern of their journey is more apparent to us than its inner meaning to them. Even Rosetta's renunciation somewhat later of Emble and her acceptance of her father—and symbolically of her race— are tepid and passive. *Angst* for her is wearying, not a challenge. Granted she achieves illumination, her struggles to attain it are perfunctory.

As in most of Auden, there are true profundities and passages

---

[10] "The Means of Grace," *New Republic*, CIV (June 2, 1941), 766 (review of Niebuhr's *The Nature and Destiny of Man*).

[11] *The Living Thoughts of Kierkegaard*, ed. W. H. Auden (New York, 1952), p. 21.

of incandescent beauty. There are, for example, such deeply felt lines as Emble's wish to revive "the primitive pact with pure feeling," Rosetta's despair at the prospect "of more deaths/ And worse wars, a winter of distaste/ To last a lifetime," and her description of a fallen world, with her comment upon it: "The significant note is nature's cry/ Of long-divided love." Witty passages alleviate the lugubrious atmosphere: Rosetta's description of modern superficiality ("to grosser ears/ In clubs and cabarets crooners wail/ Some miserere modern enough/ In its thorough thinness") and Malin's exposé of Utopian shallowness (as we go "forward into/ Tidy utopias of eternal spring,/ Vitamins, villas, visas for dogs/ And art for all").

The best part of the poem is the Epilogue over which Malin presides. His portrayal of the modern age—its lack of purpose and its need for Christian values—has the combined emotional depth and intellectual conciseness of Auden at his best:

> We would rather be ruined than changed,
> We would rather die in our dread
> Than climb the cross of the moment
> And let our illusions die.
> .   .   .   .
> We're quite in the dark: we do not
> Know the connection between
> The clock we are bound to obey
> And the miracle we must not despair of . . . .

III

Distressed by the spiritual failure of a "low dishonest decade," Auden analyzed in "New Year Letter" the political, social, and ethical situation in the late 1930's. Generally critics have regarded the poem as a success; Marianne Moore, in particular, has been enthusiastic, calling it a "landmark in literature." [12] In his humanistic phase, which preceded and included the composition of "New Year Letter," Auden had adopted the Christian principle of original sin, but had denied the existence of a God separate from man's own spirit.[13] The notes in the original edition of "New Year Letter" indicate Auden's eclectic uses of thinkers like Pascal, Kierkegaard, Kafka, Blake, Rilke, Nietzsche, Goethe, Spinoza, Baudelaire, Jung, Tillich, Freud, and Dante. All these writers, even the most religious, were interested in speculation of a more general sort, particularly in defining the basis upon which man may exist in society and build his ethos. It was this freer philosophical—as opposed to the doctrinal—aspect of these thinkers which attracted the unconverted Auden.

In "New Year Letter" Auden shows a sympathy for Christian postulates but does not wholly accept them. If from the standpoint of his later views the poem is an incomplete statement, still it contains in embryo the ideas which Auden was to develop as he became more orthodox. "New Year Letter" has, then, the interest of being a germinal work. It is concerned, basically, with the difficulty of attaining order in a disordered world. There are two possible sources of order: art or altruistic love. Art can take us only so far (this idea Auden explored again in "The Sea and the Mirror"). In contrast to the parlous, almost hopeless situation outside, Auden in the poem admits, somewhat reluctantly perhaps, to a sense of fulfillment in the arts and in the act of writing. Like Auden, most modern intellectuals have felt the same split

[12] *Predilections* (New York, 1955), p. 98.

[13] See the contrast between his review of John MacMurray's *The Clue to History, Nation,* CXLIX (September 9, 1939), 273, and his review of Niebuhr's *Christianity and Power Politics, Nation,* CLII (January 4, 1941), 24–25.

in their lives between the validity of the private life and the horrors of history, and like him they have also felt their own insignificance in influencing the refractory present.

The poem is rich in other ideas basic to an understanding of the later Auden. In the prologue, modern man is seen as condemned to an isolation from which he must try to escape. The war only partially unites us. Throughout the poem Auden is oppressed by the modern age: "The situation of our time/ Surrounds us like a baffling crime." We are responsible for our situation; we must therefore try to alleviate it by facing, in all humility, our guilt, pride, and egotism:

> How hard it is to set aside
> Terror, concupiscence and pride,
> Learn who and where and how we are,
> The children of a modest star,
> Frail, backward, clinging to the granite
> Skirts of a sensible old planet,
> Our placid and suburban nurse
> In SITTER's swelling universe,
> How hard to stretch imagination
> To live according to our station.

This whimsical (note the pun "Sitter's," the earth seen as a "modest star," and mankind described as clutching the "skirts" of earth) yet serious application of scientific fact to man's spiritual crisis is a consistent feature of the poem. A similarly wry yet spacious view of earth informs this passage from Part III:

> Eccentric, wrinkled, and ice-capped,
> Swarming with parasites and wrapped
> In a peculiar atmosphere,

> Earth wabbles on down her career
> With no ambition in her heart.

The assimilation of astronomy and topography is often more intensively, less playfully, accomplished. Thus in the introductory paragraph in Part II, Auden envisages the uncertainties of the new decade in terms of mankind as a traveler high in the mountains trying to decipher a signpost, while he sees in the valleys below the flashing fires destroying his "lost existence." Then in Part III Auden affectionately describes localities in the limestone Midlands associated in his mind with developments in the race or in himself.

There are similarities both to the mock epic and to the epical drama of Goethe in parts of "New Year Letter." There is a studied disparity between sprightly style and sobriety of subject; there are catalogues (the poets whom Auden considers his peers and the captive nations in Part I, the British places Auden has known and loved in Part III) ; and there is the lively dramatization of Mephistopheles in Part II, whom poets almost always make more engaging than they should. It is as if Auden could not resist the opportunity, put in his way, of making Mephistopheles a living character of some stature. As in Goethe, Mephistopheles misleads man by encouraging him to be cynical and negative; he is "the Spirit-that-denies," who works through "fear and faithlessness and hate." He is a "realist" and opportunist as well who uses facts for his own designs, even to the point of adopting for the moment views contrary to his own. That he is skilled in duplicity this zestfully heightened, colloquial account of his ends and means attests:

> To say two different things at once,
> To wage offensives on two fronts,
> And yet to show complete conviction,
> Requires the purpler kinds of diction,

> And none appreciate as he
> Polysyllabic oratory.
> All vague idealistic art
> That coddles the uneasy heart
> Is up his alley, and his pigeon
> The woozier species of religion,
> Even a novel, play or song,
> If loud, lugubrious and long . . . .

"A fascinated listener," he carries all before him by his affability and complaisance. Generally he tries to confuse us more by half-truths than by outright lies; still we may choose not to become "the moral asymmetric souls/ The either-ors" which he would have us be. He can even be of use to a mind critical of his ideas and activities by suggesting to it the paradox that truth is an amalgamation of partial views. Several half-truths comprise the full truth: "hidden in his hocus-pocus," we may find an ultimate reality through our own God-given "gift of double-focus."

As opposed to "Cartesian mechanism" and a rigid "Hegelian idealism," [14] Auden follows Kierkegaard and the other "existentialists" he cites in his notes and asserts an intuitive, subjective, transcendental scale of values. When we proclaim these values of the spirit, Auden would say, we justify our faith and deny the denier, Mephistopheles: "Against his paralysing smile/ And honest realistic style/ Our best protection is that we/ In fact live in eternity." Auden insists that all inordinate claims by the logical intellect be rejected as tending to increase man's pride in his powers: "And all our intuitions mock/ The formal logic of the clock./ All real perception, it would seem,/ Has shifting contours like a dream."

For Auden, as we have seen, truth emanates from the reconciling

14 "A Preface to Kierkegaard," *New Republic,* CX (May 15, 1944) , 683.

of opposed ideas, intuitions, states of mind, or aspects of personality. The shifting moods of "New Year Letter," as well as the
subtlety of the argument, support this view. In Part I, the time-
less world of art is set against the chaotic world of the political
present. The poem keeps turning its conspectus from the individual's inner life outward to his life in society, and back again.
If structurally Part I deals primarily with art and the intellectual
life, Part II with man's life in society, and Part III with man's
spiritual life where the public and private worlds intersect,[15] still
each section of the poem reveals a fortuitous—or skillfully
planned—juxtaposition of all these aspects of man's life rather
than a concentration upon any one of them. As befits a discursive
poem, the structure is not absolutely demarcated; one paragraph
flows into the next, as ideas suggest by association still other ideas.
Unity, we shall see, is a matter of tone and texture. The alternation of the playful and the solemn implies that both extremes con-
tribute to the integral fabric of life and must be accommodated
to each other. The abstract life of the mind is also counterpointed
with the autobiographical confession, completely specific in reference. Even our inevitable isolation works in two directions and is
simultaneously cause for regret and elation. The absolute nature
of man's isolation paradoxically makes more frenetic and inspirit-
ing his sense that in all humility he must love his neighbor; alienation may thus sharpen his sense of social responsibility. Auden is
aware, too, of the pernicious effects of splitting man's nature
apart, of simplifying the conflict among his loyalties, of denying
the claims of either mind or heart. Auden perceives that science
has all too often led, with its dependence upon the logical processes of mind and its technological aim, to the death of the soul.

[15] See Auden's review of Charles Norris Cochrane's *Christianity and Classical Culture,* "Augustus to Augustine." *New Republic,* CXI (September 25, 1944), 374:
"There can, for the Christian, be no distinction between the personal and the political, for all his relationships are both."

The result is that on "An earth made common by the means/ Of hunger, money, and machines," the faculty of "natural intuition" perishes. The spiritual man of the Middle Ages has been disastrously replaced by the economic man of the Renaissance, "the urban, prudent, and inventive/ Profit his rational incentive." The machine has also destroyed tradition and the basis of society in personal relationships; "the effect of technological progress has been to make power impersonal and to divorce it completely from excellence." [16]

In the concluding lines of the poem, Auden regards the love of our fellow man as more important than the need we feel to be loved for ourselves; thus renewal comes from the Holy Spirit within, but only as it is ultimately directed outward to others: "O every day in sleep and labour/ Our life and death are with our neighbour,/ And love illuminates again/ The city and the lion's den/ The world's great rage, the travel of young men." The attainment of Agape, which Auden defines elsewhere as "Eros mutated by Grace," is all-important.[17] If man is a fallen creature, he is also potentially divine; a too-easy belief in original sin without a belief in the possibility of redemption is a fallacious "Homeric" pessimism.[18]

Technically the poem is remarkable for its fusion of seriousness of content with irony and humor, with pace and verve, with a casual and equivocal manner. The informality works in the direction of emphasizing Auden's humility as he gropes for the truth. Written in what he calls "the middle style" (Dryden in the poem is denominated "the master of the middle style"), "New Year Letter" ranges upward without sentimentality into beauty

[16] "Speaking of Books," *New York Times Book Review* (December 20, 1953), p. 2.

[17] "Eros and Agape," *Nation*, CL (June 28, 1941), 757.

[18] See "Religion and the Intellectuals," *Partisan Review*, XVIII (February, 1950), 123.

or downward without triviality into satire, humor, and banter. Thus at various points in "New Year Letter" there are richly evocative lines, for example, "As on the evil Aryan lives/ Descends the night of the long knives," "For we are conscripts to our age/ Simply by being born; we wage/ The war we are," or the concluding prayer quoted in part in the last paragraph. At other points, there is quizzical commentary upon such salient subjects as the music of Wagner:

> The genius of the loud Steam Age,
> Loud WAGNER, put it on the stage:
> The mental hero who has swooned
> With sensual pleasure at his wound,
> His intellectual life fulfilled
> In knowing that his doom is willed,
> Exists to suffer; borne along
> Upon a timeless tide of song,
> The huge doll roars for death or mother,
> Synonymous with one another;
> And Woman, passive as in dreams,
> Redeems, redeems, redeems, redeems.

The range of "New Year Letter" and Auden's virtuosity counteract Hoggart's charge that the poem is "painfully slack and drumming." [19] The upper and lower reaches of Auden's intellect and sensibility are yoked by a vigorous wit which harmonizes opposing states of sensibility. Wit and irony give distance to the ideas in the poem, sustain Auden's objective presentation of them, and prevent the false intensities, the solemnity, and the pompous dignity which the direct presentation of ideas sometimes involved in mid-Victorian verse. Austerity in thought is not contradicted

---

[19] *Auden: An Introductory Essay,* p. 95.

but reinforced by Auden's comic sense of disproportion; and this disproportion is expressed in the contrast between ideas verging toward the portentous and a language verging toward the ridiculous. The linguistic flexibility of "New Year Letter" is remarkable, accommodating slang, macaronic tags, and colloquial rhythms, at the same time that this ingenious informality escapes too overt an intellectual relaxation. The whole is a marvel of stylistic animation and carefully maintained intellectual stance: the right distance is kept between grave idea and wry presentation. Auden extends the provenance of the four-beat couplet, used for humorous and satiric effects by Butler and Swift, to include, in varying degrees of formality, discussion of weighty subjects. Browning's "Christmas Eve and Easter Day" had anticipated such use of this form. The regularity of the rhyming couplets also compensates for the rapid, sometimes startling movement of the argument, and serves to anchor Auden's finespun homiletics. The expression of his all-embracing curiosity has been adjusted to the restrictions imposed by a well-defined medium; the couplets make for tautness and discipline Auden's intellectual exuberance. The poem expresses a luminous intelligence which knows its own limitations but which has nevertheless thought deeply enough about the situation of modern man to achieve an objective—but not a ponderous—exposition of its values.

The unusual nature of the thought is partly reinforced by the unusual rhymes "in which the element of chance in language seems to predominate over the element of fate and choice" (W. H. Auden, in *The New Yorker* of April 26, 1958).[20] The deliberate nature of the ideas is always then in running contrast with the seemingly haphazard, fortuitous fashioning of the couplets. Auden is fond of feminine rhyme, which suggests the comic,

[20] Auden's description of Byron's "doggerel."

as it often does in Byron's "Beppo" and "Don Juan" and Browning's "Christmas Eve and Easter Day." Furthermore, he will often rhyme one long word with several short words to achieve the double or triple rhyming syllables of feminine rhyme. At times, as in Marianne Moore's poetry, he rhymes accented with unaccented syllables.[21] Startling also is Auden's placing of prepositions, conjunctions, and adjectives at the end of a line. Thus a phrase or a clause will be broken in two, the introductory element occurring at the end of the first line of the couplet. In "New Year Letter" we have an insistent regularity in form with multifarious irregularities in the rhyme scheme; thereby, the impression of diversity within unity is achieved. Auden often uses the extended, ingenious comparison of metaphysical poetry: in Part I, for example, the ominous quality of the present age is conveyed by Auden's comparing it to a corpse and the men of the time to suspected murderers, and in Part III, the partial errors of Rousseau and Plato (idealization of the common man versus idealization of the state) are envisaged as two streams fed by one source, a lowering cloud in "ego's" atmosphere.

As in Pope and Swift, the couplet often becomes an epigram or an aphorism. Thus Auden describes the poets presiding over the tribunal of art in Part I with pungency and individuality:

> But even as a child [Blake] would pet
> The tigers Voltaire never met . . .
> And heard inside each mortal thing
> Its holy emanation sing.
>
> .   .   .   .
>
> Black TENNYSON whose talents were
> For an articulate despair.

[21] Auden admits such indebtedness to Marianne Moore in a review of *Nevertheless, New York Times Book Review* (October 15, 1944), p. 7.

Auden's control of his diverse materials and a varied style are perhaps the most noteworthy aspects of "New Year Letter." Irony, wit, and humor do not call attention to themselves except for the pleasure inherent in a display of versatility. Rather they help define and throw into relief the abundant ideas: note, in this regard, Auden's view ten years later that "verse is . . . perhaps superior to prose as a medium for the lucid exposition of ideas because in skillful hands the form of the verse can parallel and reinforce the steps of the logic." [22] From the standpoint of fertility of idea and the modulation of form to express his thought, "New Year Letter" is one of Auden's best poems, and it has the concentration of Pope's "Epistle to Dr. Arbuthnot." "New Year Letter" is a like epistle for the modern age.

IV

"The Sea and the Mirror" in scope and beauty is, as some critics have maintained, Auden's masterpiece. [23] Tautly organized, its components balance and interweave with one another. The pleasure to be had from the whole supplements, in the Coleridgean sense, the pleasure to be had from its parts. The Stage Manager's short prologue parallels Ariel's brief epilogue spoken to Caliban; Caliban's earthy but involuted prose address to the audience complements Prospero's dignified and colloquial address to Ariel; and the short speeches of the other characters collected under "The

---

[22] *Poets of the English Language,* ed. W. H. Auden and Norman Holmes Pearson (New York, 1950), III, xiii.

[23] Mark Schorer, "Auden, Shakespeare and Jehovah," *New York Times Book Review* (September 17, 1944), p. 4; Francis Scarfe, *W. H. Auden* (Monaco, 1949), p. 49; Edward Callen, "The Development of W. H. Auden's Poetic Theory since 1940," *Twentieth Century Literature,* IV (October, 1958), 84; and Bent Sunesen, "'All We Are Not Stares Back at What We Are': A Note on Auden," *English Studies,* XL (December, 1959), 439–49.

Supporting Cast, Sotto Voce" are enclosed in the center of the poem. These people form not only the pivot of psychological interest but are centrally located so as to seem accessible to the influences acting upon them from outside, notably those of Prospero, Ariel, and Caliban.

The Stage Manager asserts that the abstractions of the logical mind are not the full truth and that intangible values, which supplement those given us by the intellect, exist:

> Well, who in his own backyard
> Has not opened his heart to the smiling
> Secret he cannot quote?
> Which goes to show that the Bard
> Was sober when he wrote
> That this world of fact we love
> Is unsubstantial stuff:
> All the rest is silence
> On the other side of the wall;
> And the silence ripeness,
> And the ripeness all.

This passage reveals Auden's skill in making fresh poetry from familiar Shakespearean phrases. The last four lines, moreover, convey an acceptance and a reconciliation, linked with Ariel's wisdom in the postscript. There Ariel, who is the artistic impulse in essence, wants Caliban as he is, and welcomes "reality," epitomized in Caliban, no matter how gross or grotesque. The ripeness is all, both for Ariel who welcomes Caliban's "drab mortality" and for Caliban who, in his long prose speech, disparages the production he has just witnessed and by implication the whole human performance, but who still perceives through it intimations of the "Wholly Other Life."

"Prospero to Ariel," the first section, is Audenesque in its easy but sinewy style, its colloquial charm, and its vigor of idiom. The naturalness of diction and rhythm in these lines combines with a dignity of tone appropriate to Prospero's dedication as artist and with an intellectuality which supports the closely reasoned aspect of his ideas:

> Stay with me, Ariel, while I pack, and with your first free act
>   Delight my leaving; share my resigning thoughts
> As you have served my revelling wishes; then, brave spirit,
>   Ages to you of song and daring, and to me
> Briefly Milan, then earth.

Auden describes the meter for this speech as couplets with thirteen syllables in the first line, eleven syllables in the second, and consecutive vowel sounds elided.[24] His accomplishment is not only to write well in a constricted meter but to achieve in it a spontaneous rather than a studied effect.

Upon leaving his isle, Prospero is concerned with his double destiny as retired artist and emergent human being. As an old man he now wishes to recover his humanity, somewhat aborted by his excessive concern with art and study; but he is also reluctant to give over his magician's reputation. If art introduces us to an ideal realm of order ("godlike in its permanence and beauty, providing a picture of life which is worthy of imitation as far as it is possible") ,[25] it may prevent us from acquiring knowledge of undistorted reality. Art may not only bring out latent values for the maker and the percipient, but it may corrupt the uncritical maker by encouraging moral expediency and the uncritical percip-

---

[24] Letter from Malcolm Cowley, *Poetry*, LXV (March, 1945) , 345.

[25] "The Dyer's Hand: Poetry and the Poetic Process," *Anchor Review: Number Two* (New York, 1957) , p. 257.

ient by suggesting that the harmonies of art are easily attained in life and sufficient to regulate it. Prospero has thus been led by Ariel to forget the two promises he had made as an apprentice: "To hate nothing and to ask nothing for its love." There is Antonio, whom Prospero, by his intellectual withdrawal, encouraged in evil and then could not help hating; and there is Caliban, whom Prospero molded so as to enjoy the satisfaction deriving from the "absolute devotion" of a created object. The failure with Caliban is particularly disturbing, for it undermines Prospero's achievement with the other characters and his spiritual confidence: "his wreck/ That sprawls in the weeds and will not be repaired:/ My dignity discouraged by a pupil's curse,/ I shall go knowing and incompetent into my grave." A further irony is that Prospero is blind to what he needs for a completed wisdom, the refractory realities present in Caliban whom he symbolically rejects by leaving him behind on the isle. The rejection of Caliban is fateful for Prospero because he evades the truth about himself, because he will not recognize the ugly and grotesque, and because he lacks the imagination to understand a sinister being he has himself in part engendered. In the Kierkegaardian sense, Prospero has insight at the aesthetic and moral levels, but lacks insight at the religious. Intellectually to be admired, Prospero in Auden's view lacks the radical charity—or Agape—discernible at times even in reprobates like Falstaff: "Agape requires that we love our enemies, do good to those that hate us, and forgive those who injure us, and this command is unconditional." [26] The formidable Prospero pays lip service to Agape, but does not "unconditionally" embrace it. As Auden says in another connection, "Prospero's forgiving is more the contemptuous pardon of a man who knows he

[26] "The Fallen City: Some Reflections on Shakespeare's 'Henry IV,'" *Encounter*, XIII (November, 1959), 28.

has his enemies completely at his mercy than a heartfelt reconciliation." [27]

Still Prospero has been able to change for the better the attitudes of the remaining characters. The exaltation and harmonizing power, common to art and religion, can work positively on people nearer to the normal manifestations of conscience than are Antonio and Caliban. The people on board the ship returning to Milan have "been soundly hunted/ By their own devils into their human selves." With a creator's satisfaction, Prospero views the lovers Ferdinand and Miranda whose "eyes are big and blue with love; its lighting/ Makes even us look new." Possibly their love is too much like the harmonies to be found only in art and too little like the actuality. He wonders what may happen when Miranda becomes to Ferdinand "familiar as a stocking." For himself Prospero is glad to have got beyond the possibility of a disillusioned awakening from the dream of romantic love. At the same time he may have become too subtly corrupted by pride and egotism to experience with abandon the ecstasy of selfless passion.

As for the other chief philosopher in the work, Caliban, his opinions on similar subjects are extensions of Prospero's own. Auden conceived Caliban's address as a virtuoso piece, exploiting Jamesean involutions of syntax to secure added nuances of meaning. From our knowledge of *The Tempest,* it represents a comic reversal of expectation for the slave to be an even more subtle philosopher than the master and a more suave man of the world. It is also the proud Prospero's just fate to be surpassed in insight and sophistication by a contemned underling. It is an added irony that no one, except Caliban himself and his audience, recognizes his superiority. Since in their different realms they are both in-

[27] "Balaam and the Ass: On the Literary Use of the Master-Servant Relationship," *Encounter,* III (July, 1954) , 45.

trepid, it is not fortuitous that Caliban's conclusions resemble Prospero's. Both agree that the world of art is several removes from the real world. As Caliban says, it presents us with "the perfectly tidiable piece of disorder" but only that. In life something always resists being tidied up: in the second section ("Supporting Cast") the demonic Antonio thus refuses to be reconciled with the spiritual Prospero, and Sebastian's repentance, though real, has been due to accident. Caliban himself is a discordant entity in an artist's universe, except for the artist who has made an honest endeavor to assimilate Caliban's reality. Still, almost all art represents an attempt to reconcile the real and the ideal ("the sounded note is the restored relation") ; and we ignore at our peril what art can teach us. In his monologue Caliban describes two types of people who falsify experience by denying the harmonies between the tangible and the intangible to be found in art. There are those who slavishly follow himself and deny Ariel, and those who are lifted to Ariel's rarefied atmosphere and deny the gross reality embodied in himself. Art has a complex and subtle relationship to life; in itself, it can neither be accepted nor rejected as a guide to experience.

The middle section of the poem entitled "The Supporting Cast, Sotto Voce" reveals Auden's virtuosity and insight at their most complex and steady. The form Auden uses for each speaker is appropriate, either directly reflecting the speaker's qualities or providing an ironic commentary upon them. As in Prospero's and Caliban's discourses, form and substance are inseparable.

Antonio dominates this part of "The Sea and the Mirror," in some respects the poem as a whole, because he is the unreconciled figure who threatens to undermine the hard-won peace of the other characters. To convey the involutions of his hatred for Prospero and for the light, Antonio sullenly meditates in the elaborate pattern of *terza rima*. Antonio will prevent Prospero from attaining, first, pure "Being" and, secondly, a perfect grouping of human beings, whereby the harmonies of art might be approximated in life. Antonio's is the motiveless malignity in the background that bides its time to destroy because it must. Antonio will constantly threaten the serenity of Prospero and tempt him to resurrect the wand he has broken and the books he has destroyed. Antonio, evil as he is, has the positive function of checking the pride of Prospero, insidious because of its very benignancy. Antonio's appended comments to each of the speeches in Part II imply that he exists as a challenge in the spiritual lives of his fellows, all the more sinister because no one pierces beneath his appearance to see him as he is. He is a figure no one reckons with until his influence is perhaps disastrously entrenched. In toughness of fiber and strength of purpose he equals Prospero; and just as he formerly wrenched the dukedom from his brother, Antonio is only waiting his opportunity to destroy and humiliate his brother spiritually.

The soliloquies of the other members of the supporting cast also reveal an organic union of idea and form. Thus Ferdinand in the intricate pattern of the sonnet struggles to express his deep but tangled emotions, to crystallize depths of feeling almost inexpressible in words. Subject to the limitations imposed by the sonnet, the welter of his inner being is at last ordered to the point that he can define in the concluding line what Miranda means to him: "The Right Required Time, The Real Right Place, O Light." The hedonist and sensualist, Stephano, speaks through the ballade: the elaborate metrical pattern is in satiric contrast with the plainness and crudeness of his emotions. He finds it difficult to achieve identity apart from his mother; despite his simplicity, his quest is the same as that of his peers: "A lost thing looks for a lost name." The couplet conveying the befuddlement of Adrian and Francisco is engaging nonsense and its brevity a comment upon their vacuity of mind: "Good little sunbeams must learn to fly,/ But it's madly ungay when the goldfish die." For the lyrical expression of simple emotion the master and the boatswain use the popular ballad meter modified into a six-line stanza. As in Stephano's ballade, a universal theme is established, despite the ignorance of the speakers: the isolation of each individual. Describing their liaisons, they not only define their own loneliness but that of the rest: "And two by two like cat and mouse/ The homeless played at keeping house." Trinculo is no intellectual, but his perceptions are more complex than those of the master and boatswain. Accordingly, a form more complex than theirs is necessary, but one not too complicated. Auden therefore assigns him quatrains in iambic trimeter with lines two and four rhyming. Like the master and boatswain, Trinculo knows the overwhelming isolation expressed by the other characters when they are honest with themselves. Trinculo perceives that the clown, like the artist, is subject to fits of "fine frenzy" and to terrors which do not strengthen him spiritually but which do provide him with materials for sardonic humor whereby he can entertain others.

Gonzalo's address in rhyming trochaic tetrameter is well-adapted to weighty ideas. In the service of the intellect, he had denied the mystery of being and the provenance of the contingent and the absurd. He is now restored in spirit, has overcome "doubt and insufficient love," and admits the all-importance of a transcendent reality. His opening lines convey the grave beauty and solemnity of his discourse as a whole:

> Evening, grave, immense, and clear,
> Overlooks our ship whose wake
> Lingers undistorted on
> Sea and silence.

In Gonzalo's speech Auden reveals his marked ability to modulate the moods of his characters. Sobriety yields by degrees to subdued rejoicing as Gonzalo in the last stanza accepts with humility his deliverance:

> Even rusting flesh can be
> A simple locus now, a bell
> The Already There can lay
> Hands on if at any time
> It should feel inclined to say
> To the lonely—"Here I am,"
> To the anxious—"All is well."

Alonzo's address to his son Ferdinand, who will soon be ascending the throne of Milan and perhaps of Naples, is subtle in idea, informal in tone, and solemn in sentiment. Again a somewhat artificial meter, this time of counted syllables, is entirely natural and spontaneous. In the opening stanza the starkly concrete yet somewhat discordant details ("fish see sceptres descending," "broken-down sofa," "mutilated statue") go beyond the realistic to convey a suggestion of the sinister, the foreboding, and the unpredictable, as Alonzo warns his son of the uncertainties even of a royal existence:

> Dear Son, when the warm multitudes cry,
> Ascend your throne majestically,
> But keep in mind the waters where fish
> See sceptres descending with no wish
> To touch them; sit regal and erect,
> But imagine the sands where a crown
> Has the status of a broken-down

> Sofa or mutilated statue:
> Remember as bells and cannon boom
> The cold deep that does not envy you,
> The sunburnt superficial kingdom
> Where a king is an object.

The sea and desert imagery in these lines is developed in every stanza to signify the dreariest ranges of desolation; the sea and the desert are free places, but they are wildernesses and therefore places of alienation from the rest of humanity.[28] Apart from the implications of this imagery, Alonzo's philosophical meaning would not exist. Ferdinand should be warned, Alonzo thinks, that a human being is subject to extreme pressures: the sea and the desert, ice and fire. The sea and the desert—"The sea . . . the symbol of primitive potential power as contrasted with the desert of actualized triviality, of living barbarism versus lifeless decadence"[29]—comprise opposing forces never far from each other nor far from "the temperate city" of man's residence. They are only horrors to the unreconciled heart which lacks confidence in itself and power to reconcile these discordant entities. By enduring all they may subject us to, "the scorching rocks" and "the bitter treatment of the tide," one may achieve clarity, serenity, wisdom, salvation:

> the whirlwind may arrange your will
> And the deluge release it to find
> The spring in the desert, the fruitful
> Island in the sea, where flesh and mind
> Are delivered from mistrust.

[28] Auden, *The Enchafèd Flood: or, The Romantic Iconography of the Sea* (London, 1951), pp. 25 ff.

[29] *The Enchafèd Flood*, p. 28.

Auden projected the elaborate psychology of the repentant Sebastian through a sestina. In an arresting flash of memory, Sebastian sees himself as he was only a little while before: "To think his death I thought myself alive/ And stalked infected through the blooming day." He now welcomes the negative experiences of failure, exposure, and defeat as positive states which have prevented him from committing a crime. He sees that projected evil in the mind is much more alluring than the actual evil deed: "In dreams all sins are easy, but by day/ It is defeat gives proof we are alive;/ The sword we suffer is the guarded crown." The sestina leaves unsolved to what extent Sebastian's repentance derives from weakness of will or from conscience.

In her villanelle Miranda sees nature, art, and humanity in harmonious unity: "we/ Are linked as children in a circle dancing:/ My Dear One is mine as mirrors are lonely,/ And the high green hill sits always by the sea." On this note of partial reconciliation the speeches by the supporting cast end. The characters have achieved some of the harmony to be found in the completed art work; Miranda's description of the characters "in a circle dancing" is similar to Caliban's description of art as "the excellent order of the dancing ring." In life, of course, an absolute harmony is impossible; witness Antonio's rejection of the virginal Miranda's spirituality in his comments which follow her villanelle. The "restored relation" between the human and the divine—celebrated in Caliban's concluding words—has at least been adumbrated through Prospero's aesthetic magic. Antonio's consistent menace may ultimately make the "restored relation" more genuine by his very threat to it.

"The Sea and the Mirror" is a philosophically unified and skillfully constructed work of art, much more carefully wrought than "For the Time Being" and "The Age of Anxiety," in which Auden was too explicitly Christian perhaps for the requirements of his art to be uppermost in his mind. The transcendental sub-jectivism and the Christian values, expressed or implied in the poetry of this period, form the complex, however, out of which Auden was to write during the late 1940's and 1950's. If none of his volumes is individually as significant as *On This Island* or *Another Time*, still when we consider as an entity *Nones* (1950), *The Shield of Achilles* (1956), and *Homage to Clio* (1960), we are impressed by the continuing vitality and relevance of Auden's poetry. The bulk of first-rate work during the last fifteen years is less than in the period 1930–45, but there are a number of poems written in late years which may achieve a classic status: "In Praise of Limestone," "Prime," "Nones," "The Fall of Rome," "The Chimeras," "A Walk After Dark," and "A Duet" from *Nones;* "The Shield of Achilles," "Fleet Visit," "The Proof," and "Nocturne I" from *The Shield of Achilles;* and "Reflections in a Forest," "First Things First," "Sabbath," "Friday's Child," and "Secondary Epic" from *Homage to Clio.*

If Auden's poetry of the last fifteen years were to be compressed into a single volume, the solidity rather than the slenderness of the accomplishment would be more apparent. In writing on Ber-nard Shaw, Auden once stated that a writer is great when he tran-scends both simple acceptance and revolt; [30] this has been, I feel, the source of Auden's own enduring interest since the early 1940's for most readers. If from some points of view, Auden's recent work represents a falling off from the exuberant fertility of the late 1930's, from another point of view we witness a deliberate reaching out to extend the provinces of poetry.

The keeping alive of the poetic impulse may have been the re-sult of a transplantation to a new environment in the early 1940's. In America Auden renewed the powers which had been ex-

---

[30] "The Fabian Figaro," in Louis Kronenberger, ed., *George Bernard Shaw: A Critical Survey* (New York, 1953), p. 153. This essay was written in 1942.

hausted in the England of the 1930's; in becoming, as it were, a citizen of the world, his vision was widened and made more firm. America exposed him more closely to the leveling processes of a technological civilization and forced him to come to terms more quickly with violent pressures from without. To Auden's stay in America we owe some of the poems in *Another Time*, the long poems of the 1940's, and some excellent poetry composed more recently. As he felt his isolation intensify in an alien environment, his need for philosophic and spiritual assurance increased, and he turned to existentialist thinkers and the work of Reinhold Niebuhr for guidance during this time of crisis. Possibly as an American citizen, since 1956 residing part of the year in England, Auden may again achieve some of the radical reorientation of his views which the move to America once gave him. He may yet give us another poem of the freshness and vigor of "The Sea and the Mirror"; and he once again may exemplify to the full his own definition of the great poet as simultaneously a realist, romanticist, and ironist.[31]

[31] Howard Griffin, "Conversation on Cornelia Street: A Dialogue with W. H. Auden," *Poetry*, LXXXIII (November, 1953) , 97.

Mr. Tate:
Whose Wreath Should Be
a Moral

Radcliffe Squires

ALTHOUGH I see Allen Tate as a poet deprived (by circumstances both within and without his control) of his fullest potential, I see him as one of the dozen or so American poets of the century worth reading more than once. Pleasanter, less grievously afflicted poetry has been written by younger men than Tate, and while it is unfair to pronounce upon careers that have not finished up, still, at the moment, the anthologies seem almost to change season when one leaves Tate's poetry to read newer lines. One moves from the impression of a vision, a belief, and profundity, to a poem by poem separateness, a prettiness of craft, a domestic pretense which saves the poem from life. About such poems and such poets I cannot imagine that much can ever be said. I can mention two exceptions, Robert Lowell and Stanley Kunitz; however, both these poets owe something of their opulent strain and haggard resolution to Allen Tate.

And while it is scandalous that Tate has not received certain public prizes, one may be comforted in reflecting that in the last fifteen years several awards have been made to poets whose poetry is respectable because Tate's poetry helped create respect for the kind of poetry it is.

Indeed, if men of genius may ever be called "typical," Allen Tate may fairly be said to present a template of an American poet in this century. There are other and different patterns, but none so common and none so instructive. Whatever one may conclude about Tate's poetic achievement he may also conclude about much of the poetry written between 1920 and 1950.

Only slightly this side of the first cause of Tate's kind of poetry stands the urgency to effect moral responsibility which, though balancing upon the precarious and the improbable, has wide ambition: a moral responsibility devoted to itself, yet by the most sober and appealing implications obtaining to the ambient order of society. Or, rather, to the whole disorder of society, for such is the assumption. The assumption of disorder presses about the poetry, forcing it into some essential design of resistance against disorder. A crystal in the magma. That is to say, this poetry assures its life by powerful disciplines, a faith in tradition and the civilizing virtues of wit and learning. The poetry stands then on an aesthetic legal code backed up by a common law of criticism. Such a poetry, moral in aim and rationalistic in method, might properly expect to have the protection of the academy.

My words are intended to be general, for I am speaking of a type of poetry and a type of poet, and it is only of passing interest to me that the archetype is that of T. S. Eliot. Had Eliot never existed, Tate's diction might well have been different, but his poetic scheme and career would not have altered greatly. Both had been formed, I gather from his correspondence with Hart Crane, before he read Eliot's poems. It seems now historically inevitable that when the poet abandoned all hope of being the legislator of the world, he would decide to become its conscience, to take up the only role left to the voice but little heeded. Power, however, never corrupts an unacknowledged legislator, whereas an unacknowledged conscience is in constant danger of becoming neurotic.

What is the form that conscience takes in Allen Tate's poetry? I wish to confess at once that I do not know all the boundaries, but I think that I know where it begins and where it ends. It begins, suitably enough, with introspection at an intensely personal, almost private level. And the introspection, or at least the ancillary discoveries of the introspection, would appear to be the primal ooze of all of Tate's poetry, the gaze of its bliss, the shape of its originality. "Sonnets at Christmas" and "Sonnets of the Blood" are among the richest and most polished sonnets of our time. Being Tate's, they would of necessity be polished, but conscience rather than craft gives fiat to their richness. In the second of the Christmas group (1934) he tells us:

> When I was ten I told a stinking lie
> That got a black boy whipped; but now at last
> The going years, caught in an accurate glow,
> Reverse like balls englished upon green baize—
> Let them return, let the round trumpets blow
> The ancient crackle of the Christ's deep gaze.
> Deaf and blind, with senses yet unfound,
> Am I, untutored to the after-wit
> Of knowledge, knowing a nightmare has no sound;
> Therefore with idle hands and head I sit
> In late December before the fire's daze
> Punished by crimes of which I would be quit.

Punished? Not finally, for eight years later in "More Sonnets at Christmas" he must add that the "lying boy of ten . . . was not

. . . left uneasy by his fall." These poems suggest that the present must serve as an atonement for the past, for the act is not understood at the time of its commission. Time does not necessarily bring comfort, but it may bring reality or realization.

Some years ago I wrote that Tate's elaboration of guilt belonged to the consciousness of a "temperate manichee." That phrase now seems smart aleck. I retract it here. I am certain that Tate is not masochistically calling attention to his "sins." I am certain that he is not exorcising his devils through a luxury of pain. It is more nearly as if he were unwilling to accept forgiveness until he has clarified his transgression; and, more importantly, until he has rescued his transgression from the jargon of the confessional box. Above all, never to accept forgiveness easily, either for himself or for mankind. For in "The Wolves":

> Now remember courage, go to the door,
> Open it and see whether coiled on the bed
> Or cringing by the wall, a savage beast
> Maybe with golden hair, with deep eyes
> Like a bearded spider on a sunlit floor
> Will snarl—and man can never be alone.

Even so, Tate is content neither with identification and analysis of guilt nor with confining it to a recrudescent memory. On the contrary he sees sin solidly occupying the self's past and future. Or so he seems to say in the first part of "Records":

> The boy-man on the Ox Road walked along
> The man he was to be and yet another,
> It seemed the grandfather of his mother,
> In knee-breeches silver-buckled like a song,
> His hair long and a cocked hat on his head,
> A straight back and slow dignity for stride;

The road, red clay sun-cracked and baked,
Led fearlessly through scrub pines on each side
Hour after hour—the old road cracked and burned,
The trees countless, and his thirst unslaked.
Yet steadily with discipline like fate
Without memory, too ancient to be learned,
The man walked on and as if it were yesterday
Came easily to a two-barred gate
And stopped, and peering over a little way
He saw a dog-run country store fallen-in,
Deserted, but he said, "Who's there?"
And then a tall fat man with stringy hair
And a manner that was innocent of sin,
His galluses greasy, his eyes coldly gray,
Appeared, and with a gravely learned air
Spoke from the deep coherence of hell—
The pines thundered, the sky blacked away,
The man in breeches, all knowledge in his stare,
A moment shuddered as the world fell.

That this notion of guilt's pervasion of time is thematic is revealed by the fact that Tate's novel *The Fathers* contains a situation similar to the whipping of the black boy and to the dream in "Records." One supposes that the discovery of moral error or its re-discovery, those punitive examinations of the past, have been extended to a near abstraction wherein one's present and future are linked inconsolably with the past or with the ancestor. For example, compare "Records" with the corresponding passage in *The Fathers* where the characters are the same and where the language links, such as "silver-buckled like a song" and "hair stringy above the cold gray eyes," tell us that in Tate's mind the scenes are identical and that even more importantly, he is not faking the scene:

I tried to think of the first man who had ever walked that road, but I could see only the face of my grandfather Buchan in the portrait hanging in the front parlor at Pleasant Hill. His black silver-buckled shoes printing the brown dust; the black stockings below the tight broadcloth kneebreeches . . . over the long chestnut hair the black cocked hat, silver-buckled; and after seeing it I heard the shining silver of the shoe-buckles, the knee-buckles, the hat-buckle, like a song. But it was only a deep contrapuntal bass without any treble that I heard as we walked side by side upon the old road, cracked and burned, through the countless trees, old-field pine and blackjack, big chestnut and whitethorn locust, and I knew that our thirst was not slaked. Presently we came easily to a two-barred gate and we stopped to look over it and saw a big fat man standing in a dog-run, his hair stringy above the cold gray eyes. When we were standing on the porch and I was getting a drink from the cedar bucket he gave me a crooked stare. It is a good thing I thought that I have somebody to look to for guidance on this road, and then the man spoke: "The State of Virginia ain't in the Union no more. The people voted her out yestiddy. The Yankees are comin'." My grandfather and I said nothing but thank you as we turned away and, going out, leaned a while to rest upon the bars of the gate. I couldn't see anything; I heard a noise in the air, but it was only the fat man talking in a language that I could not understand.

This same passage further illuminates the configuration of motives surrounding Tate's preoccupation with the sins of the past. The ghostly grandfather makes a parable of the story of Jason who, he says, "caused all the evil by means of his own privation of good." And earlier: "No, it was not the intention of your brother-in-law to kill your brother. It is never, my son, his intention to do any evil but he does evil because he has not the will to do good." At the end of the book, the hero, Lacy, decides to take on the burden of moral responsibility which the brother-in-law cannot. "I'll go back and finish it. I'll have to finish it because he could not finish it. It won't make any difference if I am killed. If I am killed it will be because I love him more than I love any man." He will not "love" the less, we see, for his knowledge of evil. And Lacy's moral position is, as we might expect, precisely the position of Allen Tate. He assumes the guilt of his fellow man as well as his own to be his responsibility. Whatever solvency may come must come as a result of a resolution to act. The insight, the courage for the decision—somehow—comes to him through a contemplation of the past.

But I am speaking now too sanguinely. I am speaking of theory. Does action or resolution inevitably consummate the rite of examination and evaluation of the past? Does action ensue, for example, in "Ode to the Confederate Dead"? While unlikely that Tate would be happy to hear it, his ode is less like any neoclassical or romantic English ode than it is like Whitman's "When Lilacs Last in the Dooryard Bloom'd." More strongly than in even Keats's or Shelley's odes, the theme seems knotted and confused with a personal experience, something that actually happened in ordinary time and space. So, too, with the symbolic materials. Whitman's bird and flowering tree, Tate's plunging leaves and revenant wind come from personal history rather than the requirements of theme. They are simultaneously definite and yet rimmed with a hypnotic blur. Ultimately, however, the impression is that Whitman's poem assumes that it is transferring feeling as directly as it can, whereas Tate's ode seems to assume that direct transfer is an impossibility. Hence,

> . . . you know the rage,
> The cold pool left by the mounting flood,
> Of muted Zeno and Parmenides.

We remember Zeno (not the Cypriot founder of the Stoic school but the Eleatic philosopher of the fifth century B.C.) argued that Achilles could never overtake the tortoise. The intent of his argument was really to prove the opposite or to disprove the hypothesis that being is infinitely divisible. Within the framework of Tate's poem the reference to this dealer in stunning contradictions becomes freighted with irony if we further remember that Aristotle called Zeno the inventor of dialectic. For in a sense the ode despairs of dialectic resolution. This is hardly to say that "Ode to the Confederate Dead," which mounts steadily with compactness and power, is not a fine—possibly a great—poem. But it is a way of insisting that the reader observe that it finishes in questions that seem not even rhetorical, which have no answer and lead not to motion but to paralysis:

> What shall we say who have knowledge
> Carried to the heart? Shall we take the act
> To the grave? Shall we, more hopeful, set up the grave
> In the house? The ravenous grave?

Perhaps to have asked terrifying questions is an expression of moral decision. But I think not; and I think further that the reason for Tate's impotence to state a resolution, in the poem generally supposed his most ambitious, is ironically embedded in the nature of his very desire to do so.

One is aware of a certain tendency toward divisiveness in Tate's work. I do not mean anything so cosmic as his fascination with good and evil, for such a division is so ineluctable in the moral temperament that it discourages comment. I mean his proclivity, for example, to conceive of literature as based upon bellicosities—"tensions" which more effectively nourish the poem if they remain unreconciled. I mean his proclivity toward confronting an alter ego disguised perhaps by time or as a father or grandfather. I mean, too, the disparity of the psychic directions of his poetry. I shall consider two of his better-known poems.

The first three quatrains of "Death of Little Boys" and the fifth (terminal) quatrain are difficult poetry, for almost all the mood and movement of death and the wake and the implicit funeral are contained in images which are rather disassociated, though intensified for that very reason. Difficult though these sections are, they are easier than the fourth stanza:

> Till all the guests, come in to look, turn down
> Their palms, and delirium assails the cliff
> Of Norway where you ponder, and your little town
> Reels like a sailor drunk in a rotten skiff.

One wonders how the "you" of the poem, who is present in the room, got to Norway. But I cannot concur with John Crowe Ransom that Tate is merely "playing with important predication" or with Yvor Winters who thinks the poem merely bad. I suggest that one may turn for edification to the opening of Poe's "A Descent into the Maelstrom," where the narrator enacts a motive dear to the heart of Poe. Gazing from a cliff toward the sea and becoming giddy, he is tempted to throw himself into the churning sea below—a sea which in one of the few examples of submarine gothic in literature is easily perceived to be related to Poe's rather elaborate concept of death. As to the "sailor drunk in a rotten skiff," one may turn to A. Gordon Pym's friend who attempts while drunk to pilot a little yacht (which, if not rotten, needs bailing out) and in so doing adumbrates in an early chapter the whole rhythm of *The Adventures of A. Gordon Pym* —a rhythm running from the literary joke, the tedium of formulated adventure, to the ultimate blanchedness of spiritual immolation. To the degree that both these allusions are associated with the sea, they have had their entry fees paid for them by the third line of the poem which reads: "The event [death] will rage terrific as the sea." Before any further comment let me adduce the other poem.

"The Mediterranean" is an ironical yet passionately conceived poem about the American who, picnicking in a cove of the sea of the middle earth, contrasts himself with a hero-traveler of the past:

> What country shall we conquer, what fair land
> Unman our conquest and locate our blood?
> We've cracked the hemispheres with careless hand!
> Now, from the Gates of Hercules we flood
>
> Westward, westward till the barbarous brine
> Whelms us to the tired land where tasseling corn,
> Fat beans, grapes sweeter than muscadine
> Rot on the vine: in that land were we born.

This terminal picture of a land of disastrous plenty (which smothers the soul) is prepared for earlier in the poem by two references to the *Aeneid,* the later of which reads:

> Where we feasted and caroused on the sandless
> Pebbles, affecting our day of piracy,
> What prophecy of eaten plates could landless
> Wanderers fulfil by the ancient sea?

Tate renders *mensa* rather freely as "plates," but his reference to the *Aeneid* is clear. When Aeneas finally arrives upon the shores of Italy, Virgil tells us of the poor feast served on "disks" of hard bread which hunger drives them to eat. Then:

> "Ho!" cried Iulus, "We are eating our tables!"
> A boy's joke, nothing more. But the spoken word
> Meant something more, and deeper, to Aeneas,
> An end of hardship. He caught up the saying,
> Felt the god's presence. "Hail!" he cried, remembering,
> "Hail, O my destined land! All hail, ye faithful
> Gods of our homeland! Here our country lies.
> Now I remember what Anchises told me:
> *My son, when hunger overtakes you, driven*
> *To unknown shores, and the food seems so little*
> *You find it best to gnaw the tables also,*
> *There hope for home, there build, however weary,*
> *The city walls, the moat, the ditch, the rampart.*
> (VII, 115–27. Trans. Rolfe Humphries)

Hence, a contrast between Aeneas' austere hunger and American satiety.

There is no reason why a person of erudition might not turn at will to Poe or Virgil. One is not the least tempted, particularly with a Southerner, to mumble about romanticism or classicism. But I would submit that "Death of Little Boys" and "The Mediterranean" represent extremes in Tate's effort to establish a moral position. The extremes loosely correspond to what we might attribute as connotative "values" to Virgil or to Poe. "The Mediterranean" is a relatively public poem. Its quest and argument are essentially open; the criticism is clear. "Death of Little Boys" is another matter. It is a poem which desires less to reach a moral position than to find a proper moral *feeling*. It assumes the involvement of all things in death; it urges an awareness of death's gravity and draws back fastidiously from the inadequate social formalities (wake and funeral) surrounding the "ultimate dream." And here is the significant problem: These poems in a final sense fail to bring together position and feeling. They fail to consolidate a public vista with a private vision. "Death of Little Boys" does not become a universal (public) poem; "The Mediterranean" is unable in the final analysis to generate much feeling. In Tate's work there are public triumphs as open as Virgil and private ones as arcane as Poe, but surely a supreme poetry will not admit of such a separation of sensibility, such a segregation of commitment. It is this failure I agonizingly apprehend in the ending of "Ode to the Confederate Dead."

> Leave now
> The shut gate and the decomposing wall:
> The gentle serpent, green in the mulberry bush,
> Riots with his tongue through the hush—
> Sentinel of the grave who counts us all!

The gentle serpent in an earlier version was, I believe, a "worm." Tate tells us that the serpent is "the ancient symbol of time" (see "Narcissus as Narcissus"), but it is more likely to make us reflect upon the corrupted world. Yet, however we construe the image, we are apt to see it finally as only an image-extension of a silkworm, and the "sentinel of the grave" is apt to seem after all only "the conquering worm." The poem which pleads for its life to be expressed in position and concept finally drifts away into an allusive impression. (Again, fairness demands that one acknowledge that Tate himself says that the poem is about "solipsism," in which case I must urge that only a poet who despairs of convening public and private vision would entitle a poem about solipsism "Ode to the Confederate Dead.") Possibly for this reason John Crowe Ransom upon the occasion of Tate's sixtieth birthday spoke of Tate's conversion to Catholicism, as if to suggest that the step was both inevitable and desirable for Tate's poetic health. It is noteworthy that Ransom turns, then, in a seeming contradiction to his aesthetic beliefs, to biography, to life itself, as a precedent of poetry, but I shall not try to judge Ransom's words.[1] Besides they are made untouchable by that charming old trick of the Fugitives of beginning by claiming ignorance of the subject and a trashy laziness about doing homework—so that whatever erudition emerges, and much usually does, leaves the reader dazzled and sure of his own stupidity.

But I have stated that it is the nature of Tate's inclination to reach a moral position which makes it ultimately difficult for him to do so. In part, the explanation lies in the split between position and feeling. In larger part, the explanation lies in the assumption of what Ransom has with maddening cheer called "a fallen world." Or what I have called Tate's assumption of social disorder. His assumption creates the desire to forge moral order as an obvious need; the intensity of the assumption leads him into a fatalistic despair that finally vitiates his faith in his ability to create a moral order for any but himself. It is as if the twentieth-century despair were nothing new but only a belated harvest of nineteenth-century doubt. Doubt was a minor strain in the nineteenth century, but now one can scarcely hear the sea of faith straggling out between the pebbles for the roar of the poets crying, "Love, let us be true to one another."

Tate's position with all its vague but omnipresent despair seems to have dictated certain possibilities for poetic procedure and certain impossibilities. It has supposed, somewhat sourly, that the failures of history were to be associated with an idiotic

[1] See *Sewanee Review*, LXVII (1959), 528–39.

romantic faith in progress and perfectability which had been expressed in a language of largess and drafty generality, or with the baggy, general didacticism of the nineteenth century. Hence, away with any technique which might encourage the vasty or the yeasty. In other words, Tate has inherited the estate of the Rhymer's Club, Hulme, and Pound, whereby one decides to admire the small rather than the big, the object rather than the statement. The true nightmare is a yawp barbaric.

What happens when what Wordsworth called "lofty speculations" may not be openly arrayed, when sentiment and conviction must be disguised—so that for students "understanding poetry" has come to mean "translating poetry"? I think that while there are some advantages, several other than happy results ensue. In the broadest sense, if conviction must be transfigured, if belief must be masked, then conviction and belief tend to become guilty and devaluated. When this occurs, the poet, whose truest instincts would instruct him to regard conviction and faith with pride, extends his devaluation of these matters to poetry itself. If poetry cannot speak but may only incant, if it may not state, then poetry has only an aesthetic function. Have no fear—I am not about to re-open the dreary debate about the "Irresponsibles." I do not believe that poetry has any particular obligation to the world. But to the strategist I say that the poet loses psychological power when he cannot believe with Kant that his act is of the utmost importance. And to the moralist I would put the question if it is not immoral to suppose that any human act or gesture—even a poem—is without effect.

Furthermore, when the poet's attention is driven almost exclusively to object, there often results a rather naturalistic blurring of the poem. That is to say, whether we call upon correlatives or images, things are only things. They can, to be sure, be chosen ill or well, but the esemplastic imagination, alas, never existed—there is no faculty charged with the duty of fusing detail into a single meaning or effect. Fusion takes place in a poem, as in other forms, because of syntax within language; or because of a guiding concept which may be openly postulated or allegorized by a symbolism; or, less probably, because it is implied by the historicity of the poem—its time, its place, its characters, its fashion.

All the modern talus slide of wily detail imposes a weary burden on the reader. It leans upon him, compounding its pressure until it creates a glaucoma, and all goes gray. For this reason too many poets seem more alike than perhaps they really are. With the result that the critic often forces his opinion into being and against his better judgment, so that we succeed often in honoring the poets whose names we shall have forgotten in a few years. Conversely, we fail to honor those whom we should honor.

And all this passion for the object makes me feel that too frequently the contemporary poet is merely playing the percentages. I am reminded of those amusement park devices where you put in a coin for the privilege of guiding a toy steam shovel toward cameras and binoculars reposing, like Rimbaud's pianos in the Alps, upon crests of penny candies. I had an acquaintance (he now works for a computer company) who, on the perfectly correct theory that one had almost no chance to scoop up a camera, fiercely avoided the prizes and craftily maneuvered so as to gather in a profitable amount of the candy which he said was not so bad. The poet refuses to try for the prize. Indeed he is made to blush furiously by the very idea of the "great line." But I think he should try. I believe that "Ode to the Confederate Dead" ought not to have decided to be about solipsism or to have given itself at the end to a silkworm.

My remarks are finished, but as I look back on the last paragraphs it seems to me that I have too readily put on the moderately useful but immoderately silly mask and domino of the critic. If in the end the mask must come off I shall stand by my conclusion, but I cannot entirely stand by my phrasing. There was always a better way to say the last paragraphs anyway. That was to make the wonderful confusion of Pindar—so perfect for him that surely he was unaware of it—that confusion of poet and athlete, poem and a test of strength. In this confusion I should only generously want to root for a favorite whose performance in the race has made me doubt the outcome: "Come on, Allen, come on!"

Deliberate Exiles:
The Social Sources
of Agrarian Poetics

Wallace W. Douglas

HISTORY indeed has many cunning passages, if I may use the famous words in a sense that their author did not mean. Once upon a time even Mr. Eliot was only "an American at present living in England," "whose performances are not yet . . . exciting much attention in his native country, except of a few bold and adventurous critics who see important possibilities in them." [1] And once (it was not so long ago as might be thought—only 1943) Cleanth Brooks could "personally" assure Alfred Kazin "that the new formalists have next to no influence in the universities." [2] In fact history is so fractious, reality so impure, and human experience of such a rich and uncontrollable fullness that *Understanding Poetry* was treated by the re-

[1] W. S. Knickerbocker, "The Fugitives of Nashville," *Sewanee Review*, XXXVI (1928), 213.

[2] Cleanth Brooks, "Mr. Kazin's America," *Sewanee Review*, LI (1943), 58–59.

viewer in the *English Journal* as an instance of "the anthology which garbs the text with a heavy drape of editorial introduction and commentary."[3] So it was—without omen or portent— that the New Criticism was introduced to the college classroom teacher.

How difficult to recapture that innocent world now, after the battles, after the skirmishes, after the angry or grumbling *feuilletons* that defended historical, biographical, and editorial accuracy, literary appreciation, and even the value of dialectical materialism as an analytical tool. All that was a long time ago; and for many years the values and techniques of the New Critics have been commonplaces of writing and conversation in the "wider and less speculative circles" to which they were disseminated "through the various media of literary magazines, colleges, and Chautauqua platforms."[4] Now Ransom has retired, and Tate tells his friends and us that he feels "very little interest in the literary scene."[5] Another group of sensitive, passionate, and prejudiced men have found it possible or necessary to issue another Southern manifesto, twenty-seven years after *I'll Take My Stand*.[6] And the New Critics, who once spoke only to "the ears of the most toughened students of the theory and condition of contemporary poetry," have become subjects for research, a ritual reunion (made possible by a grant from the Rockefeller Foundation to the American Studies Association), and even a revolt.[7]

[3] *English Journal* (College Edition), XXVI (1938), 870–71.

[4] Knickerbocker, "The Fugitives of Nashville," p. 220.

[5] Rob Roy Purdy, ed., *Fugitives' Reunion* (Nashville, 1959), p. 132.

[6] Louis D. Rubin, Jr. and James Jackson Kilpatrick, eds., *The Lasting South* (Chicago, 1957).

[7] Purdy, *Fugitives' Reunion*, p. 220. For the revolt, see Hyatt Waggoner, "The Current Revolt Against the New Criticism," *Criticism*, I (1959), 211–25; the reunion is recorded in Purdy.

Yet the world, at least the academic world, is still very much under the influence of general ideals and values that were imported with the theories of the New Criticism. The result can be seen in the attitudes of our most fashionable professional humanists, who have been constructing their public and pedagogical personalities, with tight little good taste, on a sub-Pascalian posture full of languishings and flutterings about sin and the implacable world which makes impossible or at least unwise any attempts to improve the living conditions of those who are so unfortunate as still to be unassimilated to the new genteel bourgeoisie.

"The sense of crisis," a scholar-critic writes, "helps to explain [the New Critics'] neglect of such writers as Chaucer, Pope, and Whitman, in whose works anxiety is not conspicuous." [8] The American Council of Learned Societies makes a grant for a study of "Views of the origins of coercive government: the fall of man and the emergence of lordship." [9] A Ph.D. candidate in English writes his dissertation "to exert upon the commonplaces of contemporary liberalism the critical pressure" which is generated by the theories of the Southern Agrarians that are found in the work of R. P. Warren.[10] A lecturer in sociology begins an article on "Alienation and the Decline of Utopia" by saying, "This is an age that inspires little enthusiasm." [11] Just the other day I learned that "the feeling of anxiety is a significant aspect of our

[8] Robert Daniel, "The Critics of Nashville," *Tennessee Studies in Literature* (Knoxville, 1956) , p. 24.

[9] *ACLS Newsletter*, X (1959) , 9.

[10] Mark Linenthal, Jr., "Robert Penn Warren and the Southern Agrarians" (Doctoral dissertation, Stanford University, 1957) , *Dissertation Abstracts*, XVII (1957) , 2611.

[11] Keith Keniston, "Alienation and the Decline of Utopia," *American Scholar*, XXII (1960) , 161.

total lives and perhaps the very center of the affective tonality through which we address the universe and our fellow-men." [12] I have even read that "there seems to be an increasing willingness on the part of many—and, in particular, the 'intellectuals'—to entertain seriously the fundamental Christian doctrine of Original Sin." [13] Indeed perhaps we may soon be comfortable again, for "now that Roosevelts, Tafts, and Rockefellers not only accept the responsibility of their class to lead the common voter but are in turn accepted by him, it is evident that we once again have an established upper class with privileges and duties roughly equivalent to those of the eighteenth-century gentry." [14] A short while ago I discovered that at the second conference of the Frank L. Weill Institute for Studies in Religion and the Humanities, which was held in Cincinnati, there was a paper entitled "Can There Be a New Christian View of History?"

What is clearest in literary history today is "the massive impact on the course of American letters" that was exerted by the Fugitive-Agrarian-New Critic group.[15] But for several reasons the implication of Agrarian social and political theory in the poetic theory of the New Criticism has been generally overlooked or forgotten. The New Criticism became popular among English teachers only after its originators had stopped writing openly

[12] William A. Madden, "The Burden of the Artist," *1859: Entering an Age of Crisis,* ed. Philip Appleman, William A. Madden, and Michael Wolf (Bloomington, Ind., 1959) , p. 249.

[13] Robert Y. Drake, Jr., review of Randall Stewart, *American Literature and Christian Doctrine, Shenandoah,* XI (1959) , 31.

[14] Rowland Berthoff, "The American Social Order: A Conservative Hypothesis," *American Historical Review,* LXV (1960) , 511.

[15] W. K. Wimsatt, review of Rob Roy Purdy, ed., *Fugitives' Reunion* and Louis D. Rubin, Jr. and James Jackson Kilpatrick, eds., *The Lasting South, Criticism,* II (1960) , 97. On the present academic value system, see Howard Mumford Jones, "Republican Humanism," *Social Research,* XXI (1954) , 164. Thirty years ago Jones was noting that we had passed into "the age of the Solemn, and the present heresy is to be gay." See Jones, "Amidst the Encircling Gloom," *Scribner's,* LXXXVII (1930) , 405.

political essays. In all their later talk about epistemology, ontology, and the rude world that refused to submit itself to scientific abstraction, it was quite possible to overlook their deep-set political convictions. Furthermore the popularity of the New Criticism coincided with the violent period of conservative reaction, in the forties and early fifties, when young teachers were escaping from present social problems into the patterns of poetry, or the criticism of poetry, where there were reflections of those better days when everybody understood about values. But the political assumptions of the New Critics are not really very far from sight. A very simple content analysis will prove that their poetic theory, even though it is notorious for defending the integrity of the poem as an organic unity, could give "one of the biggest pushes, perhaps . . . the biggest, to the mid-century American 'religio-aesthetic reaction' against progressive 'liberalism' and scientism." [16]

II

In a general sort of way we know what happened to the Vanderbilt group, the warm, simple young men from Campbellsville, Murfreesboro, Columbia, and Pulaski, in Tennessee, and Guthrie and Winchester, in Kentucky. From fugitives of an innocent revolt against the literary conventions of the plantation cult, they became political polemicists and defenders of the South, transformed by such events as the Scopes trial, Mencken's attacks on the Sahara of the Bozart, the Gastonia strike, and the Scottsboro case, as their ancestors had been by the works of Garrison and the Abolitionists. In their last period they set out to reform the

[16] Wimsatt, review of *Fugitives' Reunion* and *The Lasting South,* p. 98.

study of literature in the universities, which was perhaps not a modest objective.

Apparently these events are unified only because they occurred to the same heroes, but in fact there is a thematic or logical unity of a sort. Beneath the cluttered surface of this history, beneath this bare and uninteresting abstraction (which is a segment of experience deprived of all the rich contingencies that give life meaning), it is indeed possible to find a recondite truth for the philosopher and scholar. This unifying factor in the historical, religious, and critical ideas of the New Critics is their need to justify and validate the enormous amounts of value they invested in the social system of the South.

The foundation of the Vanderbilt mythology is in history, in a specialized, though hardly unusual, view of the South's intimate connection with or origin in European social systems. In the South, this view asserted, life had been, perhaps still was, "leisurely and unhurried"; and truly the Old South knew "a way of life, not a routine of planting and reaping merely for gain." [17] Southerners were not "intemperately addicted to work and to gross material prosperity." [18] Southern culture was homely rather than elegant, and of course it was not a patch on that of Greece or even Rome, but it stood for the agrarian way of life—"the old and accepted way of life for which Egypt, Greece, Rome, England, and France had stood." [19] The South had been a squirearchy not an aristocracy, with caste lines obscured or eased by the sedulously cultivated manners of friendliness. "It was a kindly society,

---

[17] Frank Lawrence Owsley, "The Irrepressible Conflict," *I'll Take My Stand* (New York, 1930), p. 71.

[18] John Crowe Ransom, "Reconstructed but Unregenerate," *I'll Take My Stand*, p. 12.

[19] Owsley, "The Irrepressible Conflict," p. 69.

yet a realistic one; for it was a failure if it could not be said that people were for the most part in their right places." [20] In a word, it was a stable society, of that special kind that, in the modern myth, is a necessary precondition to great poetry.

According to the Agrarians, the peculiar stability of the South was an effect of the presence of many small, independent farmers whose interests convinced them of "the virtues of establishment." [21] Here the Agrarians were borrowing, I suspect, from the old myth of the Sturdy Yeoman which had been current among British literary men during most of the nineteenth century. The Agrarians presented the South as a society much like the rural England which is supposed to have existed until the second enclosure movement. There were classes of planters, yeomen, and landless tenants, and these were equivalent to the British classes of landowners, occupiers in copyhold or customary tenure, and renting farmers. The Agrarians emphasized the small occupying owner of a family farm. The British yeoman had settled the South, and he remained the most touching and important figure in the Agrarian myth.

Like their British forebears, the Agrarians saw themselves engaged in a great struggle against industrialism. In Agrarian history, 1865 is a crucial year, the beginning of that long destruction of the Old South, the completion of which it seemed to be the Agrarians' fate to witness. It was the year when the North finally took over the political forms and committed the country to industrial and commercial expansion, diversified farming, and a fluid class structure. Accordingly, the "agrarian

[20] Ransom, "Reconstructed but Unregenerate," p. 14.

[21] Ransom, "Reconstructed but Unregenerate," p. 12; Ransom, "The Aesthetics of Regionalism," *American Review*, II (1934), 300–301; Donald Davidson, "A Mirror for Artists," *I'll Take My Stand*, pp. 53–54.

Union" of independent states was changed into "an industrial empire," and there followed a civil conflict "more deadly" than any international war.

> This conflict is between the unnatural progeny of inventive genius and men. It is a war to the death between technology and the ordinary human functions of living. The rights to these human functions are the natural rights of man, and they are threatened now, in the twentieth, not in the eighteenth, century for the first time.[22]

The Agrarians saw the stable, traditional society of small yeomen (and the descendants of some few Cavaliers)[23] being destroyed by any one or all of a number of abstractions; for example, science, technology, finance capitalism; behaviorism, progressivism, positivism, modernism, urbanism, meliorism, cosmopolitanism, New England Transcendentalism; Wall Street, Marx, New York City, the public school system, rootless intellectuals; and "people who scrub all the oil from their skins in the articles of the plumbing industry."[24] They found it harder and harder to keep a man placed, or easier for a man to get out of his place. To them it was clear

> that the people of America were losing the basic values of civilization, that we were going as a nation into materialism, that money value had become the real basic value, that the sense of community was disappearing—particularly in the North . . .

---

[22] Andrew Lytle, "The Hind Tit," *I'll Take My Stand*, p. 202.

[23] Donald Davidson, "First Fruits of Dayton," *Forum*, LXXIX (1928), 902.

[24] Donald Davidson, *Still Rebels, Still Yankees* (Baton Rouge, La., 1957), p. 3; Rubin and Kilpatrick, eds., *The Lasting South*, p. 43; Donald Davidson, "The Class Approach to Southern Problems," *Southern Review*, V (1959), 264; John Gould Fletcher, "Education, Past and Present," *I'll Take My Stand*, p. 115; Lytle, "The Hind Tit," p. 211.

that you went into a store and were insulted rather than wel-
comed . . . .[25]

Or, as Davidson put it, the "sudden advent of industrial codes
which wipe out child labor and cheap labor, and threaten at one
stroke to abolish the time-honored differences between white
and black labor, rubs hard on all the old Southern sore places."[26]
There is a degree of Spenglerian catastrophism in the Agrarian
view of history, I suspect. But also there is a lot of the plain and
simple piety and patriotism that are cultivated by the agricultural
oligarchy in the South. In their view of Southern history, the
Agrarians found very direct support for the social values they were
always talking about, such things as "stability and establishment," "a stable tradition," "a tradition of repose and *noblesse
oblige*," "a leisure which permitted the activity of intelligence,"
or the sort of provincialism "which prefers religion to science,
handicrafts to technology, the inertia of the fields to the accelera-
tion of industry, and leisure to nervous prostration."[27] In the his-

---

[25] Louise Cowan, *The Fugitive Group* (Baton Rouge, La., 1959), p. 204. Cf.
Fletcher, "Education, Past and Present," p. 119: "The inferior, whether in life or
education, should exist only for the sake of the superior." And so Robert Penn
Warren, "The Briar Patch," *I'll Take My Stand*, p. 247: Before the War the Negro
"had occupied an acknowledged, if limited and humble, place. Now he had to find
a place, and the attempt to find it is the story of the negro [*sic*] since 1865." At
p. 250: "The most urgent need was to make the ordinary negro [*sic*] into a competent workman or artisan and a decent citizen."

[26] Donald Davidson, *The Attack on Leviathan* (Chapel Hill, N. C., 1938), p. 282.

[27] Ransom, "Reconstructed but Unregenerate," pp. 3, 10, 12; Davidson, *The Attack on Leviathan*, p. 343; Davidson, "First Fruits of Dayton," p. 902; Lytle, "The
Hind Tit," p. 234. Cf. C. Hugh Holman, "Literature and Culture: the Fugitive-
Agrarians," *Social Forces*, XXXVII (1958), 19: "Now what I am suggesting about
the Fugitives is that their theme is drawn from the culture of their region; it is,
in fact, the qualities I have equated with the old order which constitute their
theme." The point is also used in C. A. Ward, "Myths: Further Vanderbilt Agrarian
Views," *University of Kansas City Review*, XXV (1958), 55: "If, as Tate and Ransom
say, a religious myth may be the sustainer of a society, may it not also be con-
jectured that a historical myth—such as the myth of the Old South—may play a
part in sustaining certain survivals from the past—including such an undesirable
survival as the doctrine of white superiority and white supremacy?"

torical myth of the South as the last form of yeoman economy, the Agrarians validated the defensive slogans of the caste-ridden society they had grown up in.

III

The Southern culture that nourished the Agrarians was not only full of history and traditions; at least since the 1830's, we are told,[28] it has been quite peculiarly orthodox, the theologically conservative successor to Puritan New England. And indeed the very foundation of the Agrarian ideology lay in the ancient sacramental-magical view of nature, with which is associated a strong feeling for the limitations of man as a creature.

To most Southerners the term "creation" comes with its literal meaning. The world is something created for man, but certainly not by him. He can understand some of its intermediate principles and relations, but its ultimate secrets are forever beyond him. He is granted some dominion over it, but not an unlimited one, since that would be setting him on a level with the Creator. Basically nature is right in being as it is. Change for its own sake is not good, and many of nature's dispositions are best left as they are. He has a degree of reverence for the natural order of things and he suspects *hubris* in a desire to change that order radically.

Toward man the Southerner takes an attitude inculcated by orthodox religion and by tragedy also.[29]

---

[28] Owsley, "The Irrepressible Conflict," p. 81. W. J. Cash (in *The Mind of the South* [Garden City, N. Y., 1954], pp. 293–94 and elsewhere) emphasizes Southern fundamentalism, but so do such wholly orthodox Southerners as Owsley (above), Richard Weaver (in "The South and the American Union," *The Lasting South*, pp. 52, 54, 64, 65), and Francis Simkins (in "The Rising Tide of Faith," *The Lasting South*, pp. 88 ff.) .

[29] Weaver, "The South and the American Union," p. 51.

The development of this attitude among the Agrarians seems to have begun quite early, and it reflects not only the persistent fundamentalism of certain sectors of Southern society, but possibly also the occultism of Sidney Mttron Hirsch.[30] Of course, the social argument is always present in the background, since, presumably, Southerners still believe that "the natural order of things" warrants the social hierarchy. Generally the Agrarians insisted that men should recognize their "precarious position in the universe," their helplessness before "the brute materiality which is nature." Any attempt to control or modify the natural world (always excepting agriculture) only "enhances too readily our conceit, and brutalizes our life." [31] Instead of "progress, or the perpetual violation of nature," men need something to stop action.[32] They should understand that human destiny is "to secure an honorable peace with nature," presumably on small family farms, where "the most ancient and the most humane of all the human modes of livelihood" can be practiced. And they should emulate the farmer, "even the farmer of comparatively new places like Iowa and Nebraska." For the farmer is not "a mere laborer" but is "among the more stable and less progressive ele-

---

[30] Sidney Mttron Hirsch: for biographical details see Cowan, *The Fugitive Group* and Purdy, *Fugitives' Reunion.* In some curious way, he was able to dominate the literary conversations in Nashville from which *The Fugitive* developed. Wimsatt, review of *Fugitives' Reunion* and *The Lasting South,* pp. 100, 102, calls him "a strange, now mysteriously patriarchal figure" but also "a solemn show-off." At the Reunion, Merrill Moore suggested that he was a non-demanding father-figure for the young men (*Fugitives' Reunion,* p. 146). He was much given to rather perverse but fascinating etymologies, which evidently captured their imaginations (*Fugitives' Reunion,* p. 120). He suggested publication and evidently also the name *Fugitive* (*Fugitives' Reunion,* pp. 124, 127; Allen Tate, "The Fugitive, 1922–1925," *Princeton Library Chronicle,* III [1942], 79). "Most of all," Davidson said, "his declaration of the high eminence of poetry somehow elevated into an almost priestly rite the consideration of the most juvenile and humble of our verses." (See Davidson, *Southern Writers in the Modern World* [Athens, Georgia, 1958], pp. 12–13.)

[31] Ransom, "Reconstructed but Unregenerate," pp. 7, 8, 10.

[32] Robert Penn Warren, "John Crowe Ransom: A Study in Irony," *Virginia Quarterly Review,* XI (1935), 99, 100. Note Warren's insistence (pp. 98, 99) on what he calls "the myth of rationality."

ments of society." And if he lives on the right kind of farm, he will not "till it too hurriedly and not too mechanically to observe in it the contingency and infinitude of nature." [33]

Today these slogans may seem to have only eschatological significance, but in fact they had pretty obvious implications in the ideological controversy of what the Agrarians may have hoped was a coming struggle for power. Perhaps no interests were threatened, or defended either, by the pseudo-definition, "Religion is our submission to the general intention of a nature that is fairly inscrutable" and "mysterious and contingent." [34] But *submission* has a clear social reference, and the function of *contingent* is to remove nature from the operations of rational analysis. Generally the Agrarians used their dogma of nature's sacrosanct incomprehensibility to warrant their attacks on science, technology, industrialism, humanitarianism, and other institutions, beliefs, and values that were charged with social significance, to use the old phrase. History, the assumption was, recorded only the universality of sin and human depravity, likewise the failure of all efforts to improve human nature as embodied in the behavior of individuals. The heavens declare the glory of God, and man is a moralist by nature, a geometrician by chance. Good works, or at least social reforms, only force nature, which had better to be left alone, except as an object of contemplation. In this strand of the Agrarian ideology, the indispensable item is "the acceptance, as fact, of an ultimate, essential condition of man: a nature which underlies and precedes his actual manifestation in particular circumstances." [35] This belief is a fruitful source for speculation or homiletic exercises, no doubt; but, unfortunately, it may also be a means to prevent or at least dis-

---

[33] Ransom, "Reconstructed but Unregenerate," pp. 19–20.

[34] *I'll Take My Stand*, p. xiv.

[35] Raymond Williams, *Culture and Society* (New York, 1958), p. 193.

courage all attempts even to think about the problems that men face as animals having to sustain life in an environment at least part of which is a result of their own actions. In effect, if not intention, Agrarian sacramentalism was also a protection for the material conditions that had created the class system—and of course also and more importantly, the caste system—in which the Agrarians invested so much psychic energy.

IV

Eventually the agrarians turned somewhat away from the Old South and the Old Time Religion and began to develop the theory of poetry as knowledge, which has become the most powerful validation of social stability that has yet been developed by American humanism. The theory assumed the existence of separate and opposed mental powers or ethical attitudes, or as Ransom put it, three kinds of minds. On one side, according to him, is the scientific mind. On the other side are the religious and poetic minds, which are metaphysical. These latter are "bigger and better" than the scientific kind of mind, or at least they are more "comprehensive and more imaginative." They are "flooded with metaphysics and a precarious but passionate concern for last things." Presumably the scientific mind is objectionable because it has a "naive confidence in the limitless power of man to impose practical abstractions on the world," for with its "incongruities and disparities" removed, life loses meaning.[36] But also, I guess, the scientific mind is bad because it is characteristic of New Englanders, who are consumed by "the rootless

[36] Allen Tate, "Three Types of Poetry," *New Republic*, LXXVIII (March 14, 1934), 126; Cleanth Brooks, "Metaphysical Poetry and the Ivory Tower," *Southern Review*, I (1936), 570, 572; Cleanth Brooks, "Wit and High Seriousness," *Southern Review*, I (1935), 332, 333; Warren, "John Crowe Ransom," pp. 93, 94.

appetites of middle-class meliorism" and are "constitutionally disposed to alter, reform, improve the world." [37]

But all the talk about metaphysics and the various kinds of minds hardly explains what knowledge there is in poetry, or what knowledge poetry is. This is a very complicated question indeed, and I do not have the skill to handle it with any assurance. What, for example, could I say of this passage from Sidney Hirsch, which is full of references to the general theory?

> And so ontologically, I'd suggest that it be considered that there's a reality—which is *paradeigma,* isn't it, the paradigms, the ideas that inhabit the realm of thought. And [Plato] calls them *ethos,* if you recall: the proper theme for a poem. I hesitate to say that, but I suppose you recall the word is a synonym for Dionysus.[38]

But in a common sense sort of way, this can be said: the ideas that the Agrarians used to explain their dogma of poetry as knowledge are loaded and charged with the same conservative and reactionary political meanings that filled their historical and religious myths.

According to Ransom, the knowledge of poetry is the knowledge felt when "we are able to contemplate things as they are in their rich contingent materiality." [39] According to Warren, the knowledge of a poem is not knowledge by report or knowledge as symptom; that is, I gather, it is not referential. Rather it is "knowledge by form. No, knowledge *of* form." Warren went on and defined "form" as "a vision of experience, but of experience fulfilled and

[37] Robert Lowell, "Visiting the Tates," *Sewanee Review,* LXVII (1959) , 558; Reed Whittemore, "Mr. Tate and Mr. Adams," *Sewanee Review,* LXVII (1959) , 583.

[38] Purdy, *Fugitives' Reunion,* p. 171.

[39] John Crowe Ransom, "Poetry: A Note in Ontology," *American Review,* III (1934) , 176.

redeemed in knowledge . . . ."[40] The way to this knowledge is through art, which, according to Brooks, may be thought of as "a description of experience which is concrete where that of science is abstract, many-sided where that of science is necessarily one-sided, and which involves the whole personality where science only involves one part, the intellect."[41]

Quite evidently the Agrarians intended to persuade the world that the most important fact about the knowledge of poetry was that it was at least different from, if not better than, the knowledge of science. They seem to have believed that what they referred to as the singular and intractable images of a poem contained, pointed to, or implicated a wider, fuller, more complete, and somehow more valuable view of or feeling for experience than could be achieved by the statements or formulas of science. Apparently they thought of the degree of abstraction (perhaps as found in the languages of science and poetry) as the variable differentiating the two forms of knowledge.

> [The image] cannot be dispossessed of a primordial freshness, which idea can never claim. An idea is derivative and tamed. The image is in the natural or wild state, and it has to be discovered there, not put there, obeying its own law and none of ours. We think we can lay hold of the image and hold it captive, but the docile captive is not the real image but only the idea, which is the image with its character beaten out of it.[42]

Now I think I can understand William James's crab which refused to be classified by phylum, order, family, and so on, but

---

[40] Robert Penn Warren, "Knowledge and the Image of Man," *Sewanee Review*, LXIII (1955), 191.

[41] Cleanth Brooks, "The Christianity of Modernism," *American Review*, VI (1936), 439.

[42] Ransom, "Poetry: A Note in Ontology," p. 175.

kept asserting his own individuality: "I am myself. Myself alone." But I am not at all sure that I know, for example, what Tate was talking about when he said, "Religion pretends to place before us the horse as he is," the "complete and self-contained horse [that exists] in spite of the now prevailing faith that there is none simply because the abstract and scientific world cannot see him." [43] Somehow or other I keep missing the significance of the Agrarian argument. I know, of course, that scientists are not interested in individual cases but rather in statistically significant populations. But then what? Sometimes the Agrarians sound as if they had hoped to disprove science, repeal the twentieth century, or exorcise the whole modern temper by the common sense observation that the world of immediate observation is concrete and insubordinate. Perhaps they believed in Johnson's legendary way of disproving Berkeley. But what is so special about treating the individual as an individual? Of course the Agrarians did not mean to object to the use of "general properties and large appearances" in poems. They seem to have thought—at least eventually they did—that they were talking about epistemology, not style alone. But could they really have believed that knowledge may be limited to individual propositions about particulars? Could they really have believed that modern men have been "so transported by the abstractions of science that [they] require something [*sc.* "poetry"] to restore [them] to awareness of the world in which [they] live"? [44]

The questions can be answered by examining the world and

---

[43] Allen Tate, "Remarks on Southern Religion," *I'll Take My Stand*, p. 157.

[44] Francis X. Roellinger, "Two Theories of Poetry as Knowledge," *Southern Review*, VII (1942), 697, 700. Note Cleanth Brooks, "The Formalist Critics," *Kenyon Review*, XIII (1951), 72: "That the general and the universal are not seized upon by abstraction, but got at through the concrete and the particular." This is item seven in Brooks's critical "credo." I have no idea what, precisely, it means. Perhaps it represents an extreme, and naive, extension of Baconian empiricism. Or maybe it goes back to Whitehead's remarks on Wordsworth.

life that the Agrarians created, or that they saw, when they were expressing their opposition to science and to the great abstractions that they associated with science and industrialism.[45] In the fashion of modern reactionary humanism, they created a world of eternal and irremediable conditions of sin, pain, and deprivation. There was a vision of quality, also a vision of quantity. Thought and feeling were split. Men no longer had that "appreciative concern with persons, objects, and events of this world," which may become art, and which is more meaningful and intensely human than the mere chart of experience that is provided by science.[46] The world could no more be seen in all its "concrete fullness," with all its "natural and contingent materials." [47]

For the Agrarians, the most obvious fact of experience, when "fulfilled and redeemed in knowledge," [48] was its "discordant and contradictory" materials, by which man's powers are defined and limited. Irony itself, which some have thought the Agrarians turned into the necessary and sufficient condition for "poetry," was only "a qualifying recognition of the negative aspects of experience." [49] Perhaps these "negative aspects" are such things as man's "rhythm of destiny, his tonality of fate." [50] At any rate, they seem to have something to do with evil, "the tragic pathos of life," "the tragic experience [which] is universal and a corollary of man's place in nature," or the "immense complication of life as

---

[45] Davidson, "A Mirror for Artists," pp. 43–44, 49; Davidson, " 'I'll Take My Stand': A History," *American Review*, V (1935) , 313; *I'll Take My Stand*, pp. xi, xv, xvi; Purdy, *Fugitives' Reunion*, p. 91.

[46] Robert Penn Warren, "A Note on Three Southern Poets," *Poetry*, XL (1932) , 110; Warren, "John Crowe Ransom," p. 98.

[47] Ransom, "The Aesthetics of Regionalism," p. 306.

[48] Warren, "Knowledge and the Image of Man," p. 191.

[49] Cleanth Brooks, "The Modern Southern Poet and the Tradition," *Virginia Quarterly Review*, XI (1935) , 311. See also Brooks, "Metaphysical Poetry and the Ivory Tower," p. 576.

[50] Warren, "Knowledge and the Image of Man," p. 192.

a whole." [51] And I suppose they may be recognized in what Brooks called "the successful blending of opposites," as in Hardy's "The Convergence of the Twain": "The great ship and the iceberg, in man's purposes so utterly dissociated," Brooks said, "are actually meant for each other in the larger purposes of fate." [52] Or as Lytle said much earlier, "Each meal [at a typical Southern farm] is a victory over nature, a suitable union between the general principles of cookery and the accident of preparation." [53]

When the Agrarians treated poetry as the knowledge of, or as an expression of reverence for, the sacramental wholeness of "the World's Body, the tensional completeness, the impure reality, the paradoxical confrontation," they seemed to be recognizing the abstract principle or myth of Evil as a constitutive force of the universe. But as one of their interpreters has noticed, the doctrine was not without social overtones, for the "concrete fullness of human experience" somehow always included "the land, the history, the stabilizing tradition, the responsibility, the au-

---

[51] Warren, "Knowledge and the Image of Man," p. 187; Brooks, "Metaphysical Poetry and the Ivory Tower," p. 575.

[52] Brooks, "Metaphysical Poetry and the Ivory Tower," p. 583.

[53] Lytle, "The Hind Tit," p. 220. I wonder if the description of the meal (pp. 226 ff.) does not, perhaps, fit the organic definition of a poem: "There is no puny piddling with the victuals, and fancy tin-can salads do not litter the table. The only salad to be seen on a country table is sallet, or turnip greens, or if further explanation is necessary, the tops of turnips cut off and cooked with a luscious piece of fat meat. It has the appearance of spinach; but unlike this insipid slime, sallet has character, like the life of the farmer at the head of the table." Perhaps this is a place to introduce my favorite comment on the Agrarians. It is from the *Letters of Sherwood Anderson*, selected and edited by Howard Mumford Jones in association with Walter B. Rideout (Boston, 1953), p. 389. In the late summer of 1937, Anderson had attended the Writers Conference at Boulder; in September he wrote to a friend in the Veterans Administration, "Between ourselves, I think the real sour bird out there [at the Conference] was Ransom. That one has that thing so aggravating about many Southerners, a wholly unjustified feeling of superiority. He [is] so damned softly and gently superior that it makes me want to shout, 'Balls.'"

thority"—all very powerful conservative abstractions.[54] Brooks could speak, with rather surprising jauntiness, of "the teasing mixture of good and bad which makes up the world—the mixture of qualities in the concretion of reality" that is "rendered for us through Huck's vision in the Grangerford episode." But later he used this same "moral complexity" of the "complicated world" represented in the novel to explain not merely Colonel Sherburn's theatrical and immensely effective actions, but also what he saw as a shift of the reader's sympathy to the Colonel, occurring when he stands off the townspeople: "He is a brave man, the mob is poor-spirited." [55] The device was one that Shakespeare found effective, but perhaps Brooks was aware of what I call Fletcher's principle, after its discoverer, John Gould Fletcher:

> . . . underneath unions and industrial progress there are always people, and people are not like figures in a ledger, or debit and credit columns in an account book. They are beings acted upon continually by the sun, the soil, the wind, the rain, and by the persistent habits of mind which these engender: irrational hatreds and impossible loyalties.[56]

[54] Wimsatt, review of *Fugitives' Reunion* and *The Lasting South,* p. 98.

[55] Cleanth Brooks, "The Teaching of the Novel: *Huckleberry Finn,*" *Essays on the Teaching of English,* ed. Edward J. Gordon and Edward S. Noyes (New York, 1960), pp. 209, 211, 213–14.

[56] Fletcher, "Section versus State," *American Review,* I (1933), 483–89. Cf. Davidson, " 'I'll Take My Stand': A History," p. 310, on the "indelible impressions" made by those latter-day condottieri, the Confederate captains, who surrendered only in the military sense. Warren, "The Briar Patch," p. 257, speaks of the Southerner's "naive distrust of most types of organization"; it would be interesting to know just what types do not merit distrust. This gross frontier individualism was expressed very clearly in the Introduction to *I'll Take My Stand:* "It is strange, of course, that a majority of men anywhere could ever as with one mind become enamored of industrialism: a system that has so little regard for individual wants. There is evidently a kind of thinking that rejoices in setting up a social objective which has no relation to the individual. Men are prepared to sacrifice their private dignity and happiness to an abstract social ideal, and without asking whether the social

The following rather rich moment in Ransom's life is another example of the "ambiguous" content of the Agrarian world-model. Once, on a Santa Fe train out of Albuquerque, Ransom saw some Indians threshing, and laughing as they threshed. This, I take it, was one of those fresh, free, wild, primordial, and self-willed images in which the wholeness of the world is revealed in concrete form. To Ransom what was revealed was nothing less than the creative power of the social organization that the Agrarians asserted had existed in older days, when sturdy yeomen plowed their independent ways. The Indians made Ransom reflect on the aesthetic response to living which is possible when life is organized by ancient patterns and in full consciousness of tradition. He added, "The superiority of Indians, by which the philosophical spectator refers to their obviously fuller enjoyment of life, lies in their regionalism." Evidently the poetic view of reality has its abstractions and generalizations, though reason knows them not.[57]

The conclusion seems to be that the Agrarian theory of poetry as knowledge was a validating myth for the social values and forms that the Agrarians were constantly defending against the American industrial ideal. The material of the theory may have been drawn from epistemology, eschatology, and even criticism. Its form and content, however, were simply expressions of the old political and social grievance that the Agrarians had suffered

---

ideal produces the welfare of any individual man whatsoever. But this is absurd. The responsibility of men is for their own welfare and that of their neighbors; not for the hypothetical welfare of some fabulous creature called society." This is simply the language of Tory localism, and the Agrarians are perfect illustrations of the fear that countrymen and small-townsmen feel for the city and government. Nowhere in all their writing did the Agrarians ever recognize the sense of social responsibility which has been developed in Western bourgeois societies in the last century and a half or so, and of course they had no liking for the governmental and political mechanisms that have been developed to express that consciousness or simply to make living possible.

[57] Ransom, "The Aesthetics of Regionalism," p. 293.

from in their very earliest days. Perhaps the best proof of this is the very basic tenet of the theory—the famous opposition between the bare abstractions of science and the qualitatively rich statements, expressions, structures, or forms of poetry, history, and myth. This distinction was adapted from or based on a polemic device that had been developed in the South during the slavery controversy of the nineteenth century, that period of social change which for Southerners was even more corrosive and traumatic than the one the Agrarians found themselves lost in.

Perhaps no Northerner can ever understand all the reasons for the enormous quantity of negative affect that the notion of "abstraction" evokes from Southern intellectuals like the Agrarians. As nearly as I can make out, however, William Lloyd Garrison and the Abolitionists may be more responsible for the peculiar attitude than Bergson, Whitehead, or Burtt. Garrison, according to Owsley,

> knew no moderation. He had no balance or sense of consequence. His was the typical "radical" mind which demands that things be done at once, which tries to force nature, which wants to tear her up by the roots.

The substance of the charge is that Garrison and the Abolitionists were radicals who were committed to action in the name of abstract human rights and moral principles. Southerners, on the other hand, were realists, and they appealed to the realities of Southern environment, history, tradition, and social system in order to defend political and juridical rights whose reality was attested, for their defenders, by their existing in written form in certain clauses of the Constitution. Thus the slavery controversy and the Civil War itself were simply the results of the clash between the theoretical radicalism of the North and the historical realism or expediency of the South. For Southerners even today words like *abstraction, theoretical, general principle* seem to arouse all their loyalties to the Old South, all the defenses of their paranoid regionalism.[58]

Sometimes the Agrarians used this polemical distinction in its pure political form. "In order to study the Negro problem," Davidson once wrote, "the sociologist must abstract it. That is always the first act of science." [59] The observation is true enough, I suppose. In one sense or another, scientists must "abstract" what they want to study and comprehend; and presumably their results may be called "abstractions." To most people the process would seem fairly inoffensive; but to Davidson it must have meant a direct attack on the social stereotypes which (in these scientific days) have to be the chief validations for the ideals, sentiments, and habits of the Southern white. To deflect the attack, Davidson adopted the polarity of history and science.

> To the conservative white man such a [sociological] study will seem distorted and partial. But to all who would like for various reasons to avoid and ignore the lessons of history . . . the sociological study is a boon from Heaven, which they are much pleased to accept uncritically and to exploit without limit.[60]

[58] Owsley, "The Irrepressible Conflict," p. 79. Note Davidson, "First Fruits of Dayton," p. 896: "People do not like to think, of course, that the truth may be more sober and complex than a story in the New York *Times* or an editorial in the *Nation* would encourage them to believe. They prefer a simple myth to a complicated truth." See also James McBride Dabbs, *The Southern Heritage* (New York, 1958), pp. 170 ff., who argues that Southerners fear abstractions because they need to defend the unjustifiable abstraction, Negro-as-servant. Furthermore, the development of sociological abstractions means an investigation of and hence a threat to the stability of society.

[59] Donald Davidson, "Preface to Decision," *Sewanee Review*, LIII (1945), 396.

[60] Davidson, "Preface to Decision," pp. 396–97. Cf. Owsley ("The Irrepressible Conflict," pp. 62, 68, 77) on the complexity of the Negro problem: "the North can never understand the importance of slavery among the causes of the Civil War until the negro [sic] race covers the North as thickly as it does the lower South."

Warren used the same polarity to define the bad effect of Negro emigration from the South. Migrants, he said, forget the reality of their homeland and come under the influence of abstract social theories.

> Moreover, the [Negro] leader himself loses his comprehension of the actual situation; distance simplifies the scene of which he was once a part, and his efforts to solve its problems are transferred into a realm of abstractions. The case is not dissimilar to that of the immigrant labor leader or organizer who has in the past left the life he understood and come to this country whose life he did not wholly understand. Both have shown a tendency toward the doctrinaire.[61]

Signs of the anti-slavery polemic can also be found in even the high, remote places of Agrarian poetics and criticism. I take for an example this innocent, though headlong, section from the famous "Note in Ontology," in which Ransom is discovered, as it were, struggling to define the exact nature of the image. Considering his intense commitment to the concrete, some might consider the problem *ultra vires,* but the careful reader will notice that the ground of Ransom's description is a shadowy but none the less "concrete" picture of some sort of grapple between "science" and "image."

> Every property discovered in the image is a universal property, and nothing discovered in the image is marvellous in kind though

---

In Reconstruction the South "was turned over to the three millions of former slaves, some of whom could still remember the taste of human flesh and the bulk of them hardly three generations removed from cannibalism." "For the negroes [sic] were cannibals and barbarians, and therefore dangerous."

[61] Warren, "The Briar Patch," pp. 251 ff. Fletcher, "Education, Past and Present," p. 121, notes that Tuskegee and Hampton Institutes "are adapted to the capacity of that race and produce far healthier and happier specimens of it than all the institutions for 'higher learning' that we can give them."

it may be pinned down historically or statistically as a single instance. But there is this to be understood too: the image which is not remarkable in any particular property is marvellous in its assemblage of many properties, a manifold of properties, like a mine or a field, something to be explored for the properties; yet science can manage the image, which is infinite in properties, only by equating it to the one property with which the science is concerned; for science at work is always *a science,* and committed to a special interest.

In the remainder of the passage Ransom rather subtly drew into his general attack on science all the associations that go with attacks on freedom.

It is not by refutation but by abstraction that science destroys the image. It means to get its "value" out of the image, and we may be sure that it has no use for the image in its original state of freedom. People who are engrossed with their pet "values" become habitual killers. Their game is the images, or the things, and they acquire the ability to shoot them as far off as they can be seen, and do.[62]

Since being engrossed with values was certainly one characteristic of the Agrarians, it is hard to know what keeps them out of Ransom's company of villains. Perhaps their values were not "pet." But no doubt a question like that is simplistic, and one should rather note the extreme richness of Ransom's figure, by which he is able to move from defining a term to expressing all the feelings of his Southernness against those Northern doctrinaires who, in the name of freedom, would destroy all the ancient ways and manners, all the formal systems that man has invented to cope with his painful but inevitable state of sin.

[62] Ranson, "Poetry: A Note in Ontology," p. 176.

The power that the anti-slavery polemic exercised over the minds of the Agrarians must have been quite enormous. It could dominate not merely how they "read" the world but also how they managed works of art. Even the moral content of *Huckleberry Finn* could be affected by this patterning of Agrarian thought. In a discussion addressed to high school teachers, Brooks looked at the book from the notion that a person who recognizes all the complexity of the real world will select for attention such events as suggest "the personal and concrete" in human relations. For evidence he used Huck's feelings about Jim:

> Huck's own resolve to help the slave Jim escape comes as the result of concrete judgments and experiences. . . . It is the concrete experiences that shift Huck's ideas, not the power of an idea which changes his sentiments. Huck is the vagabond, not the reformer.[63]

Indeed, as Brooks said, "Huck is not the doctrinaire Abolitionist." But alas, in this unfortunate world, it is very difficult indeed to exercise such selectivity among symbolic systems as Brooks argued for. Mr. Phelps "comes into Jim every morning to read the Bible to him and pray with him." But he also holds Jim "in confinement as a runaway slave." [64] Of course Mr. Phelps is not to be condemned or disparaged because he cannot keep himself thinking about Jim as Jim, as the primordially fresh image of himself, himself alone. Everyone realizes the great power that is possessed by the low-order abstractions of folksay and individual observation, especially over men like Mr. Phelps. And indeed the

---

[63] Brooks, "The Teaching of the Novel: *Huckleberry Finn*," p. 213.
[64] Brooks, "The Teaching of the Novel: *Huckleberry Finn*," pp. 213–14.

abstraction of Jim to "runaway slave" may have more power
than most of the formulas by which common living is carried on.
"Privately," Davidson once remarked, the Southerner "does not
for one moment forget that the grandfathers [of Negro college
students], no matter how highly educated, were his or somebody's
grandfather's slaves." [65] "Negro as grandfather's slave" and "Negro as runaway slave" are quite as much abstractions as "Negro as
item in sociological study," "Negro as citizen," or "Negro as human being," putting aside for the moment all differences in level
of generalization. But perhaps the Agrarians did not see them as
abstractions because they somehow expressed or were charged
with "the strongly marked character of the South, that deep provincialism buttressed by homogeneity of stock and the stubborn
defenses of a group isolated by defeat in war." [66]

As Ransom once remarked, "the peculiar institution of slavery
set [the South] apart from the rest of the world, gave a spiritual
continuity to its many regions, and strengthened them under the
reinforcement of 'sectionalism,' which is regionalism on a somewhat extended scale." [67] At every stage of their development, including the last, the aesthetic stage, the thought of the Agrarians
was shaped and filled by their Southernness. The impelling
problem in their approach to experience was the material
changes in Southern life that, it seemed to them, were opening
the social system of the small town to turmoil and confusion.
"How may the little agrarian community resist the Chamber of
Commerce of its county seat, which is always trying to import

[65] Davidson, *The Attack on Leviathan,* p. 309. Cf. Warren, "The Briar Patch,"
pp. 260–61: The proper "place for the Negro is the small town or farm, where he
is less a problem and more a human being who is likely to find in agriculture and
domestic pursuits the happiness that his good nature and easy ways incline him to
as an ordinary function of his being."

[66] Josephine Pinckney, "Bulwarks Against Change," *Culture in the South,* ed.
W. T. Couch (Chapel Hill, N. C., 1935) , p. 41.

[67] Ransom, "The Aesthetics of Regionalism," p. 303.

some foreign industry that cannot be assimilated to the life-pattern of the community?"[68] was the central question of experience, to which they addressed their writing throughout their careers. They feared such a clash of values as the South experienced in the fifteen years before 1932, when it was "violently and suddenly" drawn into the national life,[69] and such as they themselves perhaps suffered as they moved on in the academic world, where, at least in their early career, they must have met many upholders of "cosmopolitanism, progressivism, industrialism, free trade, interregionalism, internationalism, eclecticism, liberal education, the federation of the world, or simple rootlessness."[70] It is sometimes hard to keep from thinking that the Agrarians just wanted to make the whole world take on the ineluctable and subtly graded social distinctions of the small town.

In their earliest days they found validations for their desire in the historical myth of the yeoman and in the fundamentalist myth of man's sin and nature's holiness. In the last stage of their career, when their influence on academics was greatest, they absorbed their earlier myths into the subtle and powerful theory of poetry as knowledge. And surely of all the critics who have collapsed the ancient Greek distinction between art and knowledge, none have found so few yet so subtle meanings in the high realm of poetry. For the Agrarians, poetry's vision of quality meant being mature, in the sense of having a capacity for "an ironical contemplation" that will not "over-simplify the human predicament," but will rather accept such things as the mysterious Old Testament God "of contingency, of the unpredictable,"

---

[68] *I'll Take My Stand*, p. xix. And note Ransom, "Reconstructed but Unregenerate," p. 20, where he acknowledges a struggle between the city and the village-rural cultures in the South in the Twenties.

[69] Warren, "A Note on Three Southern Poets," p. 113.

[70] Ransom, "The Aesthetics of Regionalism," pp. 293–94.

and "the wisdom of untruths or double truths in which the ancients often shadowed their greatest mysteries." [71] They explained the dissociation of sensibility as an effect of the disappearance, in their uniquely troubled days, of "a more stable way of life and a more ordered structure of ideas," which in the past had been the means of reconciling the discord of angelic and brute in man. The content of Agrarian poetic theory, which was drawn from their religious and historical myths, gave very powerful support to its central dogma, the disvaluation of abstraction. At the same time, all the connotations of "poetry" worked in support of the political and social ideals that were expressed in the content. Together content and connotations were combined in a most powerful instrument of conservative polemic. As Wimsatt has said, "The recognition of the whole [is] a refusal of abstractionism; it [entails] above all the difficult recognition, the acceptance of evil, and hence [is] no less a refusal of meliorism." [72] It is surely a real irony of this intractable world that the doctrine of the poem's organic wholeness should be transformed into a doctrine in which "poetry" becomes a name for the "whole" view of experience that insists not only on the meaningfulness of the notion of "sin" but also on its relevance to problems of social change and, above all, of social control. I find myself wanting to ask, as Professor Jones did, thirty years ago, "Must we never live because we have to die?" [73]

---

[71] Brooks, "Metaphysical Poetry and the Ivory Tower," p. 574; Warren, "John Crowe Ransom," pp. 96, 97; Davidson, "A Mirror for Artists," p. 30.

[72] Wimsatt, review of *Fugitives' Reunion* and *The Lasting South*, p. 98.

[73] Jones, "Amidst the Encircling Gloom," p. 411.

A Bibliography of Howard Mumford Jones

(From 1913 through December, 1961)

Books

America and French Culture, 1750–1848. Chapel Hill: University of North Carolina Press, 1927.

American Humanism: Its Meaning for World Survival. New York: Harper and Brothers, 1957.

The Bright Medusa. Urbana: University of Illinois Press, 1952.

Contemporary Southern Literature: An Outline for Individual and Group Study. Chapel Hill: University of North Carolina Press, 1928.

Education and World Tragedy. Cambridge: Harvard University Press, 1946.

The Frontier in American Fiction: Four Lectures on the Relation of Landscapes to Literature. Jerusalem: Magnes Press (Hebrew University), 1956.

Gargoyles and Other Poems. Boston: The Cornhill Company, 1918.

Guide to American Literature and Its Backgrounds Since 1890. Cambridge: Harvard University Press, 1953. Second edition, revised, 1959.

The Harp That Once—A Chronicle of the Life of Thomas Moore. New York: Henry Holt and Company, 1937.

Ideas in America. Cambridge: Harvard University Press, 1944.

The King in Hamlet. Austin: University of Texas Press, 1918.

The Life of Moses Coit Tyler. Ann Arbor: University of Michigan Press, 1933.

A Little Book of Local Verse. LaCrosse, Wisconsin: Inland Printing Company, 1915.

The Masque of Marsh and River. [LaCrosse, Wisconsin], 1915.

One Great Society: Humane Learning in the United States. New York: Harcourt, Brace and Company, 1959.

The Pursuit of Happiness. Cambridge: Harvard University Press, 1953.

Reflections on Learning. New Brunswick: Rutgers University Press, 1958.

The Theory of American Literature. Ithaca: Cornell University Press, 1948.

They Say the Forties. New York: Henry Holt and Company, 1937.

Writing a Technical Paper (with Donald H. Menzel and Lyle G. Boyd). New York: McGraw-Hill and Company, 1961.

Pamphlets

A Brief History of the United States (Kurze Geschichte der Vereinigten Staaten). [Printed for Distribution to German Prisoners of War in the United States, 1945].

A Brief Survey of American Schools (Eine Einführung in das Amerikanische Schulwesen). [Printed for Distribution to German Prisoners of War in the United States, 1945].

A Friendly Guide into the Graduate School. Birmingham, Alabama, 1946.

An Introduction to American Government (Eine Einführung in die Amerikanische Verfassung und Verwaltung). [Printed for Distribution to German Prisoners of War in the United States, 1945].

A Little Guide to America (Kleiner Führer durch Amerika). [Printed for Distribution to German Prisoners of War in the United States, 1945].

Editions

American Poetry, Percy H. Boynton, editor, with the assistance of Howard Mumford Jones *et al.* New York: Charles Scribner's Sons, 1918.

The College Reader, Robert M. Lovett and Howard Mumford Jones, editors. New York: Houghton Mifflin Company, 1936.

A Descriptive Catalogue of an Exhibition of Manuscripts and First Editions of Lord Byron . . . , compiled and annotated by R. H. Griffith and Howard Mumford Jones. Austin: University of Texas Press, 1924.

The Letters of Sherwood Anderson, selected and edited with an introduction and notes by Howard Mumford Jones, in association with Walter B. Rideout. Boston: Little, Brown and Company, 1953.

Literary History of the United States, Robert E. Spiller *et al.,* editors; Howard Mumford Jones *et al.,* associate editors. 3 vols. New York: Macmillan, 1948.

Major American Writers, Howard Mumford Jones and Ernest E. Leisy, editors. New York: Harcourt, Brace and Company, 1935. Second edition, 1945. Third edition, with Richard M. Ludwig, 1952.

Modern Minds: An Anthology of Ideas, Howard Mumford Jones, Richard M. Ludwig, and Marvin B. Perry, Jr., editors. Boston: D. C. Heath and Company, 1949. Second edition, 1954.

Oliver Wendell Holmes: Representative Selections, with introduction, bibliography, and notes by S. I. Hayakawa and Howard Mumford Jones. New York: American Book Company, 1939.

Plays of the Restoration and Eighteenth Century as They Were Acted at the Theaters-Royal by Their Majesties' Servants, Dougald MacMillan and Howard Mumford Jones, editors. New York: Henry Holt and Company, 1931.

Poems of Edgar Allan Poe, Howard Mumford Jones, editor. New York: Random House, 1929.

Primer of Intellectual Freedom, Howard Mumford Jones, editor. Cambridge: Harvard University Press, 1949.

Syllabus & Bibliography of Victorian Literature, Parts I, II, III, and IV, Howard Mumford Jones *et al.,* editors. Ann Arbor: Trial Edition, Printed by Brumfield and Brumfield, 1934.

Introductions

Army Life in a Black Regiment, by Thomas Wentworth Higginson. East Lansing: Michigan State University Press, 1960. Pp. vii-xvii.

Dark Laughter, by Sherwood Anderson. New York: Liveright Publishing Corporation, 1960. Pp. 1–7.

Davy Crockett: American Comic Legend, edited by Richard M. Dorson. New York: Rockland Press, 1939. Pp. xi-xiv.

The Expedition of Humphry Clinker, by Tobias Smollett. New York: E. P. Dutton and Company (Everyman's Library) , 1943. Pp. v-xi.

French Fiction, compiled by Albert L. Rabinovitz. (*New York University Index to Early American Periodical Literature, 1728–1870,* No. 5.) New York: William-Frederick Press, 1943. Pp. 8–9.

A History of American Literature: 1607–1765, by Moses Coit Tyler. Ithaca: Cornell University Press, 1949. Pp. v-viii.

The History of the Adventures of Joseph Andrews and His Friend Mr. Abraham Adams, by Henry Fielding. New York: The Modern Library, 1939. Pp. v-xxii. Slightly revised for the 1950 edition.

James Fenimore Cooper: A Re-Appraisal, by Lyman H. Butterfield *et al. New York History,* XXXV (October, 1954) , 369–73.

The Jew in the Literature of England to the End of the Nineteenth Century, by Montagu Frank Modder. Philadelphia: Jewish Publication Society of America, 1939. Pp. xiii-xvi.

The Rise of Silas Lapham, by William Dean Howells. New York: Oxford University Press, 1948. Pp. v-xi.

A Traveler from Altruria, by William Dean Howells. New York: Sagamore Press, 1957. Pp. 1–11.

Articles in Books

"The Aims of Literary Study" (with L. M. Rosenblatt and O. J. Campbell), *Modern American Vistas,* ed. H. W. Hintz and B. D. Grenbanier. New York: Dryden Press, 1940. Pp. 443–48.

"Cather, Willa," *Chambers's Encyclopedia* (new edition). New York: Oxford University Press, 1950. Vol. III, p. 182.

"The Comic Spirit and Victorian Sanity," *The Reinterpretation of Victorian Literature,* ed. Joseph E. Baker. Princeton: Princeton University Press, 1950. Pp. 20-32.

"Development in Humanistic Scholarship," *Both Human and Humane: The Humanities and Social Science in Graduate Education,* ed. C. E. Boewe and R. F. Nichols. Philadelphia: University of Pennsylvania Press, 1960. Pp. 81–93.

"The Drift to Liberalism in the American Eighteenth Century," *Authority and the Individual* (Harvard Tercentenary Publication). Cambridge: Harvard University Press, 1937. Pp. 319–48.

"Edgar Allan Poe," *The Unforgettable Americans,* ed. John A. Garraty. New York: Channel Press, 1960. Pp. 141-45.

"Education and One World," *Goals for American Education,* ed. Lyman Bryson *et al.* New York: Harper and Brothers, 1950. Pp. 213–33.

"1859 and the Idea of Crisis: General Introduction," *1859: Entering an Age of Crisis,* ed. Philip Appleman, William A. Madden, Michael Wolff. Bloomington: Indiana University Press, 1959. Pp. 13–28.

"The European Background," *Literary History of the United States,* ed. Robert E. Spiller *et al.* New York: Macmillan Company, 1948. Pp. 3–15.

"The European Background," *The Reinterpretation of American Literature,* ed. Norman Foerster. New York: Harcourt, Brace and Company, 1928. Pp. 62–82.

"The General Educational Stream of the Liberal Arts," *Readings for Citizens at War,* ed. Theodore Morrison *et al.* New York: Harper and Brothers, 1943. Pp. 358–67.

"Historical and Humanistic Values," *The Humanities: An Appraisal,* ed. Julian Harris. Madison: University of Wisconsin Press, 1950. Pp. 67–74.

"Holmes, Oliver Wendell, Senior," *Chambers's Encyclopedia* (new edition). New York: Oxford University Press, 1950. Vol. VII, p. 177.

"Horace Mann's Crusade," *America in Crisis: Fourteen Crucial Episodes in American History,* ed. Daniel Aaron. New York: Alfred A. Knopf, 1952. Pp. 91–107.

"A Humanist Looks at Science," *Science and the Modern Mind: A Symposium,* ed. Gerald Holton. Boston: Beacon Press, 1958. Pp. 100–8.

"The Humanities and the Common Reader," *The Humanities: An Appraisal,* ed. Julian Harris. Madison: University of Wisconsin Press, 1950. Pp. 22–39.

"The Image of the New World," *Elizabethan Studies and Other Essays in Honor of George F. Reynolds.* Boulder: University of Colorado Press, 1945. Pp. 62–84.

"The Land of Israel in the Anglo-Saxon Tradition," *Israel: Its Role in Civilization,* ed. Moshe Davis. New York: Harper and Brothers, 1956. Pp. 229–50.

"Lewis, Sinclair," *Chambers's Encyclopedia* (new edition). New York: Oxford University Press, 1950. Vol. VIII, pp. 498–99.

" 'Literature' and the Economic Order," *Saving American Capitalism: A Liberal Economic Program,* ed. Seymour E. Harris. New York: Alfred A. Knopf, 1948. Pp. 346–54.

"Literature as an Aid to Intercultural Understanding," *Conflicts of Power in Modern Culture,* ed. Lyman Bryson *et al.* New York: Harper and Brothers, 1947. Pp. 309–17.

"Literature: Truth, Fiction, and Reality," *Frontiers of Knowledge in the Study of Man,* ed. Lynn White, Jr. New York: Harper and Brothers, 1956.

"A Little Learning," *New World Writing, Ninth Mentor Selection.* New York: New American Library, 1956. Pp. 273–83.

"Longfellow," *American Writers on American Literature,* ed. John Albert Macy. New York: Liveright, 1931. Pp. 105–24.

"Longfellow, Henry Wadsworth," *Chambers's Encyclopedia* (new edition). New York: Oxford University Press, 1950. Vol. VIII, pp. 683–84.

"A Modest Caveat About the Curriculum," *Essays on the Teaching of English in Honor of Charles Swain Thomas,* ed. Robert M. Gay. Cambridge: Harvard University Press, 1940. Pp. 11–30.

"Murat, Achille," *Dictionary of American Biography,* ed. Dumas Malone. New York: Charles Scribner's Sons, 1934. Vol. XIII, pp. 339–40.

"Museums Are Not Encyclopaedias," *Art Across America.* Utica: Munson-Williams-Proctor Institute, 1960. Pp. 9–12.

"The Peccant Humors of the Graduate School," *The Inauguration of Rufus Carrollton Harris as President of Tulane University and a Series of Symposia on Current Trends in University Education.* New Orleans: American Printing Company, 1939. Pp. 164–78.

"The Pre-Raphaelites," *The Victorian Poets: A Guide to Research,* ed. Frederic E. Faverty. Cambridge: Harvard University Press, 1956. Pp. 161–95.

"Realism in American Literature," *American Story: The Age of Exploration to the Age of the Atom,* ed. Earl S. Miers. Great Neck, New York: Channel Press, 1956. Pp. 275–79.

"The Relation of the Humanities to General Education," *Proceedings of the Institute for Administrative Officers of Higher Institutions, Volume VI,* ed. William S. Gray. Chicago: University of Chicago Press, 1934. Pp. 39–52.

"Religious Education in the State Universities," *Religion and Education,* ed. Willard L. Sperry. Cambridge: Harvard University Press, 1945. Pp. 57–71.

"The Role of Higher Education in America," *A Handbook for College Teachers: An Informal Guide,* ed. Bernice B. Cronkhite. Cambridge: Harvard University Press, 1950. Pp. 216–32.

"Royster, James Finch," *Dictionary of American Biography,* ed. Dumas Malone. New York: Charles Scribner's Sons, 1935. Vol. XVI, pp. 212–13.

"The Study of American Culture," *The Harvard Reading List in American History.* Cambridge: Harvard University Press, 1949. Pp. 1–3.

"Tyler, Moses Coit," *Dictionary of American Biography,* ed. Dumas Malone. New York: Charles Scribner's Sons, 1936. Vol. XIX, pp. 92–93.

"We Shall Not Overthrow Communism by Suppressing the Critical and the Creative Mind," *Crucial Issues in Education,* ed. H. Ehlers. New York: Henry Holt, 1955. Pp. 36–39.

"Whittier, John Greenleaf," *Chambers's Encyclopedia* (new edition). New York: Oxford University Press, 1950. Vol. XIV, p. 573.

Articles in Periodicals

"A. E. Housman, Last of the Romans," *Double Dealer,* III (March, 1922), 136–41.

"Albrecht Von Haller and English Philosophy," *PMLA,* XL (March, 1925), 103–27.

"American Comment on George Sand, 1837–1848," *American Literature,* III (January, 1932) , 389–407.

"The American Concept of Academic Freedom," *American Scholar,* XIX (Winter, 1959–60) , 94–103.

"American Democratic Tradition," *Hadassah Newsletter,* November, 1953, pp. 4, 12.

"American Forces in Action," *Saturday Review of Literature,* XXX (April 26, 1947) , 15–16.

"American Literature and the Melting Pot," *Southwest Review,* XVI (Spring, 1941) , 329–46.

"American Malady," *Saturday Review of Literature,* XXXII (August 6, 1949) , 24–27.

"American Prose Style: 1700–1770," *Huntington Library Bulletin,* VI (November, 1934) , 115–51.

"The American Scholar Once More," *Harvard Alumni Bulletin,* XXXIX (March 26, 1937) , 732–39.

"American Scholarship and American Literature," *American Literature,* VIII (May, 1936) , 115–24.

"Amidst the Encircling Gloom," *Scribner's,* LXXXVII (April, 1930) , 405–11.

"Are the Cultural ABC's Softening Our Brains? A Debate [with William James Durant]," *Forum and Century,* LXXXIII (January, 1930) , 8, 14–18.

"Are Translators People?" *Pacific Spectator,* II (Autumn, 1948) , 479–84.

"Are We the East's Victims?" *Chicago Sun Book Week,* December 3, 1944, p. 49.

"Are Women's Colleges for Women?" *Agnes Scott Alumnae Quarterly,* XXIII (Spring, 1945) , 3, 7–15.

"Arnold, Aristocracy, and America," *American Historical Review,* XLIX (April, 1944) , 393–409.

"Art and General Education," *College Art Journal,* VII (Spring, 1948) , 157–60.

"Art as a Social Force," *College Art Journal,* X (Summer, 1951) , 317–32.

"The Attractions of Stupidity," *Tuftonian,* IV, N. S. (Summer, 1944) , 78–79.

"The Author of Two Byron Apocrypha," *Modern Language Notes,* XLI (February, 1926) , 129–31.

"Betrayal in American Education," *Scribner's,* XCIII (June, 1933) , 360–64.

"Books," *College and University,* XXVII (October, 1951) , 5–13.

"The Byron Centenary," *Yale Review,* XIII (July, 1924) , 730–45.

"A Case of Plight," *Atlantic Monthly,* CLXXXVII (June, 1951), 51–52.

"Certain Unalienable Rights," *Nation,* CLXXVII (December 12, 1953), 483–84.

"The Chinese State of America," *Common Ground,* I (Winter, 1941), 40–44.

"Citizen or Mechanic?" *Saturday Review of Literature,* XXVI (September 18, 1943), 3, 26.

"The Colonial Impulse: An Analysis of the 'Promotion' Literature of Colonization," *Proceedings of the American Philosophical Society,* XC (May 10, 1946), 131–61.

"The Confused Case of Upton Sinclair," *Atlantic Monthly,* CLXXVIII (August, 1946), 148, 150–51.

"The Creative Intelligence—The World of Ideas," *Harvard Educational Review,* XXII (Summer, 1952), 203–17.

"Critics and Intellectuals: The Fenced-In Variety," *Saturday Review of Literature,* XXIV (October 11, 1941), 3–4, 20.

"Dark Days Ahead," *Forum,* LXXXIV (October, 1930), 200–7.

"Desiderata in Colonial Literary History," *Publications of the Colonial Society of Massachusetts,* XXXII (1937), 428–39.

"The Direction and Future Responsibility of Graduate Training," *Proceedings of the Southern University Conference* (1947), pp. 103–15.

"A Discussion of Southern Poetry," *Westminster Magazine,* XIX (June, 1929), 5–13.

"Do Foreign Languages Improve Your Own," *Books Abroad,* XX (Winter, 1946), 19.

"Do You Know the Nature of an Oath?" *American Scholar,* XX (Autumn, 1951), 457–67.

"Faiths for a Complex World," *American Scholar,* XXVI (Autumn, 1957), 437–41.

"Fiction and the Art of Fiction," *New York Times Book Review,* July 28, 1946, pp. 2, 8.

"Fifty Guides to American Civilization," *Saturday Review of Literature,* XXIX (October 12, 1946), 15–16, 57.

"The Fine Arts Are Essential Too," *Independent School Bulletin,* Series of 1947–48, No. 3 (February, 1948), 7–9.

"Football in French; or, The Game Isn't What It Used to Be," *Harvard Alumni Bulletin,* LVII (October 9, 1954), 49.

"The Forgotten Professor," *Yale Review,* XX (Summer, 1931), 778–87.

"The Founders of Phi Beta Kappa," *Journal of Higher Education*, XXII (October, 1951), 381–83.

"The Future of Southern Culture," *Southwest Review*, XVI (Winter, 1931), 141–63.

" 'The Gay Science,' " *American Scholar*, XIV (Autumn, 1945), 393–404.

"The Generation of 1830," *Harvard Library Bulletin*, XIII (Autumn, 1959), 401–14.

"Gibbon, Wickedness, and the Atom Bomb," *Sequoia*, I (Winter, 1956), 1–7.

"Goal for Americans," *Saturday Evening Post*, CCXXXIV (July 1, 1961), 32–33, 62–64.

"Good People of New Orleans . . . ," *Tulanian*, XXV (June, 1952), 2–5, 15.

"Graduate English Study: Its Rationale," *Sewanee Review*, XXXVIII (October–December, 1930), 464–76; XXXIX (January–March, 1931), 68–79; XXXIX (April–June, 1931), 200–8.

"The Graduate School and the Problems of Training Teachers," *Journal of Proceedings and Addresses of the Association of Graduate Schools* (1949), 52–75.

"Graduate Work," *Saturday Review of Literature*, VI (August 3, 1929), 30.

"The Greatness of the Nineteenth Century," *Harvard Library Bulletin*, XI (Winter, 1957), 5–20.

"Have College Women Let Us Down?" *Mademoiselle*, XXXIV (January, 1952), 128, 155–56.

"The Historical West," *Dial*, LXVI (May 17, 1919), 508–9.

"How Much Academic Freedom?" *Atlantic Monthly*, CXCI (June, 1953), 36–40.

"A Humanist Looks at Science," *Daedalus*, LXXXVII (Winter, 1958), 102–10.

"The Humanities and Research," *Harvard Foundation for Advanced Study and Research News Letter*, May 16, 1955, pp. 6–8.

"Humanities Research as Creation," *The CEA Critic*, XVIII (January, 1956), 1, 6.

"The Idea of a Franciscan Academy," *Americas*, I (October, 1944), 160–65.

"Ideas, History, Technology," *Technology and Culture*, I (Winter, 1959), 20–27.

"If I Were a Scandinavian," *American Scandinavian Review*, XXXV (Summer, 1947), 135–38.

"The Image of the Scholar," *Mills Quarterly*, XXXIX (February, 1957), 83–87.

"An Impartial Pro-Democrat," *Nation*, CLXXXI (November 12, 1955), 424.

"The Importation of French Books in Philadelphia, 1750–1800," *Modern Philology*, XXXII (November, 1934), 157–77.

"The Importation of French Literature in New York City, 1750–1800," *Studies in Philology*, XXVIII (October, 1931), 235–51.

"The Influence of Byron," *Texas Review*, IX (April, 1924), 170–96.

"The Influence of European Ideas in Nineteenth-Century America," *American Literature*, VII (November, 1935), 241–73.

"Inside a Tradition," *Catholic World*, CLIX (July, 1944), 366–67.

"Is There a Southern Renaissance?" *Virginia Quarterly Review*, VI (April, 1930), 184–97.

"James Fenimore Cooper and the Hudson River School," *Magazine of Art*, XLV (October, 1952), 243–51.

"A Letter to the Editors of *American Literature*," *American Literature*, XII (March, 1940), 108.

"The Letter Writers of Seventeenth-Century Virginia," *Shenandoah*, VIII (Summer, 1957), 16–23.

"The Letters of Sherwood Anderson," *Atlantic Monthly*, CXCI (June, 1953), 30–33.

"The Limits of Contemporary Criticism," *Saturday Review of Literature*, XXIV (September 6, 1941), 3–4, 17.

"Literary History and Literary Plenty," *Saturday Review of Literature*, XXV (October 31, 1942), 5–6.

"Literary Scholarship and Contemporary Criticism," *English Journal*, XXIII (November, 1934), 740–58.

"Literature and Orthodoxy in Boston after the Civil War," *American Quarterly*, I (Summer, 1949), 149–65.

"The Literature of Virginia in the Seventeenth Century," *American Academy of Arts and Sciences Memoirs*, XIX, Part 2 (1946), 3–47.

"Local Literature and the State of Michigan," *Michigan Alumnus Quarterly Review*, XL (March, 1934), 28–32.

"The Longfellow Nobody Knows," *Outlook*, CXLIX (August 8, 1928), 577–79, 586.

"Masterpieces Weekly," *Atlantic Monthly*, CLXXVIII (October, 1946), 152, 154.

"Men—Not Cattle," *Atlantic Monthly*, CLXIII (April, 1939), 492–98.

"Methods in Contemporary Biography," *English Journal*, XXI (January, 1932), 43–51; (February, 1932), 113–22.

"A Minor Prometheus," *Freeman,* VI (October 25, 1922) , 153–55.

"A Mississippi Holiday," *Mid-West Quarterly,* III (October, 1915) , 45–48.

"Mother Love Is Not Enough," *Saturday Review of Literature,* XXVII (October 28, 1944) , 16.

"New England Dilemma," *Atlantic Monthly,* CLXV (April, 1940) , 458–67.

"The New Frontier Recognized—and in an Old Tradition," *Life,* L (June 23, 1961) , 58–59.

"Nine Glimpses of Ourselves," *Saturday Review,* XXXVIII (February 12, 1955) , 11–12.

"Nobility Wanted," *Atlantic Monthly,* CLXIV (November, 1939) , 641–49.

"Notes on the Knowledge of French in Eighteenth-Century America," *Studies in Philology,* XXIV (July, 1927) , 426–37.

"On Leaving the South," *Scribner's,* LXXXIX (January, 1931) , 17–27.

"On the Conflict Between the 'Liberal Arts' and the 'Schools of Education' " (Report of the Committee on the Teaching Profession of the American Academy of Arts and Sciences: Frank Keppel, Robert Ulich, Howard M. Jones, Chairman) , *ACLS Newsletter,* V, No. 3, n. d., 17–38.

"On Rereading *Great Expectations,*" *Southwest Review,* XXXIX (Autumn, 1954) , 328–35.

"Opportunities and Support for College and University Libraries," *College and Research Libraries,* XIV (January, 1953) , 9–21.

"Origins of the Colonial Idea in England," *Proceedings of the American Philosophical Society,* LXXXV (September 30, 1942) , 448–65.

"The Orphan Child of the Curriculum," *English Journal* (College Edition) , XXV (May, 1936) , 376–88.

" 'Outside Look' at the AAUP," *Publishers' Weekly,* CLXIX (June 25, 1956) , 2735–39.

"Patriotism—but How?" *Atlantic Monthly,* CLXII (November, 1938) , 585–92.

"Patterns of Writing and the Middle Class," *American Literature,* XXIII (November, 1951) , 293–301.

"Paul Green," *Southwest Review,* XIV (Autumn, 1928) , 1–8.

"The Place of the Humanities in American Education," *English Leaflet,* XXXVII (June, 1938) , 81–95.

"Poe, 'The Raven,' and the Anonymous Young Man," *Western Humanities Review,* IX (Spring, 1955) , 127–38.

"Portrait of a Mid-Westerner Lonely but Happy, Simple but Complex," *New York Herald Tribune Book Review,* April 12, 1953, pp. 1, 19.

"Possible Changes in Policies Concerning Admission to Graduate Schools," *Bostonia,* XVII (April, 1944) , 37–38, 73–74.

"Press Neglect of the Humanities," *Nieman Reports,* XI (April, 1957) , 11–12.

"Professor Babbitt Cross-Examined," *New Republic,* LIV (March 21, 1928) , 158–60.

"Prose and Pictures: James Fenimore Cooper," *Tulane Studies in English,* III (1952) , 133–54.

"Pro-Semite," *America-Israel Bulletin,* I (December 1, 1956) , 1, 4.

"Publishing Time, Literary Time," *New York Times Book Review,* June 29, 1947, pp. 1, 24.

"The Recovery of New England" (within "The Withering of New England") , *Atlantic Monthly,* CLXXXV (April, 1950) , 51–53.

"Reflections in a Library," *Saturday Review,* XLIII (April 9, 1960) , 34, 52–53.

"Relief from Murder," *Atlantic Monthly,* CLXII (July, 1938) , 79–85.

"Remarks on Chair Day," *Harvard Alumni Bulletin,* LXIII (June 10, 1961) , 676–77.

"Remarks on Concluding a Course in Recent and Contemporary American Literature," *Archive,* LXVII (December, 1954) , 5–11.

"The Renaissance Man Today," *Saturday Review,* XLII (June 20, 1959) , 10–12.

"Salvaging Our Literature," *American Scholar,* II (May, 1933) , 347–62.

"The Scholar and the World," *Journal of Higher Education,* XXII (October, 1951) , 345–52, 399.

"The Scholar Can't Have It Both Ways," *Saturday Review of Literature,* XXVII (June 17, 1944) , 22.

"Sculpture of Nathaniel Burwash," *Chrysalis,* VII (1954) , 3–12.

"The Service of the University," *ACLS Newsletter,* VII (Winter, 1956–57) , 3–13.

"Shaw as a Victorian," *Victorian Studies,* I (December, 1957) , 165–72.

"The Social Responsibility of Scholarship," *PMLA,* LXIV (March, 1949) , 37–44.

"Sousa," *New Republic,* XXXVIII (February 27, 1924) , 14–15.

"The Southern Legend," *Scribner's,* LXXXV (May, 1929) , 538–42.

"The Student South," *New Student,* VIII (October, 1928) , 12–13.

"Telemachus and Ulysses," *Texas Quarterly,* I (February, 1958) , 42–54.

"Theodore Dreiser: A Pioneer Whose Fame Is Secure," *New York Times Book Review,* January 13, 1946, p. 6.

"They Knew Not Joseph," *Atlantic Monthly,* CLXXVII (April, 1946), 120–23.

"This Business of Teaching," *Harvard Educational Review,* XIV (March, 1944), 136–48.

"Those Eminent Victorians," *Scribner's,* XCIII (February, 1933), 89–93.

"The Three Traditions," *Texas Publication of the Conference of College Teachers of English,* XVII (December, 1952), 13–22.

"Tombs of the Tar Heels," *Carolina Play-Book,* I (June, 1928), 9–13.

"Tribalism," *Atlantic Monthly,* CLXX (October, 1942), 87–93.

"The Two Harvards," *Harvard Alumni Bulletin,* XLVI (May 13, 1944), 461–62.

"The Undergraduate and Political Responsibility," *American Scholar,* XVII (Autumn, 1948), 395–406.

"Undergraduates on Apron Strings," *Atlantic Monthly,* CXCVI (October, 1955), 45–48.

"The Vultures of Peace," *Saturday Review,* XXXI (February 21, 1948), 9–10, 24–25.

"What Has Become of Laughter?" *Freeman,* VI (January 24, 1923), 467–69.

"What Is Literary History?" *Saturday Review of Literature,* XIV (August 8, 1936), 10.

"What Kind of Science?" *Harvard Alumni Bulletin,* LXI (October 25, 1958), 113–15.

"What's the Matter with Literary Scholarship?" *Saturday Review of Literature,* XIX (March 18, 1939), 3–4.

"What's Wrong with *The Nation?*" *Nation,* CXXVII (December 19, 1928), 678–79.

"Whitman and the Immigrant: 'Salut au Monde,'" *Saturday Review of Literature,* XIII (November 30, 1935), 9.

"Whittier Reconsidered," *Essex Institute Historical Collections,* XCIII (October, 1957), 231–46.

"Who Remembers Sparta?" *Columbia Engineering Quarterly,* Special Issue, October, 1954, pp. 22–25, 40–42.

"William Ellery Leonard," *Double Dealer,* VIII (May, 1926), 332–38.

"William Vaughan Moody: An American Milton," *Double Dealer,* IV (August, 1922), 79–86.

"Writers and American Values," *New York Times Book Review,* August 5, 1945, p. 2.

"Wycherly, Montaigne, Tertullian, and Mr. Summers," *Modern Language Notes,* XLVII (April, 1932) , 244–45.

Addresses

"The American Concept of Academic Freedom," *The Conference on University Education and Student Life.* Ithaca: Cornell University Press, 1958. Pp. 28–38.

"The Assault on Culture" (excerpts from a commencement address at the University of Colorado) , *Colorado Alumnus,* XXVIII (July, 1938) , 7–8, 9–10.

"The Bible from a Literary Point of View," *Five Essays on the Bible: Papers Read at the 1960 Annual Meeting of the American Council of Learned Societies.* New York: American Council of Learned Societies, 1960. Pp. 45–59.

Books and the Independent Mind (address at the dedication of the Memorial Library) . Madison: University of Wisconsin, 1954. Pp. 1–22.

"Campus: Echo or Criticism?" (excerpts from an address to the National Association of Student Personnel Administrators) , *Harvard Alumni Bulletin,* LVIII (November 5, 1955) , 161–64.

"Commencement Behind the Barbed Wire" (address at Fort Getty School for German Prisoners of War) , *Harvard Alumni Bulletin,* XLVIII (October 20, 1945) , 120–22.

"Education for the Professions" (excerpts from an address at Case Institute) , *Case Alumnus,* XXXV (March, 1956) , 9–11, 23.

Emerson Once More: The Ware Lecture Delivered at the Emerson Sesquicentennial Observance Sponsored by the American Unitarian Association in Concord, Massachusetts, May 25, 1953. Boston: Beacon Press, [1953]. Pp. 1–25.

"The Faith That Is in You," *Bulletin of the University of Wisconsin: Address Given During the Ninetieth Annual Commencement of the University of Wisconsin May 28–29, 1943.* [Madison: University of Wisconsin Press, 1943.]

"The Fear of Books," *Addresses Made Before the Friends of Howard Tilton Memorial Library of Tulane University.* New Orleans: Friends of the Howard Tilton Memorial Library, 1944. Pp. 5–15.

"The Fetish of the Classics" (address at a meeting of the Northwestern Teachers Association of North Carolina), *English Journal* (Regular Edition), XVIII (March, 1929), 221–39.

"The Future of the Academy" (presidential address), *Proceedings of the American Academy of Arts and Sciences,* LXXV (December, 1944), 131–39.

"The General Educational Stream of the Liberal Arts," *What Is a University? Four Addresses by Howard Mumford Jones, James Bryant Conant, Harlow Shapley, and James Phinney Baxter, 3rd.* Cambridge: Harvard University Press, 1938. Pp. 11–33.

"The Iron String" (address at a Leverett House Junior-Senior Dinner), *Harvard Alumni Bulletin,* LII (April 8, 1950), 540–43.

"Justice Fielding and the Novel" (address at the Law School of New York University), *Journal of Public Law,* VII (Spring, 1958), 162–74.

"Looking Around" (address at the College of Business Administration, the Tulane University of Louisiana), *Harvard Business Review,* XXXI (January–February, 1953), 133–34, 136, 138, 140, 142.

"The Mysterious West" (address at the Annual Dinner of the Iranian Institute), *Bulletin of the Iranian Institute,* VI–VII (December, 1946), 133–38.

"The Place of Books and Reading in Modern Society" (address at the Fifty-fifth Annual Conference of the American Library Association), *Bulletin of the American Library Association,* XXVII (December 15, 1933), 585–93.

Report from Outside (Commencement address at Skidmore College). N.p., 1961. Pp. 1–11.

"Republican Humanism" (Horace M. Kallen Lecture for 1953), *Social Research,* XXI (Summer, 1954), 159–78.

The Scholar As American (Abbott Lawrence Lowell Inaugural Lecture). Cambridge: Printed and Distributed by the President's Office of Harvard University, 1960.

"Scholarship and Democratic Faith" (Commencement address at the University of Kansas City), *University Review,* IX (Autumn, 1942), 12–18.

["To My Way of Thinking . . ."], *Addresses on the Bill of Rights Delivered in Commemoration of Its 150th Anniversary* . . . . Boston: Published by the Civil Liberties Committee of Massachusetts, 1939. Pp. 8–22.

["Trends of Scholarship"], *Trends of Scholarship in the Modern Language Association.* New York: Printed by the Authority of the Executive Council of the Modern Language Association of America, 1937. Pp. 15–25.

"Two Founders' Day Messages for Badger Alumni," *Wisconsin Alumnus,* LII (March, 1951), 19.

"What Our Society Is and Is Not—A Definition," *America-Israel Bulletin,* I (May 1, 1957) , 1, 6.

"What's Past Is Prologue," *ACLS Newsletter,* VI (Spring, 1955) , 18–24.

Poetry in Books and Periodicals

"Astronomy," *New Republic,* XXV (January 19, 1921) , 224.

"At the Dunes," *Forum,* LVI (August, 1916) , 158–61. Excerpt, "Night on the Dunes," *Current Opinion,* LXI (September, 1916) , 198.

"The Case Is Closed," *Independent,* LXXXII (June 28, 1915) , 533.

"The Convocation Ode," *The Quarter-Centennial Celebration of the University of Chicago June 2 to 6, 1916: A Record,* ed. David Allan Robertson. Chicago: University of Chicago Press, 1918. Pp. 110–19.

"Dead March," *American Magazine,* LXXXII (November, 1916) , 87.

"Doing Double Duty," *Harvard Alumni Bulletin,* LXIII (March 18, 1961) , 465.

"Economics," *American Magazine,* LXXV (April, 1913) , 23.

"Faculty Club" ("The Social Scientist," "The Philosopher," "The Psychoanalyst," "The Historian," "The Anthropologist") , *Atlantic Monthly,* CCIII (January, 1959) , 89.

"Fisherman," *Freeman,* VI (February 7, 1923) , 520.

"Five sonnets from *They Say the Forties," New Michigan Verse,* ed. Carl Edwin Burklund. Ann Arbor: University of Michigan Press, 1940. Pp. 13–17.

"The Garden in September," *Midland,* II (February, 1916) , 39–40.

"The Great Lakes: A Sonnet Sequence," *Canadian Magazine,* XLIII (June, 1914) , 173–74.

"Heartbreak," *Lyric,* VI (April, 1926) , 11–15.

"The Last Ride of Don Quixote," *University of California Chronicle,* XXIV (July, 1922) , 273–86.

"Librarians," *Literary Digest,* LV (July 21, 1917) , 34.

"Love Divided: A Sequence of Sonnets," *Midland,* I (September, 1915) , 281–308.

"Meditation on the Humanities," *Saturday Review,* XXXIX (May 5, 1956) , 24.

"November on the Lake Michigan Dunes," *Poetry,* IX (December, 1916) , 125–27.

"On a School Anthology," *University of Chicago Magazine,* VIII (June, 1916), 380.

"Plows," *Survey,* XXXI (February 21, 1914), 651.

"A Song of Butte," *Contemporary Verse,* VI (November, 1918), 73–74.

"Survival: Notes Out of Greece" ("To a Peloponnesian Ant," "The Astonished Fly," "To an Athenian Cockroach," "An Attic Donkey," "Nest at Knossos"), *Texas Quarterly,* II (Winter, 1959), 32–35.

"Tell Him," *Saturday Review of Literature,* XVI (May 8, 1937), 12.

"They That Dwell in Shadow," *Midland,* VI (January–March, 1920), 24.

"To a Jazz Dancer," *The Choice of the Crowd,* ed. Charles J. Finger. Fayetteville, Arkansas: Golden Horseman Press, 1922. Pp. 12–13.

"Two University Sketches" ("Librarians," "Phonology"), *Midland,* III (June, 1917), 185–91.

"University Sketches" ("The Professor Muses," "Aphrodite"), *Poetry,* VIII (April, 1916), 7–12.

Short Stories

"Concerto in A-Flat," *The Smart Set,* LXIV (April, 1921), 99–109.

"Drigsby's Universal Regulator," *Midland,* VI (September, 1920), 157–73, and *Texas Review,* VI (January, 1921), 150–62.

"The Education of Paul Gant," *Smart Set,* LVIII (February, 1919), 107–14.

"His Mother," *Smart Set,* LIX (June, 1919), 113–20.

"Mr. Ribbett Finds the Purple Field," *Woman's Viewpoint,* III (July, 1925), 24–25, 44–45, 47, 51.

"Mrs. Drainger's Veil," *Smart Set,* LVII (December, 1918), 61–75.

"The Social Engineer" (with Mildred Patterson), *Woman's Viewpoint,* II (March, 1925), 14–15, 72–73, 75.

Plays

"The Fascinating Mr. Denby: A Comedy for Four Women" (with Selwin Sage), *Drama,* XIV (February, 1924), 175–77, 187. Also published separately, New York: Fitzgerald Publishing Corporation, 1935.

"Keddra: A Play in One Act," *University of California Chronicle,* XXIII (April, 1921), 169–208.

"The Shadow," *Wisconsin Plays, Second Series.* New York: B. W. Huebsch, 1918. Pp. 87–136.

Translations

Hermit Songs, by Samuel Barber. New York: G. Schirmer, 1954.

Latin Poetry in Verse Translation, ed. L. R. Lind, with translations by Howard Mumford Jones *et al.* Boston: Houghton, Mifflin Company, 1957.

Medieval Latin Lyrics, by Philip Schuyler Allen. Chicago: University of Chicago Press, 1931.

North Sea, by Heinrich Heine. Chicago: Open Court, 1916.

The Romanesque Lyric: Studies in Its Background and Development from Petronius to the Cambridge Songs, 50–1050, by Philip Schuyler Allen, with renderings into English verse by Howard Mumford Jones. Chapel Hill: University of North Carolina Press, 1928.

Book Reviews

Abramowitz, Isidore. *The Great Prisoners. Chicago Sun Book Week,* March 31, 1946, p. 3.

Adams, John Donald. *The Shape of Books to Come. Saturday Review of Literature,* XXVII (December 2, 1944), 25.

Agar, Herbert. *The Formative Years. Yale Review,* XXXVI (Summer, 1947), 725–27.

Aldridge, John W. *In Search of Heresy. Saturday Review,* XXXIX (May 26, 1956), 21, 33.

Altick, Richard D. *The Scholar Adventurers. Graduate School Record* (Ohio State University), IV (March, 1951), 10–12.

America's Lost Plays, Vols. 1, 2, 3. American Speech, XV (December, 1940), 427–30.

———, *Vols. 4, 5. American Speech,* XVI (February, 1941), 51–52.

———, *Vols. 10, 11, 12. American Speech,* XVI (October, 1941), 212–15.

————, *Vol. 14. American Speech,* XVI (December, 1941) , 298–300.

————, *Vol. 15. American Speech,* XVII (February, 1942) , 57–58.

————, *Vol. 16. American Speech,* XVII (February, 1942) , 58.

————, *Vol. 17. American Speech,* XVII (October, 1942) , 184–85.

————, *Vols. 18, 19. American Speech,* XVII (December, 1942) , 263–64.

————, *Vol. 20. American Speech,* XVII (February, 1943) , 56–57.

Amory, Cleveland. *The Proper Bostonians. New York Times Book Review,* October 19, 1947, p. 7.

Armstrong, William M. *E. L. Godkin and American Foreign Policy. Nation,* CLXXXIII (November 24, 1956) , 463.

Ashburn, Frank D. *Peabody of Groton: A Portrait. New York Times Book Review,* November 5, 1944, p. 6.

Ashton, Helen. *Letty London. Saturday Review of Literature,* XXXIV (October 6, 1951) , 34.

Aydelotte, Frank. *The Development of Honors Work in American Colleges and Universities. Key Reporter,* IX (Autumn, 1944) , 6.

Babbitt, Irving. *On Being Creative and Other Essays. Modern Language Notes,* XLVIII (June, 1933) , 406–8.

Bailey, Marcia Egerton. *A Lesser Hartford Wit, Dr. Elihu Hubbard Smith. Modern Language Notes,* XLV (January, 1930) , 43–45.

Barnes, Margaret Ayer. *Within This Present. Virginia Quarterly Review,* X (April, 1934) , 280–83.

Basler, Roy P. *Abraham Lincoln: His Speeches and Writings. American Literature,* XIX (March, 1947) , 90–91.

Basso, Hamilton. *In Their Own Image. Virginia Quarterly Review,* XI (July, 1935) , 452–57.

Bishop, John Peale, *Act of Darkness. Virginia Quarterly Review,* XI (July, 1935) , 452–57.

Blanshard, Paul. *The Irish and Catholic Power: An American Interpretation. Nation,* CLXXVIII (January 2, 1954) , 14–15.

Bliven, Bruce, and Mezerik, A. G. (eds.) . *What the Informed Citizen Needs to Know. New York Times Book Review,* November 11, 1945, p. 4.

Bode, Carl. *The Anatomy of American Popular Culture. Journal of American Folklore,* LXXIII (April–June, 1960) , 163–64.

Bowers, David (ed.) . *Foreign Influences in American Life: Essays and Critical Bibliographies. New England Quarterly,* XVIII (December, 1945) , 547–48.

Bowle, John. *Politics and Opinion in the Nineteenth Century. Yale Review,* XLIV (Autumn, 1954) , 147–50.

Boynton, Percy H. *Literature and American Life. American Literature,* IX (March, 1937) , 97–98; also *International Journal of Ethics,* XLVII (April, 1937) , 393–95.

Brickell, Herschel (ed.). *O. Henry Memorial Award Prize Stories of 1942. Saturday Review of Literature,* XXV (December 19, 1942) , 16.

Bridenbaugh, Carl. *Myths and Realities: Societies of the Colonial South. William and Mary Quarterly,* X (April, 1953) , 263–67.

Bromfield, Louis. *Mrs. Parkington. Saturday Review of Literature,* XXVI (January 9, 1943) , 9.

Brooks, Howard L. *Prisoners of Hope. Christian Register,* CXXI (May, 1942) , 175.

Brooks, Van Wyck. *The Life of Emerson. Virginia Quarterly Review,* VIII (July, 1932) , 439–42.

———. *New England: Indian Summer, 1865–1915. Saturday Review of Literature,* XXII (August 17, 1940) , 3–4, 14–15.

———. *Opinions of Oliver Allston. Saturday Review of Literature,* XXIV (November 15, 1941) , 5, 20.

Buck, Pearl S. *Dragon Seed. Saturday Review of Literature,* XXV (January 17, 1942) , 5.

Burlingame, Roger. *Of Making Many Books. New York Times Book Review,* October 27, 1946, pp. 4, 38.

Burnett, Whit (ed.). *This Is My Best. Saturday Review of Literature,* XXV (November 7, 1942) , 14.

Burton, Katherine. *Celestial Homespun. Saturday Review of Literature,* XXVI (May 29, 1943) , 26.

Campbell, Killis. *The Mind of Poe and Other Studies. Journal of English and Germanic Philology,* XXXIII (April, 1934) , 313–14.

Canby, Henry Seidel. *American Memoir. New York Times Book Review,* August 24, 1947, pp. 1, 25.

———. *Classic Americans. American Literature,* IV (November, 1932) , 311–13.

Canfield, Dorothy. *Bonfire. Virginia Quarterly Review,* X (April, 1934) , 280–83.

Cater, Harold Dean. *Henry Adams and His Friends. Yale Review,* XXXVI (Summer, 1947) , 725–27.

Cather, Willa. *Obscure Destinies. Virginia Quarterly Review,* VIII (October, 1932) , 591–94.

――――. *The Novels and Stories of Willa Cather. Saturday Review of Literature,* XVIII (August 6, 1938) , 3–4.

Cecil, Lord David. *Poets and Story-Tellers: A Book of Critical Essays. Saturday Review of Literature,* XXXII (April 16, 1949) , 16.

Changing Patterns in American Civilization. American Literature, XXII (November, 1950) , 373.

Chew, Samuel C. *Byron in England. New Republic,* XL (October 1, 1924) , 6–7.

Clark, Harry Hayden (ed.) . *The Poems of Freneau. Saturday Review of Literature,* VI (January 18, 1930) , 651.

Cohen, I. Bernard. *Benjamin Franklin. American Scholar,* XXIII (Winter, 1953–54) , 123.

Commager, Henry Steele (ed.) . *America in Perspective. Saturday Review of Literature,* XXX (December 20, 1947) , 11.

――――. *The American Mind. Yale Review,* XXXIX (Summer, 1950) , 723–26.

Conroy, Jack. *The Disinherited. Virginia Quarterly Review,* X (April, 1934) , 280–83.

Cooke, Delmar Gross. *William Dean Howells, A Critical Study. Freeman,* VII (April 25, 1923) , 163.

Coon, Horace. *Triumph of the Eggheads. Nation,* CLXXXI (November 12, 1955) , 424.

A Correlated Curriculum: A Report of the Committee on Correlation of the National Council of Teachers of English. American Literature, IX (November, 1937) , 375–80.

Craig, Hardin. *Literary Study and the Scholarly Profession. Annals of the American Academy of Political and Social Science,* CCXLI (September, 1945) , 182–83.

Cross, Wilbur, and MacAfee, Helen (eds.) . *The Yale Review Anthology. Saturday Review of Literature,* XXV (December 5, 1942) , 36.

Curtis, Charles P., Jr., and Greenslet, Ferris (eds.) . *The Practical Cogitator. New York Times Book Review,* December 2, 1945, p. 6.

Davis, H. L. *Winds of Morning. Saturday Review of Literature,* XXXV (January 19, 1952) , 16–17.

De Voto, Bernard. *The World of Fiction. Saturday Review of Literature,* XXXIII (April 15, 1950) , 46.

De Vries, Louis Peter. *The Nature of Poetic Literature. Modern Language Notes,* XLVI (December, 1931) , 529–32.

Diekhoff, John S. *The Domain of the Faculty in Our Expanding Colleges. Annals of the American Academy of Political and Social Science,* CCCVIII (November, 1956) , 214–15.

Donham, Wallace Brett. *Education for Responsible Living. New York Times Book Review,* May 6, 1945, p. 4.

Doremus, T. E. *Flaw Dexter. Saturday Review of Literature,* XXX (June 21, 1947) , 31.

Dos Passos, John. *The Head and Heart of Thomas Jefferson. American Literature,* XXVII (November, 1955) , 428–29.

———. *Number One. Saturday Review of Literature,* XXVI (March 6, 1943) , 7–8.

Dunn, Esther Cloudman. *Pursuit of Understanding. New York Times Book Review,* December 30, 1945, p. 4.

Edel, Leon. *The Psychological Novel, 1900–1950. Saturday Review,* XXXVIII (April 23, 1955) , 18–19.

Eliot, T. S. *Essays Ancient and Modern. Saturday Review of Literature,* XIV (September 19, 1936) , 13.

Ellison, Joseph W. *Tusitala of the South Seas. Saturday Review,* XXXVI (August 8, 1953) , 11.

Erskine, John. *The Memory of Certain Persons. New York Times Book Review,* April 6, 1947, pp. 3, 29.

Eytan, Walter. *The First Ten Years. America-Israel Bulletin,* II (April 10, 1958) , 3–4.

Farrell, James T. *Literature and Morality. Saturday Review of Literature,* XXX (September 6, 1947) , 18–19.

Faulkner, William. *Knight's Gambit. Saturday Review of Literature,* XXXII (November 5, 1949) , 17.

———. *Pylon. Virginia Quarterly Review,* XI (July, 1935) , 452–57.

Fenton, Charles. *Stephen Vincent Benet. Saturday Review,* XLI (October 25, 1958) , 16.

Ferguson, DeLancey. *Mark Twain: Man and Legend. American Speech,* XVIII (December, 1943) , 286–87.

——— (ed.) . *Stevenson's Letters to Charles Baxter. Saturday Review,* XXXIX (June 9, 1956) , 19.

Fine, Benjamin. *Democratic Education. Journal of Higher Education,* XVII (April, 1946) , 220.

————. *Our Children Are Cheated. New York Times Book Review,* October 26, 1947, pp. 10, 12.

Fisher, Vardis. *Passions Spin the Plot. Virginia Quarterly Review,* X (April, 1934) , 280–83.

Fisk, Ethel F. (ed.) . *The Letters of John Fiske. Pennsylvania Magazine of History and Biography,* LXVI (January, 1942) , 139.

Fleming, Barry. *Siesta. Virginia Quarterly Review,* XI (July, 1935) , 452–57.

Floan, Howard R. *The South in Northern Eyes, 1831–1861. Mississippi Valley Historical Review,* XLV (June, 1958) , 145–47.

Foerster, Norman (ed.) . *The Reinterpretation of American Literature. Modern Language Notes,* XLV (January, 1930) , 43–45.

Foff, Arthur. *Glorious in Another Day. Saturday Review of Literature,* XXXI (January 24, 1948) , 18.

Fuller, Edmund. *Man in Modern Fiction. Saturday Review,* XLI (May 17, 1958) , 34–35.

Furness, Clifton Joseph. *Walt Whitman's Workshop. Modern Language Notes,* XLV (January, 1930) , 43–45.

Garrod, H. W. *Poetry and the Criticism of Life. Modern Language Notes,* XLVI (December, 1931) , 529–32.

Givens, Charles G. *The Doctor's Pills Are Stardust. Saturday Review of Literature,* XVIII (July 16, 1938) , 15.

Glasgow, Ellen. *A Certain Measure. Saturday Review of Literature,* XXVI (October 16, 1943) , 20.

————. *In This Our Life. Saturday Review of Literature,* XXIII (March 29, 1941) , 5–6.

————. *The Sheltered Life. Virginia Quarterly Review,* VIII (October, 1932) , 591–94.

————. *The Works of Ellen Glasgow (Virginia Edition) . New York Herald Tribune Books,* July 24, 1938, pp. 1–2.

Goris, Jan-Albert. *Strangers Should Not Whisper. New York Times Book Review,* February 18, 1945, p. 7.

Gray, James. *Wings of Great Desire. Saturday Review of Literature,* XVIII (September 3, 1938) , 10.

Green, Paul. *Lonesome Road. Yale Review,* XVI (July, 1927) , 802–4.

Greenlaw, Edwin. *The Province of Literary History. Modern Language Notes,* XLVI (December, 1931) , 529–32.

Greenslet, Ferris. *The Lowells and Their Seven Worlds. Harvard Alumni Bulletin,* XLIX (October 26, 1946) , 130.

Greenway, John. *American Folk Songs of Protest.* Midwest Folklore, IV (Spring, 1954) , 48–51.

Griswold, A. Whitney. *Essays on Education.* Journal of Higher Education, XXV (October, 1954) , 394–95.

Guérard, Albert. *Art for Art's Sake.* Saturday Review of Literature, XV (January 16, 1937) , 10–11.

———. *Personal Equation.* New York Times Book Review, May 2, 1948, p. 4.

Guéry, Susanne. *La Pensée d'André Maurois.* Erasmus, V (June 25, 1952) , 369.

Hand, Wayland D., and Arlt, Gustave O. (eds.) . *Humaniora: Essays in Literature, Folklore, Bibliography.* Journal of American Folklore, LXXIV (July–September, 1961) , 258.

Hart, James D. (ed.) . *The Oxford Companion to American Literature.* Saturday Review of Literature, XXIV (September 13, 1941) , 7.

Hatfield, James Taft. *New Light on Longfellow.* New England Quarterly, VII (March, 1934) , 180–81; also *Journal of English and Germanic Philology,* XXXIV (July, 1935) , 468.

Hauser, Heinrich. *The German Talks Back.* New York Times Book Review, September 23, 1945, pp. 1, 18.

Heilman, Robert Bechtold. *America in English Fiction, 1760–1800.* New England Quarterly, XI (March, 1938) , 193–194.

Hemingway, Ernest. *For Whom the Bell Tolls.* Saturday Review of Literature, XXIII (October 26, 1940) , 5, 19.

Herbst, Josephine. *Somewhere the Tempest Fell.* Saturday Review of Literature, XXXI (February 28, 1948) , 15–16, 31, 32.

Hersey, John. *The Marmot Drive.* Saturday Review, XLV (November 7, 1953) , 22.

———. *A Single Pebble.* Saturday Review, XXXIX (June 2, 1956) , 10.

Highet, Gilbert. *Man's Unconquerable Mind.* Saturday Review, XXXVII (March 6, 1954) , 14.

A History of the Faculty of Philosophy Columbia University. Journal of Higher Education, XXIX (June, 1958) , 345.

Hofstadter, Richard. *Social Darwinism in American Thought.* New York Times Book Review, January 21, 1945, p. 19.

Hook, Sidney. *Education for Modern Man.* New York Times Book Review, May 26, 1946, p. 6.

Howe, M. A. DeWolfe. *A Venture in Remembrance.* Saturday Review of Literature, XXIV (September 6, 1941) , 15.

Hubbell, Jay. *The South in American Literature. American Literature,* XXVII (March, 1955) , 128–31.

The Idea and Practice of General Education. Saturday Review of Literature, XXXIV (September 8, 1951) , 17–18.

"Imagination Does But Seem" [review of seven books of verse]. *Virginia Quarterly Review,* VIII (January, 1932) , 143–50.

Isherwood, Christopher. *The World in the Evening. Saturday Review,* XXXVII (June 5, 1954) , 14–15.

Jackson, Holbrook. *Bookman's Pleasure. New York Times Book Review,* April 13, 1947, p. 4.

———. *The Reading of Books. New York Times Book Review,* September 7, 1947, p. 6.

Jackson, Katherine Gauss, and Haydn, Hiram (eds.) . *The Papers of Christian Gauss. Saturday Review,* XL (February 9, 1957) , 13–14.

Jameson, Storm. *The Hidden River. Saturday Review,* XXXVIII (April 2, 1955) , 15–16.

Jefferson, Thomas. *The Papers of Thomas Jefferson, Vol. 2. American Literature,* XXIII (March, 1951) , 145–46.

———, *Vols. 3, 4. American Literature,* XXIII (January, 1952) , 517–19.

———, *Vol. 7. American Literature,* XXV (January, 1954) , 527–28.

———, *Vols. 8, 9. American Literature,* XXVII (March, 1955) , 118–20.

———, *Vol. 10. American Literature,* XXVII (January, 1956) , 589–90.

———, *Vols. 11, 12. American Literature,* XXVIII (November, 1956) , 381–82.

Jha, Amaranatha. *Literary Studies. Modern Language Notes,* XLVI (December, 1931) , 529–32.

Johnson, James Weldon, and Johnson, J. Rosamond. *The Second Book of Negro Spirituals. Yale Review,* XVI (July, 1927) , 802–4.

Jonas, Carl. *Jefferson Selleck. Saturday Review of Literature,* XXXV (January 26, 1952) , 9–10.

Justman, Joseph, and Mais, Walter H. *College Teaching: Its Practice and Its Potential. Annals of the American Academy of Political and Social Science,* CCCVIII (November, 1956) , 214–15.

Kazin, Alfred. *The Inmost Leaf. Saturday Review,* XXXVIII (October 29, 1955) , 24.

———. *On Native Grounds. Saturday Review of Literature,* XXV (October 31, 1942) , 5–6.

Kerouac, John. *The Town and the City. Saturday Review of Literature,* XXXIII (March 11, 1950) , 18.

Kimbrough, Edward. *The Secret Pilgrim. Saturday Review of Literature,* XXXIII (January 28, 1950) , 12.

Knapp, Lewis Mansfield. *Tobias Smollett: Doctor of Men and Manners. Saturday Review of Literature,* XXXII (February 26, 1949) , 19, 37.

Kronenberger, Louis. *The Thread of Laughter. Saturday Review,* XXXV (October 18, 1952) , 24.

Krout, John Allen, and Fox, Dixon Ryan. *The Completion of Independence. New York History,* XXVI (April, 1945) , 226–27.

Krutch, Joseph Wood. *The Measure of Man. Saturday Review,* XXXVII (June 12, 1954) , 21.

———. *Samuel Johnson. Chicago Sun Book Week,* November 19, 1944, p. 1.

LaFarge, Oliver. *Raw Material. New York Times Book Review,* July 22, 1945, p. 4.

Laing, Frederick. *Six Seconds a Year. Saturday Review of Literature,* XXXI (May 8, 1948) , 13.

Lane, Robert E. *The Liberties of Wit: Humanism, Criticism, and the Civic Mind. Christian Science Monitor,* November 22, 1961, p. 13.

Lanning, John Tate. *The University in the Kingdom of Guatemala. Americas,* XIII (July, 1956) , 81–82.

Laurence, William L. *Dawn Over Zero. New York Times Book Review,* August 25, 1946, p. 6.

Lauritzen, Jonreed. *Arrows in the Sun. Saturday Review of Literature,* XXVI (January 30, 1943) , 8.

Leavis, F. R. *The Great Tradition. Saturday Review of Literature,* XXXII (April 16, 1949) , 16.

Leisy, E. E. (ed.) . *The Letters of Quintus Curtius Snodgrass. Dallas Morning News: Books New and Old,* November 10, 1946, p. 19.

Le Sueur, Meridel. *North Star Country. Saturday Review of Literature,* XXIX (January 5, 1946) , 11.

Lewis, Sinclair. *Gideon Planish. Saturday Review of Literature,* XXVI (April 24, 1943) , 6.

———. *The God-Seeker. Saturday Review of Literature,* XXXII (March 12, 1949) , 11–12.

———. *Work of Art. Virginia Quarterly Review,* X (April, 1934) , 280–83.

———. *World So Wide. Saturday Review of Literature,* XXXIV (March 31, 1951) , 20.

———. *The Nobel Prize Edition of the Novels of Sinclair Lewis. Virginia Quarterly Review,* VII (July, 1931) , 427–32.

Lewisohn, Ludwig. *Expression in America. Yale Review,* XXI (Summer, 1932), 836–39.

Link, Henry C. *The Rediscovery of Morals. New York Times Book Review,* March 9, 1947, pp. 7, 32.

Lockridge, Ross, Jr. *Raintree County. Saturday Review of Literature,* XXXI (January 3, 1948), 9–10.

Lomax, John A. and Alan. *American Ballads and Folk Songs. Yale Review,* XXIV (Winter, 1935), 422–23.

Long, Orie W. *Literary Pioneers. Journal of English and Germanic Philology,* XXXV (July, 1936), 450–51.

Longaker, Mark. *Contemporary Biography. American Literature,* VII (March, 1935), 116.

Lucas, F. L. *The Greatest Problem and Other Essays. Saturday Review,* XLIV (March 11, 1961), 31–32.

Lynd, Robert S., and Lynd, Helen Merrell. *Middletown in Transition. North American Review,* CCXLIV (Autumn, 1937), 194–201.

McCord, David. *What Cheer. New York Times Book Review,* January 20, 1946, p. 8.

McCuskey, Dorothy. *Bronson Alcott, Teacher. Saturday Review of Literature,* XXIII (December 7, 1940), 36.

MacKinney, Loren C., Adams, Nicholas B., and Russell, Henry K. (eds.). *A State University Surveys the Humanities. Journal of Social Forces,* XXIV (March, 1946), 357–58.

McLean, Evalyn Walsh. *Father Struck It Rich. North American Review,* CCXLI (June, 1936), 379–81.

McMaster, Helen Neill. *Margaret Fuller as Literary Critic. Modern Language Notes,* XLV (January, 1930), 43–45.

Mahieu, Robert G. *Sainte-Beuve aux Etats-Unis. American Literature,* XVII (November, 1945), 274–75.

Maurois, André. *Byron. Book League Monthly,* IV (July, 1930), 214–17.

Mays, David John. *Edmund Pendleton. New Republic,* CXXVIII (July 6, 1953), 19–20.

Mercier, Louis J.-A. *Le Mouvement Humaniste aux Etats-Unis. Modern Language Notes,* XLV (February, 1930), 121–24.

Miller, Perry. *Roger Williams. American Scholar,* XXIII (Winter, 1953–54), 123.

Mineka, Francis E. *The Dissidence of Dissent: The Monthly Repository, 1806–1838. Saturday Review of Literature,* XXVII (November 25, 1944), 23.

Monsarrat, Nicholas. *Leave Cancelled. Saturday Review of Literature,* XXVIII (October 13, 1945), 82.

Morgan, Guy. *P. O. W. New York Times Book Review,* October 21, 1945, p. 3.

Morris, Lloyd. *Not So Long Ago. Saturday Review of Literature,* XXXII (November 19, 1949), 31–32.

Morse, H. T. (ed.). *General Education in Transition. Saturday Review of Literature,* XXXIV (September 8, 1951), 17–18.

Mott, F. L. *A History of American Magazines, Vol. IV. New York Times Book Review,* May 5, 1957, p. 5.

Muller, Herbert J. *The Spirit of Tragedy. Saturday Review,* XL (June 8, 1957), 21, 36.

Mumford, Lewis. *The Culture of Cities. North American Review,* CCXLVI (Autumn, 1938), 170–78.

Murdock, Kenneth Ballard. *Increase Mather: The Foremost American Puritan. Journal of English and Germanic Philology,* XXV (July, 1926), 450–52.

Neff, Emery. *A Revolution in European Poetry, 1660–1900. Sewanee Review,* XLIX (March, 1941), 120–25.

Neilson, William Allan, and Wittke, Carl Frederick. *The Function of Higher Education: Two Lectures on the Norman Wait Harris Foundation. Harvard Educational Review,* XIV (October, 1944), 315.

Niebuhr, Reinhold. *The Children of Light and the Children of Darkness. New York Times Book Review,* March 11, 1945, p. 4.

Nitze, William A., and Dargan, E. Preston. *History of French Literature. Freeman,* VII (March 21, 1923), 43.

Norris, Frank. *Tower in the West. Saturday Review,* XL (January 12, 1957), 13–14.

Northrup, F. S. C. *The Meeting of East and West. New York Times Book Review,* July 7, 1946, p. 1, 21.

Nuhn, Ferner. *The Wind Blew from the East. Saturday Review of Literature,* XXV (July 18, 1942), 9.

Nye, Russel B. *George Bancroft: Brahmin Rebel. New York Times Book Review,* August 13, 1944, p. 4.

O'Brien, Kate. *Pray for the Wanderer. Saturday Review of Literature,* XVIII (August 13, 1938), 11.

O'Connor, Edwin. *The Last Hurrah. Saturday Review,* XXXIX (February 4, 1956), 12.

O'Connor, Frank. *The Mirror in the Roadway. Saturday Review,* XXXIX (September 22, 1956), 12.

Odum, Howard W., and Johnson, Guy B. *Negro Workaday Songs. Yale Review,* XVI (July, 1927), 802–4.

"On the Slopes of Parnassus" [review of ten books of verse]. *Virginia Quarterly Review,* II (July, 1926), 442–50.

Persons, Stow. *American Minds: A History of Ideas. American Literature,* XXXI (March, 1959), 95–98.

Peyre, Henri. *Writers and Their Critics: A Study of Misunderstanding. New York Times Book Review,* November 12, 1944, p. 32.

————. *Observations on Life, Literature and Learning in America. New York Times Book Review,* October 22, 1961, p. 32.

"Pictura ut Poesis" [review of fourteen books of verse]. *Virginia Quarterly Review,* VI (July, 1930), 472–76.

Plekhanov, George V. *Art and Society. Saturday Review of Literature,* XV (January 16, 1937), 10–11.

"Poetry and Time" [review of fifteen books of verse]. *Virginia Quarterly Review,* VII (January, 1931), 138–43.

Pope, Willard Bissell (ed.). *The Diary of Benjamin Robert Haydon. Keats-Shelley Journal,* IX (Autumn, 1960), 138–40.

Porta, Antonio. *Byronismo Italiano. Italica,* III (August, 1926), 66–68.

Porter, Katherine Anne. *The Leaning Tower and Other Stories. Saturday Review of Literature,* XXVII (September 30, 1944), 15.

Praz, Mario. *The Romantic Agony. Modern Language Notes,* LI (June, 1936), 395–97.

Price, Lucien. *Dialogues of Alfred North Whitehead. Journal of Higher Education,* XXV (November, 1954), 448–49.

Priestley, J. B. *Literature and Western Man. New York Times Book Review,* March 13, 1960, p. 5.

Prokosch, Frederic. *Nine Days to Mukalla. Saturday Review,* XXXVI (March 21, 1953), 15.

Quennell, Peter. *The Profane Virtues. Saturday Review of Literature,* XXVIII (July 28, 1945), 14.

Rahv, Philip. *Image and Idea. Saturday Review of Literature,* XXXII (July 23, 1949), 16–17.

Raymond, Dora Neill. *The Political Career of Lord Byron. New Republic,* XL (October 1, 1924), 6–7.

Reflections on Our Age: Lectures Delivered at the Opening Session of UNESCO at the Sorbonne University. Magazine of Art, XLII (November, 1949), 274–75.

Roberts, Elizabeth Madox. *He Sent Forth a Raven. Virginia Quarterly Review,* XI (July, 1935), 452–57.

Robinson, Henry Morton. *The Perfect Round. Saturday Review of Literature,* XXVIII (October 13, 1945), 27.

Routh, H. V. *Towards the Twentieth Century. American Literature,* X (November, 1938), 355–60.

Sandburg, Carl. *Selected Poems. Virginia Quarterly Review,* III (January, 1927), 111–23.

Schönemann, Friedrich. *Mark Twain als Literarische Persönlichkeit. Journal of English and Germanic Philology,* XXV (January, 1926), 130–31.

Schorer, Mark. *Sinclair Lewis: An American Life. Christian Science Monitor,* October 5, 1961, p. 11.

Seaver, Edwin (ed.). *Cross Section 1948: A Collection of New American Writing. Saturday Review of Literature,* XXXI (May 8, 1948), 19.

Sedgwick, Ellery (ed.). *Atlantic Harvest: Memoirs of The Atlantic. New York Times Book Review,* September 28, 1947, p. 3.

———. *The Happy Profession. New York Times Book Review,* September 29, 1946, pp. 3, 30.

Shaw, Wilfred B. (ed.). *From Vermont to Michigan: Correspondence of James Burrill Angell, 1869–1871. New England Quarterly,* X (September, 1937), 592–93.

Shepard, Odell. *Pedlar's Progress: The Life of Bronson Alcott. Yale Review,* XXVI (Summer, 1937), 850–52.

Shoemaker, Ervin C. *Noah Webster: Pioneer of Learning. Journal of English and Germanic Philology,* XXXVI (October, 1937), 609–10.

Shuster, George N. *Education and Moral Wisdom. Saturday Review,* XLIII (February 13, 1960), 53.

Sinclair, Upton. *Dragon Harvest. Saturday Review of Literature,* XXVIII (June 16, 1945), 9–10.

Slade, Caroline. *Margaret. New York Times Book Review,* May 5, 1946, p. 10.

Snow, C. P. *The Light and the Dark. Saturday Review of Literature,* XXXI (March 27, 1948), 17.

———. *The Masters. New York Herald-Tribune Book Review,* October 28, 1951, p. 8.

Spender, Harold. *Byron and Greece. New Republic,* XL (October 1, 1924), 6–7.

Spira, Theodor. *Shelleys Geistesgeschichtliche Bedeutung. Journal of English and Germanic Philology,* XXIV (October, 1925), 584–86.

Spurlin, Paul M. *Montesquieu in America, 1760–1801.* Romanic Review, XXXII (October, 1941), 312–13.

Stafford, Jean. *Boston Adventure.* Saturday Review of Literature, XXVII (September 23, 1944), 10.

——. *Children Are Bored on Sunday.* Saturday Review, XXXVI (May 9, 1953), 19.

——. *The Mountain Lion.* New York Times Book Review, March 2, 1947, p. 5.

Stauffer, Donald A. (ed.). *The Intent of the Critic.* Saturday Review of Literature, XXIV (October 11, 1941), 3–4, 20.

Stegner, Wallace. *The Big Rock Candy Mountain.* Saturday Review of Literature, XXVI (October 2, 1943), 11.

Stevenson, Elizabeth. *Henry Adams.* Nation, CLXXXI (December 24, 1955), 558–59.

Stevenson, Fanny and Robert Louis. *Our Samoan Adventure,* ed. Charles Neider. *Saturday Review,* XXXVIII (September 17, 1955), 22–23.

Stevenson, Lionel. *The Showman of Vanity Fair.* New York Times Book Review, February 16, 1947, p. 6.

Stokes, George Stewart. *Agnes Repplier: Lady of Letters.* Saturday Review of Literature, XXXII (April 30, 1949), 32.

Strunsky, Simeon. *Two Came to Town.* Saturday Review of Literature, XXX (November 8, 1947), 17–18.

Styron, William. *Lie Down in Darkness.* New York Herald-Tribune Book Review, September 9, 1951, p. 3.

Sutherland, James. *Defoe.* Saturday Review of Literature, XVII (February 26, 1938), 10.

Syrett, Harold C. *Andrew Jackson.* American Scholar, XXIII (Winter, 1953–54), 123.

Tate, Allen, and Bishop, John Peale (eds.). *American Harvest.* Saturday Review of Literature, XXV (October 24, 1942), 16–17.

Thorndike, Ashley H. *Literature in a Changing Age.* Freeman, IV (February 22, 1922), 571–72.

Trilling, Lionel. *E. M. Forster.* Saturday Review of Literature, XXVI (August 28, 1943), 6–7.

——. *The Opposing Self.* Saturday Review, XXXVIII (February 12, 1955), 11–12.

Trueblood, Elton. *The Idea of a College.* Saturday Review, XLII (September 12, 1959), 37–38.

Untermeyer, Louis (ed.). *The Poems of Henry Wadsworth Longfellow. New England Quarterly,* XVII (September, 1944), 472–73.

Van Doren, Mark. *The Autobiography of Mark Van Doren. Saturday Review,* XLI (November 1, 1958), 33.

———. *The Private Reader. Saturday Review of Literature,* XXV (March 14, 1942), 9.

Waddell, Helen. *Mediaeval Latin Lyrics. Speculum,* VI (January, 1931), 165–67.

Wagenknecht, Edward. *Cavalcade of the American Novel. Mississippi Valley Historical Review,* XXXIX (March, 1953), 799–800.

Waldo, Lewis P. *The French Drama in America in the Eighteenth Century and Its Influence on the American Drama of That Period, 1701–1800. American Literature,* XV (March, 1943), 79–80.

Walker, Charles Rumford. *American City: A Rank and File History. North American Review,* CCXLIV (Autumn, 1937), 194–201.

Walker, Stanley. *Mrs. Astor's Horse. North American Review,* CCXLI (June, 1936), 379–81.

Waples, Dorothy. *The Whig Myth of James Fenimore Cooper. Journal of English and Germanic Philology,* XXXVIII (July, 1939), 463–64.

Ward, Mary Jane. *The Professor's Umbrella. Saturday Review of Literature,* XXXI (February 21, 1948), 12.

Ware, Caroline F. (ed.). *The Cultural Approach to History and Science, Philosophy and Religion: Second Symposium. American Literature,* XIV (January, 1943), 450–53.

Weaver, Richard M. *Ideas Have Consequences. New York Times Book Review,* February 22, 1948, pp. 4, 25.

Weekley, William George. *The Ledger of Lying Dog. Saturday Review of Literature,* XXX (August 16, 1947), 11–12.

Wellek, René, and Warren, Austin. *Theory of Literature. Saturday Review of Literature,* XXXII (April 30, 1949), 12.

Wertenbaker, Thomas Jefferson. *The Puritan Oligarchy. Saturday Review of Literature,* XXX (October 4, 1947), 21, 25.

"What Price Parnassus?" [review of twenty-eight books of verse]. *Virginia Quarterly Review,* IV (October, 1928), 581–91.

Willcocks, M. P. *A True-Born Englishman. Saturday Review of Literature,* XXXI (April 3, 1948), 29, 30.

Williams, Stanley T. *The Life of Washington Irving. Yale Review,* XXV (Spring, 1936), 629–31.

———. *The Spanish Background of American Literature. Comparative Literature,* VII (Summer, 1955) , 272–75.

Wilson, Edmund. *To the Finland Station. Yale Review,* XXX (Winter, 1941) , 393–95.

———. *The Wound and the Bow. Saturday Review of Literature,* XXIV (September 6, 1941) , 3–4, 17.

Wittenberg, Philip. *The Protection and Marketing of Literary Property. American Literature,* X (March, 1938) , 110–11.

Wolfe, Thomas. *From Death to Morning. Saturday Review of Literature,* XIII (November 30, 1935) , 13.

———. *The Hills Beyond. Saturday Review of Literature,* XXIV (October 25, 1941) , 7–8.

———. *Of Time and the River. Virginia Quarterly Review,* XI (July, 1935) , 452–57.

Woodress, James. *A Yankee's Odyssey: The Life of Joel Barlow. American Literature,* XXXI (May, 1959) , 201–3.

Woodward, Francis J. *The Doctor's Disciples. Yale Review,* XLIV (Autumn, 1954) , 147–50.

Woolf, Virginia. *Between the Acts. Saturday Review of Literature,* XXIV (October 25, 1941) , 7–8.

Wright, Richard. *Black Boy. Saturday Review of Literature,* XXVIII (March 3, 1945) , 9–11.

Wylie, Philip. *An Essay on Morals. New York Times Book Review,* March 9, 1947, pp. 7, 32.

Zunder, Theodore Albert. *The Early Days of Joel Barlow. Journal of English and Germanic Philology,* XXXIV (July, 1935) , 457–59.